R J SMITH

A DOCKYARD MATEY MAKES GOOD

THE LIFE AND TIMES OF ROBERT SMITH ('NIGE')

R J SMITH

A DOCKYARD MATEY MAKES GOOD

THE LIFE AND TIMES OF ROBERT SMITH ('NIGE')

MEMOIRS

Cirencester

MEMOIRS
PUBLISHING

1A The Wool Market Dyer Street Cirencester Gloucestershire GL7 2PR

A Dockyard Matey Makes Good: 978-1-86151-424-0

First published in Great Britain in 2015
by Mereo Books, an imprint of Memoirs Publishing

The address for Memoirs Publishing Group Limited can be found at
www.memoirspublishing.com

The Memoirs Publishing Group Ltd Reg. No. 7834348

The Memoirs Publishing Group supports both The Forest Stewardship Council® (FSC®) and
the PEFC® leading international forest-certification organisations. Our books carrying both the
FSC label and the PEFC® and are printed on FSC®- certified paper. FSC® is the only
forest-certification scheme supported by the leading environmental organisations including
Greenpeace. Our paper procurement policy can be found at
www.memoirspublishing.com/environment

Typeset in 12/18pt Bembo
by Wiltshire Associates Publisher Services Ltd. Printed and bound in Great Britain by
Printondemand-Worldwide, Peterborough PE2 6XD

PART 1
A Dockyard Apprentice's Story

PART 2
The Technical Progressman

PART 3
The Apprentice, the Progressman, and now the rest of it

PREFACE

To enter the Dockyard as an apprentice you took an entrance examination, and chose your preferred trade at an induction day. The highest qualified in the examination made their choices progressively until all the vacancies were filled.

Often electrical engineering apprenticeships were the first to be taken, followed by mechanical fitters, shipwrights, shipfitters, coppersmiths, boilermakers, patternmakers, carpenters, painters & so on.

When I entered the Dockyard in 1958, there were approximately 6000 people employed in a site stretching about two miles in length, and enclosing hundreds of workshops, offices and storehouses. At this time it had a dedicated police establishment, fire service, medical centre, technical college, telephone exchange, three main (and several mobile) canteens and dedicated training facilities.

The Dockyard had three large (ship refitting) basins, eight main docks, various slipways and a very large (60 tons) floating crane. A nuclear submarine refitting facility was operational from 1968 onwards, capable of '2 stream' nuclear refuelling.

Many local engineering firms in the Medway Towns benefited from the training and skills pool of the Dockyard, such as Berry Wiggins, Blaw Knox, Wingets, CAV, Elliots etc. Likewise many local suppliers were badly affected when the Dockyard (effectively) closed in 1985: eg suppliers of tools, metals, fastenings, paint, building supplies and training establishments.

The Dockyard closed in 1985/6, and the impact is still apparent in the Medway Towns.

INTRODUCTION

This story is a brief account of my working life with the MoD and it's emerging Agencies.

Having served an engineering apprenticeship and trained as a planner with the weapons section; other duties in plant maintenance/operation, logistics and production roles followed.

With the imminent closure of the Dockyard, I was first transferred to the Royal Aircraft Establishment (RAE) at Bedford; before serving at the Army establishments located at Woolwich, Ashford and Ludgershall.

This book is intended to provide a humorous insight into the working environment at these "stations", and some of the characters that I met. It is also intended to recount some of the excellent work undertaken by these people.

DEDICATION

I dedicate this snapshot of my Ministry of Defence (MoD) career to the great people that I met on these travels.

Most were hard-working, conscientious, and generally unappreciated by almost all outside of their particular 'circle'.

Although poorly paid for the most part, these MoD civilian employees did their upmost and succeeded in providing an invaluable contribution to the services. Likewise, the serving personnel I met were excellent examples of why we have been so well protected, in spite of an ever diminishing workforce, but one which still provides the best armed forces in the world.

PART 1

A DOCKYARD APPRENTICE'S STORY

BY 'NIGE'

CONTENTS

CHAPTER 1

YEAR ONE: APPRENTICES' TRAINING CENTRE

'Oi, get off that bloody bike!' Such was my introduction to the MoD in general and Chatham Dockyard in particular. It was my first day at work, Monday September 22 1958, and I had just cycled the four miles or so from my home in Rainham, Kent, to the dockyard at Chatham.

I had already done a 'recce' so that I would know where the point of entry (Pembroke Gate) into the dockyard would be, but no one had bothered to explain that you had to get off your bike and WALK through the gate entrance. The copper who shouted the order was one of the biggest blokes I had ever seen, more so as he was wearing a full-length black uniform raincoat. It was about ten to seven, and although only late September, with a strong wind and driving rain it felt more like midwinter. He looked cold, wet, and fed up and looked as if he wanted me to know about it.

He gave me my first dockyard bollocking in a broad Scottish accent, such that I could only guess at about every third word.

However, after a couple of heated minutes he did explain to me where within the 'yard I was expected to go for my induction.

The Apprentices' Training Centre (ATC) was on the south side of the engineering factory and just to the north side of the chain test house. It consisted of two parallel single-storey brick buildings, connected by an internal passageway with a corrugated asbestos roof.

The two wings were mirror image workshops and in the centre was the main entrance with clocking on/off area, instructors' offices and toilets, apprentices' toilets and a lecture room at the back. The workshop areas had two long banks of metal-topped workbenches, with a vice and a drawer every five feet or so, and at the end of the workshop was a small pillar drill. The whole facility was illuminated by bright fluorescent lighting. This was to be my home for the next 12 months.

On arrival at the ATC we were mustered together and met by our instructors, who introduced themselves as Mr Eddie Turner and Mr Joe Ward. Eddie was a big man, above average height and stocky. He had a black moustache and glasses and was balding. Joe was also tall, thinner and even more bald. Our names were checked against the entry list and we were given the following information:

■ We would clock on and off in the entrance to this building, and our hours of work would be Monday–Thursday, 0700 - 1700hrs. (One hour lunch break between 1200-1300) and Friday 0700–1600. That was a 44-hour week.

- We would be paid (a subject of great interest to us!) on Friday lunchtime at 1200, but not this first week as we had to work a week in hand.

- Our rate of pay would be £2 11s 2d (1s 3d per hour).

- If we were late, ie 'clocked on' one minute late (at 0701), this was considered to be 'absent on parade' and we would be stopped a quarter of an hour's pay. Further lateness or re-occurrences incurred additional penalties, as I was to discover later.

- We would be required to attend the Dockyard Technical College for up to two days' release weekly, to obtain appropriate technical qualifications.

- We would be granted 88 hours' paid leave (two weeks' holiday) per year.

- We would be issued with two sets of coveralls (overalls), one on and one in the wash, and the basic hand tools we would require in learning our hand tool skills.

We were told that we would be trained in this centre for the next 12 months, and during that time we would master the basic skills using hand tools, hacksaws, hammers and chisels, files and scrapers. We would be tested periodically to ensure that we were achieving the standard required by means of 'test jobs'. A test job had to be completed satisfactorily before the next stage of the training could start.

We had all left school, mostly quite thankful to have done

so, with fairly high hopes and an optimistic outlook. But that had been in July. Now, several months later, cycling into a headwind to work at 6.15 on a cold October morning to file pieces of steel plate for eight and a half hours a day, it didn't seem such a good deal after all.

Perhaps school wasn't so bad? No, on reflection, in spite of the above, school was worse.

And we were now getting paid! Even if there would be no money for the first week. We would have to work for two weeks before we secured our first pay packets. And we were getting £2 11s 2d! How on earth would we spend all that? The answer was easy: I gave my mum £1 a week for my keep (and often borrowed at least some of it back during the week) and was left with £1 11s 2d, which I promised not to waste.

After a few months we had a pay rise, to £2 13s 0d: look out high rollers, here we come! This didn't seem a lot of money for the hours we worked, especially as some of our mates were working as labourers/teaboys on building sites and getting £5 a week.

We sorted ourselves out and found positions at the workbench that we liked or alongside someone we knew. This seemed quite important, as we were to make this our home for the next 12 months. Each position had a large work-vice fixed to the bench and a big drawer to keep our bits in. The floor alongside the benches was covered with duckboards - wooden slatted floor covers which kept our feet off the cold floor.

Several schoolfriends had started with me, so at least I could recognize some of the faces, which made the whole 'new boy' experience less daunting. From the outset my real name was ignored and I was known as Nige, mainly because several years earlier I had decided that Nige (Nigel) was a far classier name, and would be a distinct advantage to me when trying to impress the opposite sex.

Although we mostly put on a brave face, none of us really knew what to expect, and were suffering more than a little with first-day nerves.

Needless to say, the first few days went very quickly as we all struggled to adapt to our new environment and culture. We were always conscious of the fact that the 'big boys' in the other workshop wing, six months ahead of us in their training, might well be looking for signs of weakness.

So the training started. The principle aim of first-year training was to ensure that we could master basic hand tool skills. We were issued with files: flat, half round, square and triangular. These came in grades, rough, medium and smooth. We were also issued with scrapers (various), chisels (various), a hacksaw, hammer, and measuring equipment (rule and calipers). More elaborate measuring equipment was issued from the stores on an as-required basis. We were encouraged to purchase any additional tools required through the Naval Stores system.

With these basic tools we were required to handcraft metal objects to make them square, flat or regular to very fine limits - thousands of an inch. This would be achieved by practice, practice, and even more practice. (I had a nasty feeling that this was going to be boring, boring, and even more boring.)

At lunchtimes we had the opportunity to investigate a bit more of the dockyard. After eating our sandwiches, which most of us ate sitting on our toolboxes alongside our workbench, we were free to wander and investigate freely as long as we remembered to clock on again before 1300 hrs.

Incidentally, about this time, I made the mistake of saying I enjoyed the cheese sandwiches my mum had packed up for me; consequently I had cheese sandwiches, with slight variations, for the next 10 years. Most of the lads took sandwiches and, like me, a bottle of milk to drink, as we hadn't yet discovered the delights of a good brew, and we certainly couldn't afford the canteen.

At the side of the ATC was a large cycle–rack, mainly for the use of the apprentices, though workmen in the area used it as well. Cycles were still the main transport for most workmen at this time, although a few of the advanced apprentices from the other workshop had motorbikes, which they usually parked outside the main entrance.

At the north end of our workshop, between the workshop and the factory, was a large old-style toilet block. These toilets had a full-length urinal on one side and about 12 cubicles on the other. The toilet doors covered only the middle section, with a gap of about 18 inches at top and bottom so that the chargemen (supervisors) could easily locate and identify any shirkers.

The other unusual design feature of these toilets was that they were 'pre-flush'. The toilet seats were located above a gulley which travelled the full length of the toilet block and was fed with running water. They worked pretty well, apparently, but were an ideal source for 'skylarking' or pranks. One particular morning when all the 'traps' were full, some joker set alight a large bundle of cotton waste and floated it down the flushing gulley. Successive shouts of surprise and obscenities followed the burning waste as it slowly barbequed the bums above. I learned a lot of new words that day!

Unfortunately one of the occupants towards the end of the stream, with the fire well ablaze, was a little slow to react and ended up with a badly-singed scrotum, so there was hell to pay. That particular toilet block was modernized shortly afterwards. Perhaps the culprit had a role to play in the modernization programme.

The nearest workshop to the ATC was the Engineering Factory. This was the largest single building in the dockyard, being approximately 150 yards square. The first entry into this workshop was very impressive. A main gangway went through the centre, wide enough to allow access for large lorries, Lister trucks (the preferred dockyard transport) and a railway track, to accommodate the really large or heavy items. In the central area were located the stores areas at ground level, and offices above. Branching out from the central area were the various sections, which performed multifarious activities.

The submarine section was where the massive diesel engines (Admiralty Standard Range, known as ASRs) were built. These were the main propulsion units in conventional (non-nuclear) submarines at that time. The section also refitted (repaired) other large associated components.

Most of the central factory area was occupied with machine tool sections, which included heavy turning, light turning, capstan and computer-controlled lathes, milling machines, slotting and shaping machines, grinders and jig borers. Other sections included a valve refitting area, turbine auxiliaries and pumps, water pressure testing, a maintenance section and a toolroom. In the north east corner additional newer offices housed the Inspections area (DDI - delegated dimensional inspection), the Foreman's office on the ground floor, and the Inspectors' offices above.

This workshop had a massive headroom, being similar in height to the Boilershop (which is now part of the Dockside shopping outlet), and it seemed alive with a banging heartbeat; running machinery, overhead crane movements and an acrid smell of oils, paint, and the burning smell of metals being machined which hung over the whole expanse like an unseen envelope.

It was daunting, but very interesting. How on earth did all of these people know what they were doing?

Just walking through this workshop was an education in itself. There were so many men, and although they were all dressed in the issue coveralls, they seemed to be of completely different appearance. There were big strong guys hauling components into place, little fellas, nimble and busy, the moustachioed, the bearded, the bald and the 'cheesecutter' adorned, all equally focused and concentrated.

At every corner were the key men in this panorama, the

section labourers, who endlessly swept the factory floor and kept the gangways clear. This then was the Engineering Factory.

The other major workshop in this area, next to the factory, was the Boilershop. When I first walked through this shop, it immediately reminded me of Dante's Inferno. As soon as you entered you heard the THUMP THUMP of the massive hammers forming red-hot workpieces into their required shapes. Then the crackling sound of welding could be heard, along with the bright flashes created, which looked like lightning, while the coarse, acrid fumes attacked the senses. Riveting was still commonplace in the Dockyard at this time and several riveters could be working simultaneously. The noise was unbelievable.

The Boilershop, like many of the other workshops, was split into two separate but complementary sections; the 'main shop' workforce and the 'afloat' gang. The latter were the gang that worked principally on the ships, although they would bring assemblies or components back to the workshop to work on.

I was to discover the dozens of other workshops which made up the dockyard facility in due course, and to learn a little of what the other trades did and how. At this early stage, however, the need to concentrate on my own training, and the limited time away from the training centre, meant that this would have to wait.

It was important to get into a routine. Endless days were spent filing pieces of steel plate. First we had to get a surface flat. The edge of a rule would be held against the filed area and it was held up to the light. If any light could be seen through the join it was unsatisfactory. Eddie Turner had a favorite saying at this stage. He would look at the apprentice offering the work with a condescending frown and say in a very loud voice 'Is it all right? No it's bloody not all right! I could drive a horse and cart through there!' It got so that the whole group could see this coming and would join in, in chorus.

The next stage was to file square. This would be checked with a set square. Once this was mastered the basics had been achieved.

Sometimes additional minor items would be required (eg chalk and emery paper) to polish and finish prepared work. These were loaned out by the instructors, who made us guard them until it was time for their return to the store room. It didn't take us long to find out that we could go to the factory next door and get these items by the handful - which we did.

One day Dick Seamark, a real joker, had a slight accident and tore his coveralls. When it was time for him to hand them in for replacement, Eddie Turner went ballistic. 'This is malicious damage, and you could well be charged with a criminal offence!' he roared. He went on and on and really laid into the lad. Dick was so terrified he almost shat himself. Although none of us really believed he was going to be shot at dawn, it left us with a feeling of unease. What could happen to us?

It was completely unnecessary for Eddie to get his pleasure like that. The rest of the lads looking on were quite concerned, but we could not believe that this incident was worth all the aggro. Of course, once we all discovered that the bollocking was unnecessary and that the instructors in reality had no teeth at all, it was payback time. And it didn't take long.

Our craft training was supplemented by regular technical lectures. These could be hard work, as the topics, such as case hardening of steels, were not always of paramount interest to a group of sixteen year olds. But there was another problem. Both instructors tried their best, but neither had even a modicum of instructional technique. Eddie in particular had a slight speech impediment (a stutter) and difficulty with long words.

The day to remember started fairly normally. The subject was metallurgy, and specifically the elements which can be added to steels to harden them. Eddie wasn't having a good day and was struggling quite early on with some of the compounds. When he stumbled and stuttered he became flustered, and when he became flustered he stuttered.

His lecture should have gone along the lines of 'Various elements can be added to steels to change their characteristics or to harden them; often used for this purpose is molybdenum, likewise chromium'. Unfortunately Eddie's problem with some of the longer words or technical descriptions had raised its ugly head and on this particular day he struggled. 'Molib… molub… molob… melobdenum…' he stuttered. By now a titter had risen among the gathered apprentices. As Eddie got more and more flustered, a cacophony of laughter shook the room.

Eddie went into a scarlet rage. 'Stop laughing! Stop, STOP!' he shouted. This only made things worse. By now most of us were barely remaining continent.

In exasperation Eddie glowered at the helpless mass in front of him and shouted 'Right, I'll have your tea-stop breaked!' (He meant tea-break stopped, of course).

Utter pandemonium followed. The instructor from the adjacent work area rushed in – I think he imagined it was a bomb scare - to find 25 apprentices paralytic with laughter and a purple-faced instructor, hair standing on end, eyes bulging and neck veins twitching.

By this time we lads had made friends and unconsciously sorted ourselves out into groups of like-minded mates. In fact most of the lads had exactly the same interests - crumpet (girls), pop music and where to go to find both. Some of the lads were natural comedians and kept the rest of us in fits of laughter. Pete Appleby and Dave Riley were particularly funny, with the most original sayings and masterful timing.

I had for my part made friends with Bernard 'Paddy' Hargan, Dave 'Panda' Campbell and Vic Salmon, with whom I shared an interest in motorbikes, as we were both to own the same model of BSA through our apprenticeships.

After the initial settling-in period, when everything was new and strange, the ensuing weeks became less and less interesting, thanks to the repeated and prolonged tasks given to us. These were jobs which necessitated cutting off pieces of material, bar or plate, with a hacksaw and then using files or scrapers to finish and smooth items as shown on engineering drawings or sketches. It soon became very soul-destroying; it was repetitive, monotonous and uninspiring. The problem was exacerbated by the time of year and the cold dark and wet weather. We hardly saw any daylight - talk about battery hens!

The boredom of doing the same tasks every day, filing, filing, and more filing to produce a finished item, created a sense of creeping death.

It was no wonder that some of the lads created amusing situations to relieve the boredom. One such incident occurred when we had a delivery of large metal bar blanks (4' bar, cut approx. 1' thick), the material required in preparation for our next (imminent) test jobs.

Dick Seamark spotted Joe Ward going into the toilet. The instructors had their own toilets, which were padlocked when not in use, but Joe had left the padlock on the outside of the door unlocked. Dick crept up to the door and quietly closed the padlock, trapping Joe inside.

Chuckling like a demented fool, Dick carried a couple of bar blanks over to the toilet and rolled them under the door. An agitated mumbling and swearing could be heard from beyond the door, and people started to enter the toilet to investigate. Dick rolled in more bars and a couple of other lads joined in, until about 12 of these blanks had been forced into the toilet cubicle with Joe. We were in stitches, and the more Joe cussed the funnier it got. He was eventually released by the other instructor.

By now we had started our technical studies at the Dockyard Technical College, which was located in what we called the 'Khyber Pass', just outside the Dockyard. I was started in the National Certificate stream, which meant attending on two days a week (Monday and Thursday).

This was good news and bad. The good news was that it was a later start and took me away from that bloody filing, but the bad news was that it was of course just the same as going back to school again. Most of the lads were not really interested, and we were not sufficiently mature to realize that any qualifications achieved would dramatically improve our career prospects. We were however sufficiently astute to show the necessary level of interest to protect the day's release - well, it was better than work, wasn't it?

I don't recall much about my time at the college, although it lasted for three years in all. The last year was a repeat year, as I had failed to pass the previous year's exam, and I had to apply to repeat the year by way of an interview with the College Principle, Mr Ferguson.

I remember 'Fergie' Ferguson for two reasons. The first was an incident that happened one day when several of us were skylarking in the corridor outside the classrooms. Exit Mr Ferguson, who was not very pleased, and told us so. As we slunk away Paddy mouthed off 'silly old bastard, just because he's past it!' Unfortunately it was just loud enough for Fergie to hear.

I'm sure he caught up with Paddy in two bounds. He spun Paddy round and challenged him in his broad Scots accent by saying 'Past it am I? Put 'em up and let's see how good you are!'

Paddy went to put his mitts up but was thumped so hard on the shoulder, that he staggered back and ended up on his bum, red faced and sheepish. We later found out that in his younger days 'Fergie' had been a very talented amateur boxer.

The second reason was really very sad. I had met Fergie's daughter Pat through one of my ex-girlfriends, Sandra Levene. Pat struck me as being very friendly and highly intelligent. Tragically, not long afterwards, while out on a hen night, she was killed. The accident happened halfway down the old Bluebell Hill road, a notorious blackspot. Fergie was never the same again.

This is not the whole story though, as this was the accident which triggered off dozens of ghost stories and sightings around the bus stop near the spot where it had happened. There have been so many over such a long period of time that I am convinced there is something unexplained here. Pat, or one of the hen party, appeared on a fairly regular basis, for varying lengths of time and different circumstances, and some of the people who made these contacts were left severely traumatized.

Soon it was time for our first test job, made from the bar steel which had been used to trap Joe in the toilet. This male hexagon, which we had just made, had to be rotated through its six positions, fitting accurately into the female so that no light could be seen through the joints at any of the positions. We all passed fairly easily, although a few of the lads had to do a bit of rework.

When we had our mini-breaks during the day, we would be busy scrounging cigarettes off each other. 'Tailor mades' were a rare commodity (except perhaps the odd packet of Weights on a payday), so invariably this would mean 'roll-ups'. Most of the lads smoked Golden Virginia, Hearts of Oak or Old Holborn, and could roll the ciggies as thin as the matches they lit them with. The tobacco was sold in vending machines outside the main (No. 3) canteen. Golden Virginia was two shillings for half an ounce.

The other main topic of interest during the day was where we were going that night. Usually we would arrange to go to a youth club, as there seemed to be one available most nights of the week and they were cheap. Looking back, perhaps it wasn't cutting-edge entertainment - a game of table tennis, listen to the latest records and a chance to meet a few girls - but it gave us a chance to exaggerate last night's successes, and something to look forward to for the night ahead.

The relationship with our instructors was now on a much more mature level. They were not threatening us with hanging or keelhauling any more and we were showing them the respect that we now realized they deserved.

Eddie Turner was still a problem, in so far as he was extremely prone to exaggeration concerning his wartime exploits. Of course his stories got ever more exaggerated through successive telling by apprentices to other apprentices, the classic being when he supposedly saw a torpedo homing in on the ship he was on. He had jumped overboard, straddled the torpedo and guided it safely passed his ship! The age-old problem, of course, was that as he told these stories over and over again, in the end he started to believe them himself.

The time went past quite quickly. It soon was almost Christmas, and we were all looking forward to our first bank holiday. We had heard that the factory organized some sort of celebration, so a few of us decided that we would go missing for a short while to investigate.

When we entered the factory in mid afternoon the change that had taken place was impressive. Obviously it was much quieter than usual and there was no banging or loud machinery operating, but most of the sections had put up a few paper chains, tinsel, or some other kind of decoration. As the daylight was already failing, the glimmering bench lights reflecting off the decorations transformed the place. In the central area were large marking out slabs (metal tables), and a crowd was gathering here, all in good humour.

Suddenly there were shouts of 'Keith! Keith!' and clapping. Apparently Keith, one of the workshop labourers, had been encouraged to sing a few carols for us. It should be explained that he had severe learning difficulties. Short and bald, he wasn't a very commanding figure. Although it started as a 'piss-take', when this lost soul stood up on the table and sang *Silent Night* (very badly), the mood gradually changed, and most of us had lumps in our throats.

Getting to work in the winter months wasn't much fun. It might be useful here to explain that things were a lot different in those days. My home was not in a neglected state or even in a 'poor' neighbourhood, but we did not have the luxuries that we take for granted now.

We lived in a three-bedroom semi- detached house which had been privately built but acquired by the Council when the builder got into difficulties. It had two rooms plus a kitchen downstairs, and through the kitchen a ground-floor rear extension housed the toilet and coal store.

We had no central heating, double glazing, fitted carpets or inside toilet.   Upstairs consisted of two main bedrooms, a 'box' bedroom, and a bathroom. The two main bedrooms had open fire grates, which were never used, as they were too small to be effective and the coal that was available was of extremely poor quality. The amount of smoke and ash generated, plus the need to empty and re-lay the fire each morning, made them impracticable. Only once, when my Dad was ill in bed, did I ever see these fires used as a last resort. We quite rightly considered them to be dangerous.

Neither my box bedroom nor the bathroom had electric lighting. Both had ceiling-mounted, blanked-off gas fittings (thank goodness that they were blanked off!) Presumably at the time of building gas lighting was envisaged.
The bathroom contained a bath, a wash basin and a boiling copper (which was used to heat the bath water). There was no hot water supply, and no upstairs toilet.

I mention the above to show that it was a real challenge on cold winter mornings to get out of bed, put your feet on to ice-cold linoleum and quickly dress while freezing cold. A quick slosh of cold water in the bathroom was usually a trial, and most mornings ice would form on the inside of the bathroom window. It was bloody cold.

I had started off cycling to work on my rather nice racing bike, a Rotrax: it had a lightweight frame and alloy wheels, the whole business. The problem was that the dockyard roads were not suitable for such a bike. Apart from the potholes, most roads had at least one set of railway lines, more often than not several, and hitting these at any speed usually meant that you ended up on the ground and the bike would be damaged. So it was time for a change, and reluctantly I sold the Rotrax and bought a Triumph of a more heavy-duty nature on HP.

There was a slight gap between selling and getting the new bike, which meant I had to get the bus. The bus journey was a nightmare; it had to be endured to be believed. The bus left Rainham about 6.30 and seemed to be stopping every 100 yards or so. It took forever to get to the dockyard. The bus was almost full by the time I got on, with only places left upstairs. When I got upstairs I could hardly see if any of the seats were free due to the blanket of cigarette smoke. You could not see the front of the bus! The windows were running with condensation, and every other passenger, all old boys, were coughing their lungs up. Nice.

Usually, by some miracle the bus got to its destination, outside Pembroke Gate, in time for me to run to the ATC and clock on in time. But this was not going to be my preferred choice of travel.

The newly-acquired bike was better, but hard work. It was so much heavier than my other bike, and it felt as if going to work and coming home were both uphill. Because it was always raining, several layers of clothing made things more difficult. So it was time to save up and buy my first motorbike.

My sister had a girlfriend who had a small motorbike for sale, a Royal Enfield 125cc, so I purchased this 'bag of bolts' for £18. I'm sure that bike was female! It would go if it wanted to, but not otherwise. I cleaned, repainted, and serviced it, but basically it was an old, knackered two-stroke. I went to the Dockyard College on it one day and went home to Rainham in the lunch hour, when it broke down. This time it was the cylinder head gasket that had blown, so I made a new one from an old cocoa tin, and it worked! It was still on the bike when it went to the scrapyard.

That bike was always letting me down. I had my mate Dudley Young to thank for saving my bacon by giving me a lift in on many occasions. He lived at the top of our road and when I could not start the bloody Enfield I would rush out, flag him down and beg a lift on his trusty Lambretta.

The weeks passed, and just before the Easter break we had a visitor. A mouse had been seen several times in the workshop and several hilarious attempts were made to catch it. It probably came in because we ate sitting on our toolboxes in the workshop, and it had found some scraps. A concerted effort was made to catch the little blighter by blocking off all its known exit holes and collecting a range of weapons - hammers, heavy spanners, etc – for use as missiles as and when it appeared.

About a week after his first appearance the mouse was struck by a thrown hammer and killed instantly. One of the apprentices (presumably he had planned this) went into the unoccupied instructors' office and emerged with Eddie T's tobacco pouch. The mouse, bleeding profusely, was ceremoniously buried in the tobacco and the pouch buttoned up. When we left at the end of the day the pouch was left behind a corner radiator, just out of sight.

When we came back to work after Easter the place stank. The mouse had cooked in the tobacco in the pouch, and was now decomposing. The instructors were at first at a loss to work out where the foul smell was coming from, but it didn't take them too long - they just followed their noses. The tobacco pouch was ruined, and needless to say no one ever owned up to the misdemeanour.

By this time we were all regular visitors to the factory, not just to obtain consumable stores such as chalk and emery paper for our training needs. We had also come to realize that it was a permanent source of nuts, bolts etc. for repairing our bikes or motorbikes.

On one such visit we were talking to the stores assistant, who explained that the main office above his stores had originally been the Inspector's office (there was only one for the whole of the factory at this time). The Inspector's name was Mr Batty. He was a man of the old school, only just inferior to God. He was never seen without his bowler hat, and when he descended to the factory shop floor, everybody made sure they looked busy.

By this time several of the apprentices had acquired motorcycles. I for my part had to look for another, after disaster struck the Royal Enfield. One day when it refused to start I decided to try to bump-start it; I had discovered that the flywheel magneto was knackered. I ran alongside the thing, in gear, clutch disengaged, and jumped on. As I put my foot on the footrest the whole bottom half of the engine's frame collapsed and fell with a noisy CLANG into the middle of the road. The thing had been badly repaired by brazing and painted over, providing sufficient camouflage until some sucker (me) bought it. I sold it in bits to Frank Miers, a motorcycle parts dealer in New Road, Chatham, for scrap value.

So I now needed a new motor bike, and I found just the thing, a nice 350cc BSA model B31 at Grays of Chatham. I had to sell almost everything I owned to find the deposit - record player, bike, fishing rods etc - but I raised the deposit and signed the HP agreement.

One of the apprentices, Jim Apps, got himself a rather unusual 'Indian Brave' motor bike. When he first brought it to work we all crowded around, as was the custom, to inspect this machine, and Vic Salmon and I decided that we should road test it. Jim took some persuading, but he eventually agreed, so we took it out at lunchtime and did a performance test along the Power House straight. I was 'driving', with Vic as the passenger, as at that time you were allowed to ride pillion inside the dockyard. The road test was a complete failure, mainly because the bike had a very unusual hand gear change. Although we screamed the engine, we never got it out of first gear and only achieved 17 miles per hour. I don't think it did the motorbike's gearbox much good.

Jim was a smashing fella, but he was not hot on hygiene and used to chuck up a bit, especially in summer. He invariable wore a PVC Belstaff type motorcycle jacket, which we all blamed for causing his problem. It didn't seem to worry him too much – in fact he used to refer to himself as 'BO Apps'.

My mates had also got themselves motorbikes by this time. Vic Salmon had a BSA B31 like mine, while Dave (Panda) was very lucky - his dad bought him a brand new Norton Model 50. Paddy had a 500cc Velocette Venom. We often went out as a group.

My first experiences with the BSA were not encouraging. It was delivered by Grays and left in the back garden waiting for me when I got home. Naturally both parents accompanied me out to see the new arrival. Grays had parked it for me on the centre stand on the path in the back garden. The path was raised above the garden on either side, so when I sat on the bike and pushed it forward off the stand, I could not reach the garden with my right leg. I lost my balance and the bike fell over, with me still on it. I then realized what a heavy old beast this machine was, and the importance of keeping your balance. I think it was at this time that my parents started to worry about my involvement with motorbikes.

It didn't get any better. That night was a Monday and we used to meet on Mondays at a youth club in the Central Hall at Chatham. Several guys from work knew that I would be turning up on my new bike, and were waiting outside for me to arrive, as was my current girlfriend Carol.

I wanted to make a real entrance. Although it was raining heavily, I decided to leave the braking late and stop by coming down through the gearbox. Plenty of noise - get everyone's attention - good plan. But I hadn't thought this through - first ride on the bike, wet road, no idea of the gear ratios. Guess what happened next? I changed up through the gears too quickly, the back wheel locked, the bike slid one way and me the other. My mates slid off inside the club to spare me even more embarrassment (or to have a quiet chuckle) and it was left to a couple of sailors standing outside an adjacent pub to pick me and the bike up off the road. Not an auspicious start!

The bike wasn't badly damaged (in contrast to my pride) - the footrest was bent and some superficial scratches, but otherwise it was OK. I sulked all evening and was glad when it was going home time.

I could only afford the HP for the motorbike because I still had my other job. From the age of 13, I had been working on Friday nights, Saturday all day and evenings as required at the Rainham Mark Stores, delivering groceries and greengroceries to the surrounding area. I used a tradesman's bike, which had a large carrier over the front wheel, during the week and on Saturdays and accompanied the van driver, Derek (my brother-in-law), doing the deliveries on Friday nights. It was a good job, and I met a lot of nice people including a couple of early girlfriends. The boss, Mr Settatree, was a real gentleman. While I was still at school this job had proved a real boon, as the Christmas tips given to me by the customers used to largely pay for exchange trips to Germany with my school.

The pay was 1s 3d per hour (the same as I was earning in the dockyard). This was great and I loved the job, but unfortunately the shop was soon to close, due to a new Co-Op opening up almost next door, so I just hoped that it would last until I got a pay rise at the dockyard.

One of the perks of the delivery job was that you got to see all the girls going out on Saturday, and this was how I met one of my first girlfriends, Joan. She was a lovely girl, and went on to marry one of my mates, Harry.

After several months in the dockyard we were getting to be old hands. One of the most unsettling things about the job was the routine police searches at going home time, to check we hadn't been nicking anything. Although you had nothing to hide you still felt guilty. What normally happened was that you were selected ('tapped', as it was known) and shepherded into the search station. Here another police officer would ask 'Do you have any Crown property on your person?' he would normally then 'tap you down' and search your lunch bag. Your car or motorbike would also be searched before you were allowed to proceed.

Mostly this was done quite pleasantly and quickly, but I knew it didn't pay to be a 'wise guy' with the police as they could keep you there for ages if you displayed an attitude.

On our exploratory walks around the yard we discovered all sorts of new and interesting things. As soon as you entered Pembroke Gate you saw the stables where the huge shire-type horses were stabled. These were used by a firm called Curtis, who used them to collect and carry large and heavy items within the yard, and for general housekeeping duties.

The main workshops in this area included the blacksmiths, patternmakers, painters, electrical, light plate, hose, shipwrights, no. 5 machine shop, bottle and fridge shops; the dockyard laboratory, garage and the central (no. 3) canteen. A strange mixture of other buildings housed the personnel department, the surgery, compressor and boiler houses, the laundry, no. 3 dockyard well, the bosun's blockhouse workshop, the yard services in the old power station building, and the Property Services Agency (PSA) workshops and offices. Clocking on/off sheds (muster stations) were located at strategic locations for the workforce. Police offices and search areas were located just inside the Pembroke Gate and replicated at the other entrance gates.

One of the problems when a group of young lads are together is that they will get up to mischief, and on one occasion this nearly proved disastrous. Near the training centre was a storage area for very large electrical cable drums. Some of these were 10 feet in diameter and fully enclosed on the outer rim except for a gap of about 18' where the cable had been removed. These were ideal 'toys' for some of the bigger and older apprentices in their lunch hours. One of them had the bright idea of forcing an unsuspecting 'appo' (apprentice) into one of these cable drums through the small opening, and before he could struggle out, rolling the drum away with the poor appo inside yelling and hollering. This was great fun, for when the victim was eventually released he was so dizzy that he could not stand up straight or walk in a straight line, and was sometimes sick. I believe this little prank was called 'preparing for spaceflight'.

What fun it was - until the day when it all went horribly wrong. On this particular day the usual thing happened, a lad was put inside the cable drum and several others pushed it as hard as they could. What was different on this day was that the drum was being rolled along the road beside the sea wall, and as it reached maximum speed it hit a house brick in the road and the whole drum veered off at a sharp angle towards the sea wall. Utter panic.

The drum, with the lad still inside, hit the three-foot high sea wall and rose up on to it, balancing on top and inching towards the 30-foot drop into the water on the other side. Luckily a guard chain is situated along the seawall at this point, and it was this which I am convinced saved the boy's life.

The cable drum rocked momentarily in the 12 o'clock position, then very very slowly rolled backwards into the road. The dozen or so of us watching, holding our breath, hearts pounding, could all have done with a change of underpants.

Unfortunately the problems were not over. The lad inside the drum was aware that there had been a problem, although not the magnitude of it, and decided that it was a good time to get out. Unfortunately the drum had not stopped rolling, and as he poked his head out to exit, the drum continued to roll, squashing his head between the drum and the ground. The drum did one more rotation before it was brought to a complete standstill, and the shocked, battered, and very bruised apprentice fell out. His head had been badly squeezed, and the skin on his face had been pulled and stretched very badly, but he had not sustained any serious injuries. He was unbelievably lucky; he could have died twice.

He was taken to the surgery for checks as a precautionary measure, but was passed as OK after treatment for abrasions, cuts and shock. That particular game was not played again.

There were lighter moments. Sadly at this time the actress Kay Kendall died, and this was covered in the newspapers, along with a very attractive picture of her. One of the lads, Micky Pierce, was seen going into the toilet with the newspaper, and several of the other apprentices crept up outside the toilet door to listen. The story was that there was much rustling of the newspaper accompanied by other 'suspicious' noises, so word went out that he was having a wank! He was of course, subjected to almost unbearable piss-taking concerning this for weeks after, and his denials only acted to confirm our suspicions.

I remember another incident well. Joe Ward was on the receiving end of one of Dick Seamark's pranks when he was repairing one of the workshop vices. He had supported the vice handle with a large block of wood and was using a large hammer to rivet over the nut on the opposite end, while the handle was being steadied by his free hand. Joe was taking heavy swipes at this, completely unaware that Dick had crawled underneath the bench from the other side and was waiting for him to take the next swing.

As Joe took a mighty swing at the repair he was attempting, Dick kicked away the block of wood which was supporting the vice handle. As Joe hit the top of the handle, now unsupported, it slid downwards at a rapid rate and pinched Joe's hand between the two components. The injured hand started to swell up immediately, and a very large, ugly blood blister formed at the place of impact. Joe hopped around like an agitated dervish, shaking the injured arm and shouting 'Fuck a pig lad, Fuck a pig!' This was one of his favourite expressions in times of stress.

We had difficulty making our wages last, so as the weekend approached money was usually very short. Sometimes if we had enough on a Thursday we would treat ourselves to a night at the 'Bughutch' (the Royal Cinema in Rainham), which would cost us 2s 3 ½d (two and threepence halfpenny) - two shillings to get in and three and a half pence for fruit gums. We knew how to live! Sometimes we could talk my brother-in-law into coming for a pint with us (me and Paddy Hargan at this time) at the Belisha Beacon pub, for a game of darts, but he would have to lend us ten bob each until payday. Usually Thursday evenings were spent cleaning our motorbikes at my home (Paddy was in 'digs'), meticulously cleaning every component and then polishing the chrome and aluminium with Solvol Autosol. After a couple of hours or so we would go into Mum's kitchen, up to our elbows in oil and grease, use up half her tin of Vim and leave the sink dirty.

Paddy shared his digs with Taffy Roberts, another apprentice. In the early days we would often cycle home together. One such day I had just got past Gillingham station when I caught up with Paddy, off his bike at the end of an alley and looking agitated. 'What's up?' I asked, to be told that Taff had been in an argument with someone and they had gone into the alley to sort it out.

We went into the alley to investigate, and found Taff and the other guy, who was perhaps in his forties and of medium build, squaring up to each other. 'Box him Taff!' we urged. But BANG BANG, the other bloke had hit Taff twice before he could move. 'Wrestle him Taff!' we suggested, but again the old guy had Taff squirming in pain in an arm lock, no trouble at all.

It was handbags really, and Taff wasn't badly hurt (except his pride), but I think we all learned not to mouth off to people unless we were sure of the outcome. The guy explained that he had had boxing and wrestling experience when he was in the Navy.

Towards the end of the first year I had a nasty motorbike accident and was very lucky to escape without serious injuries, or worse. Three of us were riding out to Chatham in our lunch break in convoy, racing to be the first into town. We were all travelling up Dock Road, overtaking slower vehicles, me in front. I remember overtaking a bus, and the next thing I knew I was lying on the pavement on the opposite side of the road face down. Apparently a motorcycle and sidecar had been in front of the bus, and just as I got alongside he pulled out. Our handlebars clashed and I was sent into the air, bounced once and ricocheted onto the path. My motorbike carried on up the road until it finally crashed into the dockyard wall.

I was able to sit up after a short while and check if anything was hanging off. I was obviously very badly shaken and had suffered severe abrasions to my face (no crash helmet, as these were not yet compulsory), knees, ankles, elbows and back. But nothing was broken and there was no serious injury. Lucky boy!

I had missed hitting a car travelling in the opposite direction by seconds - I would probably have gone through his windscreen.

My mates had stopped and helped me prop myself against the wall. Someone produced a cloth to cover my facial abrasions, and someone else dragged my motorbike into a safe area. An ambulance had already been called. I remember sitting on the roadside, holding the pad to my face and feeling pretty lousy, when I happened to notice one of the senior apprentices, who I knew vaguely, ride past looking at me with a huge smirk on his face. Nice fella!

The ambulance arrived quite quickly and I remember getting Vic Salmon, one of my mates on this trip, to promise to convince my parents that I was going to be OK. He was going to see them with the 'good news' before he returned to work.

One of the other apprentices, Jim Apps, had only just arrived as I was being taken away in the ambulance. He looked at my motorbike and jumped to the wrong conclusion. He went back to work and told them all I had been killed!

The first year's training was now coming to an end, with all of us having reached the required standard. We now had a feel for the role of the dockyard and our place in it. I for my part had not experienced any problems in acquiring the necessary craft and academic skills, but I was still having difficulty getting to work on time, often being late by a minute or two. I was also struggling to make our two weeks' holiday last for the whole year. These problems were to stay with me for some time yet.

YEAR TWO:
THE 'BOTTLE SHOP'

We did our second year of training in the 'Bottle Shop'. Actually it was a small corner of the workshop which had been cordoned off as an apprentices' training area. To the side through the wire-mesh partition we could often see the large high-pressure air bottles being 'rumbled'. This process is basically to fill the bottles, which were usually 9.1 cu ft. (very large) high pressure air vessels, with small pieces of sharp steel plate and rotate them on a very large turntable. The steel plates inside the bottle then would scour and clean the bottle internally.

Our dedicated area comprised much of the same equipment as we had had in the previous workshop, with benches with drawers and vices along each side and at the top of our work area.

There were also several training aids: engines, various types of valves, pumps, compressors and other major assemblies, which had sections cut away to show exploded views of the internal components. On the walls were a copy of the Factories Act and some very old, tired looking safety posters.

Immediately outside the main entrance were a large cycle rack and a toilet block. This was when I first became aware of the jealously-guarded pecking order of the toilets. The main toilet block was marked 'Workmen', but to the rear two more, smaller toilets were identified as 'Chargeman's Toilet' and 'Inspector's Toilet'.

This really annoyed me. Why was it necessary for the 'officers' to have their own dedicated toilets? Did my shit stink more than theirs? I often asked this question, but never got a satisfactory answer. Guess which toilets I used when the need arose? Perhaps I had delusions of grandeur.

My timekeeping had not improved much, and I was still very prone to being a minute or so late. This was going to be a problem, as the Time Recorder (who checks that the clock is accurate and oversees the workmen clocking in) at this workshop was a real bastard. His name was Hewson. He took a particular dislike to me, probably because of my cavalier approach and my constant enquiries concerning his parenthood. On several occasions I was dashing towards the clock to beat the 7.30 deadline (new start time), only to see him nudge the minute hand on so that I clocked on late. Again. Some of the recorders were quite sympathetic towards marginally latecomers (not only me) and would hold the clock for one or two minutes to save people being late (and losing pay), but not this one.

On one such day when I was racing to beat the clock, one of the other apprentices, Alan West, had just clocked on and was standing by the workshop entrance. When he saw me arriving in a hurry on my motorbike he grabbed the bike and said 'I've got your bike - go and clock on, you'll just make it'. I didn't - 7.31 again!

Worse was to follow. When I got outside, I saw that Alan had been unable to hold my motorbike upright and it had fallen against the cycle-rack. Disaster.

The lovely paintwork and chrome on the petrol tank had been damaged, and although most of it polished out with no dents, I was a very unhappy Teddy. Alan was also distraught; it wasn't really his fault. He had a much smaller bike, and was just not used to the extra weight - my bike weighed 420lbs.

Our two instructors for this period of our training were Tom Russell and Mr Searle. Mr Searle (I can't remember his first name, if I ever knew it) was in the standard instructors mould: average height, stocky and probably in his middle fifties. He was ex-Navy, smoked a lot, and was not of a very cheerful disposition, but this may have been because, as we had been told, he had health problems. A stomach injury sustained in wartime?

Tom Russell was something else. He believed he was the bee's knees, and had done everything and been everywhere. Some of his stories were unbelievable, and after a while we stopped listening - compared to Tom, Eddie Turner was on a truth drug! However what he did have was good technical knowledge and good instructional technique. He also had quite a cheerful personality. Again our craft training was supplemented by occasional lectures, these being held in the workshop.

One day we were given a lecture on magnetos (the component used to produce the spark for petrol engines), when one of the group discovered that if you wound the handle on the training aid and held on to its HT lead you got quite a sharp electric shock. So of course after that all of us, a group of six or more, had to hold hands while someone wound the handle as fast as they could so that we all got an electric shock. They say little things please little minds!

By this time we were starting to feel a little happier about our chosen careers. We had completed our first year of training, and the second year was less regimented, giving us, we felt, an element of freedom. Also we had the comedians to keep us happy. One of the comics was Pete Appleby. He was a naturally funny guy anyway, with a permanent smile on his face, and a nose that had been broken and now permanently looked left. His dry humour and original witticisms had us permanently amused. It wasn't just what he said that was funny, but the way that he did things.

I remember one cold winter morning Pete arrived for work a little late, seeming a bit agitated. As he took off his heavy motorcycle jacket to put on his overalls we could all see that the seat of his trousers had been ripped out, showing a shredded pair of underpants and a large expanse of muddy bum. He also had bad grazes on his bum cheeks, clearly visible through the damaged clothing, but it was such a funny sight that he got no sympathy at all. He had fallen off his motorbike on his way to work and skidded along the road on his backside. With only minor injuries to his bottom and his pride he was soon back to his old self, although he did say that it was bloody cold going home that night.

We now got occasional visits from some of the apprentices in the other intakes (entries), and when the opportunity arose they would call to catch up on all the latest happenings. This was when I first encountered Paul Kenyon ('Mad Yon'), a character who was MUCH larger than life. I still don't believe some of the things he did, although I was there!

Paul used to be very popular with the other apprentices, as he had supreme self confidence and a strong personality, and he would try anything. He also had an ever-changing supply of pornographic postcards, which were very much appreciated by us art experts. He had made friends with Tommy Nye, the 'dirty book' man in the factory, who loaned his books to Paul so that our education was improved even further; just the thing for rampant 17-year-olds!

One Monday morning Paul came to work raving about a girl he had met at the weekend. Lucy was a goddess, and Paul was in love. Unfortunately she had gone on holiday to Cornwall for a week. Paul could not stand the thought of a whole week without her, but he had no transport.

One of the senior group of lads who visited us on a regular basis was Cyril Moffat, and Cyril had a new moped. He had bought it about three weeks earlier as a cheap form of transport to work; a brand new shiny 'Norman Nippy'.

Now you might not think a 50cc moped is a suitable form of

transport to go to Cornwall on, but this didn't seem to worry Paul at all. The only problem that Paul had now was to persuade Cyril to lend him his (almost) brand new moped. It took nearly all week, but his constant pleas and cast-iron promises to respect the moped finally did the trick (no doubt some money changed hands as well), and Paul set off early on Friday morning to travel to the caravan park where his girlfriend was holidaying in Cornwall.

When Paul came in to work on the Monday morning he looked terrible. His eyes were badly bloodshot and so badly puffed up that they looked half closed. He was also in a foul mood. It took a couple of days to drag the story out of him. Roughly, this is what had happened.

He had left early on Friday morning, and the journey had been a complete nightmare. The ride down to Cornwall took 14 hours. This meant that apart from stopping twice at public toilets (we still had them then) for a quick wee, he remained all that time in a sitting position, arms stretched out in front, while the little machine beneath him was being thrashed mercilessly, the vibrations running back up his arms to his armpits. It had been like driving a pneumatic drill for two days. And he had no goggles, only sunglasses.

When at last he found the caravan site, it was completely dark. He was cold beyond description and could hardly stand after so long in the same riding position. He was also starving hungry and exhausted. He fell off the moped outside the girl's caravan, staggered up to the door and knocked. No answer - they were out! He almost cried with disappointment and fatigue.

Nearby was a large toilet block which he had noticed on the way in. He staggered over to it and found refuge in one of the cubicles. It was warm and dry, but unfortunately it meant he had to resume the sitting position he had been forced into all day long.

Paul slept, sort of, for a couple of hours, then decided to see if Lucy was back yet. He went back to the caravan and saw that a light was on. It was now 10.30. He knocked again - no answer. He knocked again, louder this time. After a couple of minutes the door was opened by a large man, with a not-too-amused expression on his face.

'What do you want?' he asked, in a less than friendly, almost aggressive manner.

'I'm Paul, Lucy's boyfriend, and I've come to see her' Paul explained pleadingly.

'Well you can just bugger off. I don't want you young boys hanging around my daughter, and if I see you again you'll be sorry. Now get lost!'

Paul was so exhausted and so disillusioned with the whole episode that he did not have the will to argue. He felt like crying. Not exactly the welcome he had been expecting. He was stuck in a caravan park, in Cornwall, late on a Friday night, knackered, cold, hungry and depressed. There was nothing else he could do but head back to the toilet cubicle again and get his head down.

He got a few hours' sleep from sheer exhaustion, and awoke with every muscle in his body screaming for mercy. He didn't bother to try to see Lucy again. Then it was back on the moped, throttle full open, to suffer the torturous miles back home. He recovered quite quickly from the ordeal, but various versions of this trip kept us lads amused for several weeks.

Now that we had motorbikes we had a choice of what to do in the dinner hour. If we had the inclination, and any money, we could go for a little ride. Alternatively, if the weather was OK, a walk around the dockyard would prove very interesting. The first time you see a ship being 'docked down' can be quite a sight. The ship is manoeuvred into dock, the caisson (the 'gate' which fits into the dock entrance) is placed into position and the water is pumped out. This must be done with the ship held in the correct location, supported at both sides and critically beneath the keel. It is quite a complicated procedure, and relies on a high level of co-ordination and teamwork. Likewise when large vessels entered through the lock gates (the main entrance from the river Medway into the Dockyard) into the main basins, it was an interesting spectacle, and you had to admire the skills required.

The full variety of workshops and activities were now opened up to us. There was a ropery, which still made all the Navy's rope (sisal and nylon) requirements, and did repayment work – making rope to be sold to industry.

The Sail and Colour loft made flags and bunting for many foreign governments as well as for the Navy. The laundry cleaned the coveralls for the workforce. The smithery, galvanising shop, covered slips, machine shops, the workshops for coppersmiths, plumbers, fitters, electricians, boilermakers, sailmakers, shipwrights, caulkers and riveters, patternmakers, joiners, painters, laggers, weapons, slingers - and no doubt some I've missed! There were vast storehouses, office blocks, yard services, MT garage, canteens and much more.

The other option at lunchtime, usually the preferred one, was to nip out on your bike. This brought pleasures twofold. First you could get away from your place of work for an hour's break, and secondly there was the sheer thrill of getting on the motorbike and blasting away in the fresh air, with no noise and fumes and no boring repetitive work.

Quite often we would visit the home of one my mates, Bob Webb. Bob and I had been to the Technical School together and had been mates since. We would call at his mum's, usually two or three of us, and she would lash us up with egg and chips – heaven. She was a really lovely lady, and far from complaining she really seemed to enjoy us visiting, albeit always at mealtimes!

Now that we were wealthy second-year apprentices we could afford to push the boat out, and we would sometimes seek out a favourite café for a quick cup of tea and do a bit of posing. One of these lunchtimes will stay in my memory forever. Our favourite haunt at that time was the Rainbow Café, near Luton Arches (Chatham). We would go there for reasons of bravado, as we were told that this was a place some of the local 'tabbies' (working girls) frequented.

We duly arrived, parked up, and sure enough one of the local girls, who with her sister was quite well known, was there sitting on a bar stool up at the counter. She didn't pay much attention to us as we went in other than perhaps to give a rather amused smile. We sat there for some time sipping our tea, smoking our tailor-made ciggies (well, it was a Friday) and trying to pretend we weren't trying to look up her very short skirt (this was before ultra-short skirts were fashionable). After we had been there for about 10 minutes, by which time we were getting rather hot under the collar, Jackie (that was the girl's name), got off the bar stool, presumably to leave. However, as she swung herself off the stool she pulled her handbag off the counter and it snagged on the back of the next stool. Her handbag opened and a flat tin spun through the air and landed in the middle of the floor with a clatter. The lid opened and three condoms rolled out in different directions. Jackie laughed, bent over and picked up the 'johnnies' to put them back into the tin, also reclaiming a brush and other items which had been thrown out of her bag. Two of us sat there with mouths open while the other went scarlet (he was good at this).

We were never quite sure if this incident was in fact an accident, or perhaps a very ingenious marketing ploy. If so it was wasted on us, as we could not have afforded her even if we had pooled our money. In fact we would have run like hell if 'it' had been offered.

Another café we used was in Canterbury Street, Gillingham, where I had an embarrassing experience one Friday lunchtime. I had bought a rather nice leather motorcycle jacket from one of the other apprentices, and customized it with a design in bifurcated rivets. Pleased with this, my next adornment to the jacket was a nice brass star, a copy of the BSA motif, which I had made at work and had engraved just like the real thing.

Now to the embarrassing bit. Having got myself seated in the café, rather proud of the bright shiny new star adorning the jacket, I was devastated to hear the biggest guy in the café, who looked like trouble, call out: 'Sheriff, hey Sheriff!' He was obviously enjoying the joke with his mates, and my embarrassment. Ignoring him didn't help. He persisted, so we didn't stop long on that day and the badge came off.

My timekeeping unfortunately had not improved. I was still late occasionally and this had resulted in warnings. Mostly this was for being just one or two minutes late, but in the eyes of my employer I was Late On Parade, and this was unacceptable. Eventually I was put on 'Prompt Muster'. This meant that no lateness at all was acceptable and that if I did not clock on before the allotted time, I would not be permitted to start work and would be sent home. This shock treatment worked to a certain extent, but I did slip up occasionally and lost a morning's pay. It was taking me a long time to see the bigger picture and to understand the rules of the game.

We did about eight months' training in the bottle shop, and then we were sent into the factory to start training on machine tools – lathes, milling machines, etc. It all started with training on centre lathes in a dedicated apprentices' training area in the centre of the factory. This was where we learned the basics of turning, facing and thread-cutting materials, and how to read, measure and manufacture items from engineering drawings. Again the training became very boring, because of the repetitive nature of the tasks, and one day it nearly ended in disaster.

We were preparing for our first machining test job, a repetitive activity which involved cutting a special multi-start thread. The workpiece was being driven by a mandrel, which as it rotated protruded above the headstock of the lathe. This job got very boring, and Dick Seamark, training on the lathe in front of me, had become almost mesmerized by the slow rotation of the machine.

He rested his forearm along the top of the lathe and was about to make himself comfortable, head on forearm, when the mandrel, spinning on the lathe, caught the sleeve of his overall and violently pulled his arm to the back of the machine. Fortunately his overalls had torn, otherwise the lathe would have tried to wind his arm around the workpiece.

He shouted out in alarm, and luckily his arm was released as the overalls tore. We had all been taught how to switch off the machines in an emergency, which one of the apprentices had done, but it would have been much too late if the overalls had not torn; Dick would have been badly injured, and possibly lost his arm. He was taken to the surgery for a check-up and treated for shock. The rest of us could well have been treated for shock as well. It certainly put a damper on proceedings for the rest of the day, and we were all extremely careful running our lathes for several days afterwards. Dick was only away from work for about a week, but he did come in to see us after a couple of days, arm in a sling, and his beaming smile returned.

Proudly, although somewhat gingerly, he showed us the

injured arm beneath the sling. The whole of the arm on the inside from armpit to wrist was a massive black bruise - ruptured blood vessels, we were told. We couldn't believe how lucky he was.

At about the same time as we started the lathe test job, the adjacent section, which was an engine testing area, began a series of test runs. This meant that the massive engines which were fitted into submarines were being run up less than 50 yards away. Can you imagine the noise they made? It was common knowledge that these engines could be heard running, if the wind was in a favourable direction, as far away as Bluebell Hill five miles away. It should also be explained that we were not issued with ear defenders, as health and safety was very basic at that time.

The other major problem created by these engines was the vibration they caused. We were trying to do precision machining work and take exact measurements with a massive engine thumping away alongside of us! I remember complaining to my family, after riding home from work on my bike, that I could still hear the noise of these engines thumping away in my ears for at least an hour after I got home.

CHAPTER 3

YEAR THREE:
IN PRODUCTION

Having successfully completed our test jobs at the end of our training on the lathes, we were all sent out to work, for the first time as individuals, under the supervision of 'skippers' in the production sections of the factory, to further improve on our basic skills.

I was sent to the milling section. My skipper, Laurie, was a small man, originally from Egypt, who spoke fairly good English but was generally very quiet and only spoke to answer. But he was a good skipper, and explained very well how to operate the machine and what to do.

It should probably be explained at this point that the majority of craftsmen were not keen to take on apprentices. There were several reasons for this. The dockyard pay scheme included provision to earn extra money by way of a bonus scheme (known colloquially as 'ticket'); the faster you completed the job to the required standard, the more money you earned. Obviously when you were training an apprentice it slowed you down, even if he was interested and able, so although you as craftsman would receive a training allowance, which I think at this time it was about £1 per week, you might in fact lose money because of the longer time it took to do your job.

The other drawback with training an apprentice of course was that they would often get bored very quickly, and if their mates came to visit they usually got into mischief. So the skipper had to be aware of what 'the lad' was up to, all of the time.

The consequence of this was that some of the skippers had very little interest in training the lads. In fact it was often the less competent fitters who took on an apprentice, purely to get the extra £1 a week. This of course is the same in every walk of life, in terms of fitters and apprentices; there are the good, the not-so-good and the indifferent.

I can only remember one job I had on the milling machines, which was to machine the hexagonal heads on some special bolts. I probably remember this as it was the first job I worked on in the bonus scheme (ticket). Laurie had given me this job to do on my own and I loved it. I worked like stink on that job, getting it finished in very good time, and about three weeks later the bonus pay, about £5, came through: an extra week's money. I was over the moon.

Funny also how you remember details. Laurie used to eat garlic by the shedload every lunchtime, and you had to keep clear in the afternoon because his breath was 'radioactive'.

The training period on this section soon passed and it was time to move on again. My next training period would be at the other end of the factory on section 34, Valves and Auxiliaries.

Two of us apprentices were sent to this section, me and Paddy Hargan. We were allocated to skippers; mine was Dick Marsh and Paddy was to work with Jack Hayter. This worked very well because Dick and Jack were great mates and so were Paddy and I. We had plenty of interesting work to keep us occupied, so the days were busy but enjoyable.

Jack was about 60 at this time, average height, quite slim, short grey hair (although mostly bald), and very thick 'Mr Magoo' type glasses. He had a wicked sense of humour and a seemingly endless repertoire of profound and usually comical expressions. One of his favourites, if he caught us on a break was 'Procrastination is the thief of time'.

The other nugget that he often offered Paddy was 'if you're going courting in the countryside boy, always make sure you know where to find a five-bar gate'. The first time he offered this advice, Paddy and I decided that we needed more information. 'Well' said Jack, 'in the country a five-bar gate is what is known as an adjustable fanny. If you are out with a short girl you sit her on the top bar when you do it, and the tall girls go on the bottom' He would then chuckle to himself as if he was reminiscing, shoulders bouncing up and down as he enjoyed the moment.

Dick was shorter and quite tubby. Usually a cheerful sort, you could see him as a favourite uncle. He was more of a listener than a talker, and you could often see his shoulders moving gently as he giggled quietly at one of Jack's pearls of wisdom. He was a pipe smoker and when he used to flash up this fearsome beast, usually at break times, he would completely disappear in a blanket of foul-smelling smoke, like some magician's stage act. A very kind man, he was also very proud of his trade skills and pleased to pass on his expertise to his apprentice 'wards'.

Both Jack and Dick used to pull our legs concerning our attempted successes with the opposite sex, requesting blow-by-blow reports the following morning. Both of us had casual, non-regular girlfriends at this time, so there was very little to report, but we both had vivid imaginations. I'm sure they realized that most of our reports owed more than a little to poetic licence.

When the valves we had refitted were finished they would be sent to an adjacent section to be tested. The item to be tested was bolted down on to a water pressure test rig and subjected to the required pressure (at least the same as that it would be working at); this was very interesting, as you could see immediately the results of your recent efforts.

After approximately four months we had refitted most types of valves that were fitted in the warships, and it was time to move to the next training section. The next section I was sent to was Auxiliary Equipments, or as I soon rechristened it, 'Land of the Dead'. Unfortunately this section had been run down to such an extent that it was now just a parking spot for the unfortunates. My skipper, one of the few on the section who was still alive, was a small North Country guy named Lou Rainer. He did his best to look after me, but the truth of the matter was that we had no work to do. If you have ever been in a situation where you have no work but have to pretend to be busy when a supervisor is about, you will understand that it is (a) hard work, and (b) soul destroying.

Others on the section were really scary. The guy who 'worked' nearest to me, on the next bench, was called Matthew Hannah, and he was obviously unwell. He was always at work by the time I got there (nothing unusual in that, so was everybody else) but he would be sitting next to a radiator resting his head on his fearnought (a seaman's jacket similar to a duffle coat) and seemed to be half asleep. He would stay like that for the rest of the day. When I asked Lou what was wrong with Matthew he would just say that he had some big problems, and was not well. To be honest Matthew used to scare me rigid, his eyes always looked haunted.

He certainly was not well. Unfortunately, while I was on this section, Matthew committed suicide. Apparently he went home one night and gassed himself. As was the custom then, his tools were sold off at work with the proceeds going to the widow or family. I still have some of his tools today, engraved with his initials. What made this situation even worse was that a few years later his son did exactly the same thing!

One of the other fitters on this section was even stranger. He was nicknamed 'blueskin' (I know not why and I certainly did not ask). The story was that he had at one time been the top diesel engine fitter in the dockyard. Some time before I had joined this section his wife had died and this had triggered off his strange behaviour. He was a large man, of scruffy appearance with a full head of grey hair, and I would estimate that he was in his late sixties.

It was his going-home ritual that we found odd. About half an hour before clocking-off time he would get his cup from a shelf in the centre of the section, and with a token attempt to shelter himself he would get his cock out and piss into it. He would take a good look at the results, then remove his dentures and give them a good flush in the urine. Satisfied that they were now properly cleaned, he would pop them back into his mouth. He would then disappear to change out of his overalls, prior to the outmuster. When he returned to the section he would be wearing a pair of women's shoes, not high heels but with a heel, and as he tottered about, not too elegantly, we could see that he had put stockings on as well. He then would complete his home-going preparations by putting on his lipstick!

It would not be unfair to say that the silly bugger was an ugly old so-and-so anyway, with a deeply craggy face, and when this lipstick was applied so very badly, a lot of it around his nose, he looked like Norman Bates' mother in *Psycho*.

This experience was quite frightening at first to a fairly green lad, but after the initial shock it left me with a feeling of great sadness that this once great old boy had become such a lost and tortured soul.

This was not a happy section; I learned little and afterwards referred to it as the 'home of the bewildered'. One consolation was that as we had little work to do, a blind eye was turned when we went missing for fifteen minutes or so to visit our mates on the other sections. There was also the possibility that this gave us a chance to find out what the other sections' work entailed, and where the various operations were carried out. One of the most popular visits was to see Tommy Nye (the dirty book man) on the Turret lathes section. His vast collection of porno magazines, postcards and books were an exciting revelation to us young apprentices. Usually somewhere on the scene Paul Kenyon would be found bartering or exchanging the latest masterpieces with Tom. Both connoisseurs, they would gladly explain the finer points!

It was at this time that we apprentices learned the details of Paul's recent absence from work from a friend of his, 'Spud' Hudson. Paul had been absent for two weeks, and no one, even the instructors, seemed to know why. Gradually the story came out, although Spud had been sworn to secrecy.

Paul had had (another) row with his parents on the Friday night before his absence, and decided to leave home. As usual it was about the lack of money available to him, and therefore his inability to lead the lifestyle that he thought he was entitled to. Paul's parents were comparatively wealthy. Dad was an executive with BT and Mum had at least a couple of hairdressing shops, but they had decided that Paul should make his own way in life, so that he would appreciate the value of money.

It suited both parties that Paul should help out, on a paid basis, by collecting the week's takings from his mother's hairdressing shops on a Friday night. This particular Friday night apparently he had said 'sod it' and headed off to London in Mum's smart Jaguar with the week's takings from the two shops. On the Saturday afternoon Spud, Paul's mate, had a visit from him, with an invitation to spend the night on the town in London, mostly all paid. They went to Paul's local pub, then on to a nightclub.

When they entered the nightclub, two of the hostesses hurried over to greet Paul with a 'Hi Paul' and kisses. These girls impressed Spud; they were gorgeous, smartly dressed and immaculately made up. It all seemed very sophisticated. They joined the boys for the rest of the evening, and of course they both drank champagne. Paul didn't seem to mind, as he obviously did not have a care in the world. It was early morning when three of them made their way by taxi, back to Paul's very nice hotel. Paul's companion was to spend the night with him. The other girl had made her excuses, much to Spud's relief, shortly before they had left the nightclub.

Spud had had a great time, which of course was the object of the exercise, and when Paul took him back home on Sunday morning he could not help feeling somewhat jealous of the lifestyle Paul had to look forward to. But he was sworn not to reveal Paul's whereabouts to his parents, or to anyone else for that matter.

How quickly things can change. When Spud got the next visit from Paul on the following Saturday morning, something was obviously very wrong. Paul was not as bouncy as usual, and looking slightly dishevelled. At the earliest opportunity Paul pulled him to one side and asked 'Got anything to eat handy?' Spud's mum rustled up beans on toast in short time, and Paul quickly put it away.

The significance did not sink in at this point. Spud again accompanied Paul up to London, but it was very different this time. He was now living in a squalid bedsit, sparsely furnished and freezing cold. On entering, Paul's opener was 'Have you got two bob for the meter, Spud?'

It was obvious that the money had all gone, with not even enough for little luxuries like food and heating. What a transformation, in just a week.

They had a walk around the local area, which wasn't very pleasant, and Paul borrowed ten shillings from Spud, which he invested in bread rolls and fillings. Paul gradually explained that he had had very little food all that week. It was, he said, only because he had befriended a couple of schoolgirls that he had managed to survive the week.

Paul had been leaving the digs early on Thursday morning when the two girls had walked past and given him the eye. Never one to miss an opportunity, he turned on his best chat-up lines. The girls were both probably both aged about fifteen, well developed, and looked to be carrying lunchbags. Neither of them seemed to be in a hurry to get to school.

Paul had explained that due to temporary, unfortunate circumstances he had run out of food and money, and asked them for food. 'What's in it for us?' the cheeky one had asked. Paul had said, not really joking 'You can have my body'. After much giggling the cheeky one said that suited her just fine, providing that her mate could watch.

Paul took them into his digs, and gave Cheeky a really good tubbing, which she made it very clear that she enjoyed, being very vocal with continuous encouragement like "That's it! Wonderful! Keep going Paul, Don't stop!', as if he needed any encouragement. He had been turned on as soon as he saw that she was wearing navy blue knickers, something which he adored. All through the action, Cheeky's mate was getting more and more agitated, and at the end of the proceedings she disappeared into the next room for about five minutes, presumably to frig herself stupid. She looked happier when she came back.

Paul had himself a decent meal for a change, and both sets of sandwiches were very nice, or perhaps it was just that he was so hungry. The next day it was role reversal. The girls arrived early. Cheeky did the watching, offering lots of encouragement and advice, while her mate was even better. Perhaps this was due to a full day's anticipation, knowing that she was soon due a really powerful sex session, or perhaps she was like that anyway; they say you have to watch the quiet ones.

Paul certainly got more than he bargained for. It was the best and most uninhibited sex he had ever had, and I doubt if even he could have maintained this standard of performance for very long.

That did not matter, because the need would not arise. Paul had already decided that he would eat humble pie, go home and ask his parents to forgive and forget. There was another reason why he wanted to leave his digs. Paul had not used condoms in his sessions with the schoolgirls, and had given them the full flood of love-juice every time. He was conscious that this might well have serious repercussions in a few months' time, and did not want to be around to discuss the merits of unprotected sex with underage schoolgirls, with their parents and/or the police.

So it was home again to face the parents' wrath, but even this couldn't be straightforward for Paul. He got into Mum's Jag and set off for home, near Sittingbourne. All was fairly routine until he got to Blackheath. Travelling along the A2 he was overtaken by an American sports car, and as it passed alongside the driver looked at Paul, smiled and waved.

This was like a red rag to a bull. The two cars raced each other all the way along the A2 and through the Medway Towns at high speeds, overtaking in dangerous situations. Paul beat the sports car away from the traffic lights at the Luton Arches and gunned the Jag up Chatham Hill, doing about 70 miles an hour. Overtaking on the white line, he got halfway up the hill to where the road narrows when he met a small car, an Austin A35, travelling down the hill. The cars clipped each other and the A35 spun around and ended up facing in the opposite direction. Disaster.

By coincidence, and the worst possible luck, a young off-duty police officer was at the bus stop where the impact occurred. He must have thought that was his moment, and pounced. Unfortunately Paul was not the typical driver who had transgressed, and he answered the officer's requests for details by saying 'Don't let's make a federal case out of it John'. This did not go down too well in court, and Paul was banned for three years.

Paul returned home and ultimately was forgiven for his little escapade. He returned to work the following Monday and made his peace with the personnel office. It took us several weeks to wheedle out most of these sordid details piece by piece.

CHAPTER 4

YEAR FOUR:
WORKING AFLOAT

The last part of our apprenticeship would end the third year of our training. When we started the fourth year, my friend Bernard Hargan (Paddy) did not come to work afloat with us but was transferred to the MPBW (Ministry of Public Buildings and Works) instead. I am not sure if this was a matter of choice, luck of the draw, or because he was Irish. It must be remembered that the 'troubles' were ongoing at this time. He was transferred to the workshop just inside Pembroke Gate.

Paddy worked in the fitters' area, where he soon made good friends with Freddie Turner from the adjacent blacksmiths' section. The lads in this workshop were always looking to play jokes on unsuspecting passers-by, and I remember two of these from first-hand experience.

One prank was to superglue pins (standard paper pins), point upwards and at an angle, to the pavement outside the workshop. The lads would then loiter outside the shop until some poor unsuspecting fool (me on one occasion), stepped on to one of the pins. Your own weight would often drive the pin right through your shoe and into the foot. It didn't cause any major injury, just a very nasty shock, and it was hilarious to watch, no doubt.

The other little trick they often played was to get a small cardboard box, ideally say 4-6 inches square, fill it with lead pellets and leave it in the centre of the path outside of the workshop. As the road outside led to the main offices it would not be long before some young lad who fancied himself as a footballer would give the little box a hearty kick. The box would hardly move, but it sure gave the foot a nasty jolt!

I like to think these pranks were not meant to injure anyone, and they didn't, as far as I know. Although there were lots of girls and women who used this road, they were not stupid enough to go around kicking little boxes! We apprentices found this workshop was very useful if we needed a 'private' welding job done, or motorcycle footrests straightened in their forge.

To start my fourth year of training I was allocated to the Fitters Afloat 3 (FA3) and sent to work at 46 shop. This was a largish workshop located at the head of No. 4 Dock, in the south area of the dockyard. The workshop was split into two halves. The front half was the workshop proper, with large double doors for equipment access, and inside against the perimeter walls were attached large workbenches with heavy duty vices. The rear of the building was the 'welfare' area, with a couple of large tables, a few chairs and a large boiler for tea making at break times. There were a few very old cast iron radiators scattered around the place, but they had little effect, and the workshop was usually very cold. Well, it wouldn't do to make it too cosy, would it? In the corner of the back section of the workshop there was a small office, which was for use by the chargeman (first line supervisor).

There were several apprentices despatched to 46 shop at this time; Mick Moad, Paul Kenyon, Aubrey Snipe, Clive Akers and me, so I was expecting some lively company over the next few months, and was not disappointed. Some older apprentices were already there, including Ron Walters, John Smith, Herbie Anders and Roy Mulford.

I was allocated to work with a skipper called Charlie Flogdale, another of the larger-than-life characters who were almost commonplace in the dockyard at that time. Charlie was of average height, had a good head of wavy hair and always looked as if he had just shaved. He was known as the 'Gentleman Fitter' by some of his bitter companions, mainly because of his tendency to wear gloves (he hated getting his hands dirty), and to try to keep himself as clean as possible. I wouldn't say Charlie was scared of hard work, but as he himself would say, he had tried it once and didn't like it!

Charlie had a very useful backup income selling TVs and watches. When we had little work we would walk around the southern end of the dockyard and invariably bump into someone Charlie knew. In no time at all he would ask if they wanted a marvellous new watch and pull up his sleeve to display five or six gleaming beauties. If they were interested, the haggling would start, but Charlie didn't give much away.

One of Charlie's favourite walks was to see an old friend of his named Jack Rolf. Jack 'lived' in a small hut on the sea wall near no. 7 Slip; we would visit quite often as it was usually nice and warm, and there was the occasional cup of tea thrown in. Once or twice when we got back to 46 shop the chargeman was waiting for us demanding an explanation as to where we had been. Charlie always claimed that we had been to the stores in search of some 'backnuts', so this then became our code for a walk to see Jack. We did do some work, though.

The first ship we went on, a coastal minesweeper, was a major disappointment. As we were preparing to do some maintenance and repair on its diesel generators, we learned that there had apparently been a cock-up somewhere and these diesels were under contract for repairs by the manufacturer, so we were told not to touch them. Charlie was not best pleased. He had a blazing row (one of many) with the chargeman, who was in any event unable to alter the situation. I'm not sure this helped us to get any good jobs for several weeks afterwards.

Work was fairly patchy, until one day a Lister truck and trailer pulled into the workshop piled high with recently galvanized large bore pipes. The chargeman allocated the job to Mick Moad and me. We were to face up the flanges and install the new pipes into the submarine now in No. 4 Dock. This seemed to be a never-ending job, for as soon as we made progress with this huge mound of pipes another load would be delivered. This was another of those jobs which, although quite important, was very boring. Eventually we had sufficient pipes prepared for installation back into the submarine.

Some of these pipes had to fitted into the submarine's compensation tanks, a job from hell! These large tanks are fitted to the sides of the sub outside the pressure hull. They are normally full of fuel oil, water or a mix of both. Even when they have been emptied and cleaned, for work to be done inside they stink to high heaven as a heavy residue of the oil (which is like a dark mustard slime and stinks of sulphur) cannot be completely removed, and the ventilation is inadequate.

The only entrance or exit from these tanks is via a manhole cover, oval in shape and approximately 18' (less than 50 cm) at its largest point. After half an hour in these tanks you had to get out into the fresh air to clear your head. This in itself was a difficult exercise, almost as if the submarine was giving birth! A couple of wandering leads were all the light available, and these were only permitted once the tanks had been subject to a 'gas free' test, to ensure that all the explosive gases inside the tanks had been extracted.

When we came out of these tanks our coveralls were almost completely covered with this filthy slime, and they would need changing after one day's work. Some of the other pipes were for deck fittings, so we finished the tank work as soon as possible to start these.

Mick Moad and I were still working as a pair. One particularly sunny morning we were working up on the deck and Mick was telling me all about the great film he had seen the previous night, *Mutiny on the Bounty*. He enjoyed the film but was particularly impressed when he read that during the shooting Marlon Brando had taken a shine to one of the leading ladies (a Tahitian beauty), and disappeared into the jungle with her for 'dirty dirties' lasting for several weeks!

We were on deck in the sunshine, filing our flanges, but Mick was obviously unhappy about something. Suddenly he asked 'How many weeks' leave do we get in the year?' Slightly puzzled, I replied 'Two weeks Mick, you know that'.

All quiet. Then he said, more to himself than to me, 'That means I'll have to work for fifty weeks to get two weeks off'. Then he went on 'That means I will have to work for a hundred years to get two years off! Sod that, I'm off to throw a few bolts at the jellyfish.' (At the head of the dock was the caisson and the sea wall ran alongside; often when we walked along here we could see jellyfish and the odd eel.) So off he went, and that's what he did. We didn't see him any more that day.

Some of the other characters working at 46 shop were quite strange in their own right. One of the senior fitters, Bill, must have been in his middle sixties and had health problems. He also had a thing about fire. Often when you were filing away at one end of a long pipe, you could suddenly smell smoke, and looking at the other end you would see Bill poking a ball of smouldering rag into the pipe end and chuckling to his heart's content. This wasn't the only place he left his 'toys', for he would put them under your seat or anywhere else as the occasion arose. Pyromaniac or what?

Another oddball was Ambrose. He was short and fat and usually quiet until going-home time. He would then make a big display of stripping off his coveralls and making sure his trousers were pulled down to his knees, revealing a pair of bright red silk underpants. He would strut around in his little area, posing and clutching his genitals, asking any apprentices present 'Do you want some of this? This is the real stuff'. We all thought this was highly amusing for the first week, but it soon became boring, as the routine was never varied. All the same we all made sure that we weren't caught alone with him in one of the confined spaces on board ship, just in case he really was a queer.

One Friday payday Charlie, my skipper, was expecting to be paid some allowances for working in filthy conditions (obnoxious conditions money). The amount would vary depending on how many hours you worked in those conditions but would usually be about £1. The other fitters on the gang drew their money and received the normal £1, but Charlie was paid just 1s 3d, and he was not amused. He stormed into the chargeman's office and demanded an explanation. He was told that as he had spent so little time on the ship, this was all he was due. He told the chargeman that the only people who received any extra money were his favourites, and he could poke his 1s 3d up his arse! With that he threw his pay packet across the workshop, saying 'One and three for working all of the week in all that shit, you must be joking, bloody good job I'm going out tonight to sell a telly!'

I didn't learn a lot while I was working with Charlie, well not about engineering skills, anyway.

Some of the other apprentices in 46 shop were working for

the Weapons Section rather than for 'our' engine room party, and although we all mingled at dinnertimes etc. we had different supervisors. The chargehand for the weapons team was 'Sarge' Patman. John Patman was an excitable sort of guy at the best of times and could change his moods quite dramatically, especially if the subject of the war came up. One day at afternoon tea break, Sarge was talking to a group of lads across the workshop from us and as usual Paul Kenyon was twittering away taking the piss in the background. Sarge heard most of the comments and ignored them, until Paul said something like 'I bet you were a real hero in the war, Sarge, fighting all those Jerries'.

Sarge snapped. Face scarlet, eyes bulging, he grabbed a broom and shoved it handle-first into Paul's stomach. 'Yes!' yelled Sarge, 'and this is how we used to bayonet the bastards!' With this he thrust the broom handle at Paul again and again until he was backed up against the far wall. Paul went white, and I'm sure he thought that his time had come. However Sarge gave him a couple more good digs with the broom handle, and then, muttering 'Yes, that's the way we did it', he stormed off. Paul was quiet and very selective with his piss taking for the rest of the day!

The work supply was very patchy, and without any work to do we apprentices soon got bored. One day, for some reason or other, we decided to re-enact the burial-at-sea ritual, the burial party consisting mainly of Mick Moad, Paul Kenyon and me. Mick and I laid Paul on the large mess table, crossed his hands, put large washers over his eyes and draped a large union jack (I don't know where we got that from) over him. We said a few solemn words and then lifted one end of the table very, very slowly so that Paul slid down onto the floor. One of the other apprentices was at the same time doing a very good impersonation of a bosun's whistle, just like the real thing. We had not seen the chargeman approaching; as Paul slid on to the floor and we all collapsed laughing, we noticed him standing in the doorway with a totally bewildered expression on his face. We tidied up hurriedly, expecting a major bollocking, but the chargeman never mentioned the escapade. I did notice that after that he often looked at us as if he was optimistically searching for a glimmer of sanity.

Funny how some silly things remain in our memories. One such incident was when one of the fitters had unfortunately died and his tools were going to be sold off, proceeds to the widow. Instead of pricing and selling the toolbox contents individually, which was the traditional way of doing things, it was decided to ask for bids for the complete toolbox, locked up and contents unseen. Most of us put in bids, as was the custom, but one of the lads who had more money than the rest of us put in a high bid and made sure that we knew about it. In fact he gloated. He duly won the prize, and tried to open the toolbox without us seeing. Some chance.

The toolbox was almost full of wooden file handles, worth only a few pence each, and a few worn and inexpensive tools. Did we ever give him a hard time! 'This is the guy that bought a toolbox full of file handles, ha ha ha!' Was the expression 'buying a pig in a poke' ever better demonstrated?

Mick Moad and Paul Kenyon had become great pals, and decided that they would go to Spain for their week's holiday. I think Mick had a somewhat calming influence on Paul, so at least they did not get into any major trouble. However Mick told us about one episode which had us in stitches.

Mick had left Paul in a bar on this night and gone back to the hotel to catch up on some sleep. He was rudely awakened at about 2 am by loud mutterings and the sound of water running in the bedroom's wash basin. This persisted, so in spite of Mick's attempts to ignore the interruption to his sleep, he raised himself up on one elbow to see what was happening. Paul had his cock in the wash basin, half full of water and the tap running. He was scrubbing away at his organ with Mick's nailbrush.

'What are you doing?' Mick asked.

'Well, that scrubber smelt pretty horrible, and she looked a bit too pleased after I had turked her' he said. 'You can't be too careful, I don't want to go home with VD.'

Mick didn't want his nailbrush back.

Our social lives had picked up a little now, as we had a little money to spend and we had found youth clubs to go to most nights of the week. These were simple pleasures - a game of table tennis, play a few records and meet up with your friends. Of course the major incentive was that you might meet some girls. The clubs we looked forward to most were Tuesday night, above the Co-op in Rainham High Street, Friday at the Central Hall in Chatham and Saturday in the school hall Rainham. Buddy Holly, Eddie Cochrane and Elvis were played of course. Skin-tight jeans and Old Spice aftershave. Happy days.

It was time to change sections again, and this time I was sent to the Crane Repair Section, on the Yard Services Department. Before you were allowed to start work you were interviewed by the Foreman, and the interview went something like this:

Foreman: 'Are you afraid of working at heights?'

Me: 'I don't know Sir, I haven't done it, but I can't say that I am keen.'

Foreman: 'Well, try it for a couple of weeks, and if you're still worried after that time, come back to see me again'.

This was all standard stuff. Experience had shown that after two weeks most people would be acclimatized to working at heights and although at that stage it was still a little daunting, it did not continue to terrify.

The workshop, to the south of no. 7 slip, was an old converted storehouse where slings and crane wire ropes were kept. It was a single-skinned building with a very high roof space, poor lighting and no heating (the chargeman's office at the far end did have a small electric heater).

The gang comprised the chargeman, Tom Hill, and fitters Fred Choke, Mick Kenny, Alan Howland and Ernie Hayes. Dave Else was the skilled labourer, and there were two apprentices, Dave Campbell (Panda) and myself. There were probably others who I cannot remember.

This 'workshop' was cold, damp and miserable and we ate our dinner sitting huddled on our toolboxes. I was allocated to work with Fred Choke as my skipper. Fred was very smart, probably because he was ex-Army. He always had nicely polished boots and a miserable expression on his face. However we got on reasonably well and were employed on repairing the overhead travelling cranes in the dockyard workshops. All was fine and dandy until, after I had been there about three weeks, my mates came home on leave (one was in the Air Force, the other in the Navy), and we went out on a bender on the Friday night. I excelled myself that night and at last showed my mates that I could drink as well as they could. We ended up in the Viscount Hardinge in Gillingham for our eighth pint!

I had to work overtime the following morning, and for some reason I didn't feel very well. After about an hour at work, feeling like a rabbit having a poop, I crept off and hid in one of the nearby railway trucks to try to get my head down and recover. I could not rest, as it was so bloody cold. I still felt sick, and when I started to doze off I had a recurring nightmare that I had fallen asleep, the train had moved and I would wake up in Portsmouth. I went back to the workshop, still feeling ill, at about 11.45.

Fred was not amused. On Monday I was transferred - no sense of humour there. I went to the other (internal) section, working on dockside cranes. This was in my opinion dangerous work. Climbing up vertical ladders at the side of the cranes was no picnic at any time, but when the ladders were wet or icy and it was blowing hard, it was even less so. It was always worse coming down. The horrible bit was to stand at the top of the ladder, turn backwards and try to find the first rung of the ladder with your foot. And of course we did not climb the ladder empty handed; you always had a bag of tools in one hand, and usually a large grease gun slung over your shoulder.

I remember the first time I went up a crane jib with one of the fitters, Mick Kenny, and halfway up the jib he stopped and asked me if I wanted to grease the bearing halfway up or do the one at the top. I said that I would do the one halfway up, but when he pointed to it I asked 'where's the ladder?' (to access the bearing in the middle of the jib). Mick laughed and said that what was required was to climb across the jib itself to access the bearing. Sod that. I changed my mind and plumped for the bearing at the top - at least I had something to hang on to!

We got extra money for working at heights. It wasn't much but we certainly earned it.

Tom Hill, the chargeman, was Welsh, and a miserable bastard. This probably wasn't all his fault as at that time he was also the Mayor of Chatham, and the word was that after particularly hard nights doing his civic duty he could be a little liverish in the mornings.

My 'tour of duty' on this section was in midwinter, and our best efforts to heat up the workshop were by lighting a fire in a modified five-gallon oil drum in the centre of the workshop. This was commonplace in the older workshops. The apprentice's job last thing before going home was to go and pinch some coal from one of the many steam cranes in the area for the next morning's fire. One very cold day most of us were reluctant to leave the comparative warmth of the workshop, and Tom Hill was obviously in a bad mood. When he came out of his office shortly after start time, he told us to get out and on the job, glared around at all and sundry and returned to his office. Most of us stirred, pulled on our heavy fearnought jackets and prepared to leave. Incidentally these fearnought jackets were great at keeping out the cold, as they were manufactured from a duffel coat or blanket type of material, but they were rubbish when they got wet, as they just soaked up the water and were very difficult to get dry again.

Dave, the other apprentice on the gang, was heating a tin of soup on the fire and was a little behind the rest of us with his preparations to leave. Within a few minutes Tom came out of his office again, in an obvious rage, and glared at the apprentice. 'I told you to get out and start work!' he shouted, and gave the tin of soup a hearty kick. It ended up halfway down the workshop, leaving a trail of tomato in its wake. Yes, Tom could have his moments.

He upset my skipper, Alan Howland, and me one day. We had just got to work and it had started to snow really hard. The job we were working on was a steam rail gauge crane at the dockyard main locks entrance, at the farthest end of the yard. We knew the dockyard bus service was due to pass the workshop within the next fifteen minutes or so, which meant that we could wait fifteen minutes in comparative warmth, catch the bus and still arrive at our workplace at the same time or earlier than if we had walked. When we suggested this to Tom he went mad and told us to get out and start walking. This meant we walked the two miles to the locks where we were to work in four inches of snow, which was coming over the top of our boots, in a bitterly cold snow storm.

Well, we did just that. We had little choice. But by the time we had got to the crane we were working on and swept most of the snow off, it was time to head back to the workshop for the mid-morning tea break!

In spite of the fact that it was hard, cold, and sometimes quite dangerous on this section I enjoyed this period of my apprenticeship, and thinking of it still makes me smile.

Our social lives had by now improved a great deal, as we were now earning slightly above desperation wages, and we all had girlfriends. One of my close mates, Dave 'Panda' Campbell, was a good-looking swine who could charm the birds from the trees. He used to travel home to Dover at the weekends and we could not wait until Monday morning when he would relay all the sordid details of his fantastic weekends.

There were always dances, and some quite well-known bands played at the Strand Palais (Deal), Leas Cliff Halls (Folkestone) or the Town Hall in Dover. I'm sure some of the escapades he related to us were to say the least highly exaggerated, and of course they became even more so as they were retold among us apprentices. If he had a fight involving two of his mates and himself against three soldiers, by the time the story had been told a few times it became Dave and two of his mates against ten marine commandos, yet Dave's side nearly always won.

One of the classic interludes was when on one Monday morning Dave came to work almost unable to walk. He was creeping about like an old man of eighty. Unusually, we had some difficulty prising information about the events which had led up to this situation from him, but not for long.

It seemed Dave and mates had been to the local 'hop' and he had ended up having the last few dances with one of the local beauties. He had secured a promise that he could walk her home. They had of course stopped halfway, and he had tried his best make her go all the way. After much heaving and grunting she had offered to 'help him out', as he had persistently put her hand on his rampant penis. She offered the 'hand shandy' alternative to full sex. Dave said that she was terrific and was giving him the wank of a lifetime when the large dress ring she was wearing turned around on her finger and began cutting into the head of his cock on each downward stroke. He was in agony, but his pained mutterings were only mistaken for indications of ecstasy.

Dave said 'It hurt like hell, but I could not tell her to stop'. Well, it certainly made us stop. We were helpless with laughter, and by the time he got to the punchline we were paralytic.

Dave really made the most of the fact that he had to stay in Medway all the week for work and then travel home to Dover at weekends, as this gave him the chance to have a girlfriend at each end. When he first started courting his long-term girlfriend at Dover he had an older girlfriend who worked in a hotel in Rochester. She would arrange for him to stay overnight at this hotel when the opportunity arose. I think he thought he had won the pools, and boy were we all jealous! Mind you it did cause him some major problems at the later stages, trying to keep the two of them unknown to each other, and the usual difficulties associated with this kind of arrangement.

Paddy and I had also got ourselves girlfriends by this time. Paddy had just started courting a girl called Barbara Kember who was one of the regulars at a local youth club, and lived fairly near to me in Rainham. Paddy used to cycle up to my house and leave his bike there. We would go out for the evening and when we returned he would cycle home. I don't think his first date was a roaring success, as when he came back to collect his bike he had a worried look on his face.

'What's up with you?' I asked. He was reluctant to answer, but eventually he looked me in the eye and asked: 'Which way do you snog, Nige?' I was at first worried, then baffled.

'What do you mean?' I ventured.

'Well,' he said, 'When I went to kiss her goodnight she went like this'. He cocked his head to one side, putting on a passable impression of a pout. 'I did the same, but our noses clashed and she ended up with a nosebleed!'

In spite of the severity of his plight I could not answer - I was helpless with the giggles. I think he sorted out that particular problem in quick time, and without my help.

At that time he must have been very fond of the name Barbara, as he had been seeing another one, Barbara Webb, for a few dates some time previously. Sadly, at about this time she was killed when she fell from a carnival float while parading as the Upchurch Carnival Queen. Although Paddy had not been courting her for long, it really upset him.

For my part I was courting a girl called Larry. I had been out with her for a few months the year previously when she had lived in Strood, but for some reason it had petered out, although we kept in touch.

We got back together again after I had been on a night out with the boys. We had been to several pubs in Chatham, and after closing time my nephew Richard (Dood) and I decided that we would walk home via Bob Webb's home in Luton. After we left Bob it occurred to me that Larry lived just around the corner and it would be rude not to visit, wouldn't it?

So we knocked. Larry and her mum were still both up and happy to let us in. Larry's mum was very tolerant and even seemed slightly amused to see us, and she offered us a cup of tea. Larry discovered that they had run out of milk, so to cut a long story short, Larry and I headed off to a vending machine in the next street. We got the carton of milk and nearly made it all the way back to her house, but unfortunately next to her house was a dark alley. We had a little peck at the entrance and that lit the blue touchpaper. We almost fell into the alley and went straight into a frantic snogging session.

Larry was doing her best to hold on to the milk, but it was becoming very difficult, and in the end she dropped it. I was randy as hell. Fired up with a belly full of beer, which always did it for me, I was as hard as a stone goat. I had three fingers inside Larry, and she was making progressively louder cooing noises: I was about to go for greatest shag of all time when the back door, just the other side of the fence, opened and Larry's mum came out, talking to herself.

Most of the alley was illuminated. That killed the moment. We went in and had our cup of tea, but I was never sure if my dirty fingers had made the milk smell funny, or if I had managed to get the smile off my face.

I was courting Larry for some months afterwards. She was really considerate. She was never content to send me home with a goodnight kiss but always insisted on giving me a good wank to 'make sure I would behave myself until I saw her again'. Who was I to argue?

I was now nearing the end of my fourth year of apprenticeship. The last section I was sent to was Fitters Afloat 1 (FA1). The fitters afloat gangs, as the name implies, work mainly on board naval ships rather than in the workshops. Their work involves the repair and replacement of all the equipment fitted to these ships.

If you have never worked on board one of the Navy's ships - DON'T. The working conditions were primitive. When a ship was called in for refit it had to run on temporary supplies from shore, and this invariably meant that there would be no heating and very poor lighting aboard. Believe me, even if a ship is not surrounded by water, ie it was in dry dock, it is unbelievably cold in the winter months. Not surprising really, when you consider that everywhere you are surrounded by cold metal. Next is the noise; the power tools used by the various trades, chipping hammers, paint-removing 'knobblers', pneumatic wrenches and other assorted hand and power tools. Deafening Jet Vac pumps were used to remove bilge water.

Welding was going on everywhere, so while you were shielding your eyes from the welding flashes you would hit your head on some overhead obstruction, or fall down a hole, or both.

Apart from welding, specialist paints, gas–cutting metals and running machinery, the fumes were probably the worst. And asbestos was everywhere. Very little care was taken to minimize exposure to this, in fact it was treated in a very cavalier way, with people throwing it about all over the place!

Everything was either wet or damp. Combine this with oil/diesel/antifreeze residue and you end up with a surface like an ice rink. The lighting provided by wandering leads was generally very poor, and as a lot of the work was undertaken in very confined spaces, it was particularly nasty in the bowels of the ship. As you can probably tell, I didn't think working under these conditions was much fun!

At this time health and safety education and implementation in Chatham Dockyard was in its infancy. Compartments on board ship were not cleared when lagging (asbestos) was being removed. Ear defenders were not available to everyone, and the effect of toxic fumes was not fully understood, or it was ignored. In fact there was a culture that it was unmanly to request any safety equipment, probably the only exception being the wearing of safety goggles, as so many workmen had lost eyes. A cynical view would be that the overriding priority of the Navy Department was to complete the ship's refit on time, sometimes to the detriment of the health and safety of the workforce.

The FA1 workshop was on the north side of No. 2 Basin, behind the Navy's MTE (Maintenance Training Establishment) workshop. I was allocated to work with my skipper, Johnny Wicks. Apparently when I first arrived in the workshop, to disguise my apprehension and nervousness I stormed up to the nearest fitter and demanded 'Where's this bloke Wicks?' No wonder they thought 'we've got a right one here'!

The rest of the gang were decent sorts. The fitters tended to work in pairs, the two main couples being Sam Legg and Alan Lewis, and Barry Obie and Paddy Banks. The chargeman on this gang was Charlie Carpenter, a great guy. He took the apprentices under his wing and treated them very fairly, with a good understanding that we were young, inexperienced and high spirited. Even a pain in the arse like me!

Johnny Wicks likewise was a gem. He would always take the time to explain things, and we became great mates. One problem with working with John though was that his timekeeping was little better than mine!

The works recorder on this section was a guy called Ray Turner, who drove a little 1939 Standard Flying 9 which had once been blue and had seen better days. It used to look funny when it was driven over the railway line on the caissons, as the wheels would wobble dramatically, but somehow it had a character all of its own.

I had seen a similar one for sale in a garage in Rainham and liked it, so I pestered Ray to sell me his, which he eventually did. My first car - it cost me £5. This was a bargain that I was happy with, although there were a few jobs which needed doing.

My brother-in-law Derek, who was a qualified driver and a mechanic, went with me to collect the little car and drove it home for me to the garage I had rented. He commented 'It drives and pulls quite well', to which I replied, 'Yes, but perhaps we ought to release the handbrake!' It obviously didn't work too well.

Over the next couple of weeks Derek fully checked the car over and did the repairs necessary to make it reasonably safe and reliable. The major repairs necessary were replacement suspension pins (this would stop the excessive wheel wobble), a new steering nut (this would only last six months as the mating part in the steering rack was badly worn as well), a new clutch plate, a pair of pre-focus headlights and from the local scrap yard a pair of part-worn tyres, on their wheels.

One incident regarding this little car will stay in my memory for all time. One Sunday afternoon my girlfriend Larry had come up to see how the repairs were progressing, and seemed reasonably impressed with what had been done in such a short time. She was a little cracker (Larry, not the car), and I was a normal teenager with a rampant sex drive. To cut a long story short we ended up in the back seat of the Standard enjoying a very intense lovemaking session. I was quite nervous because the car was up on jacks, and as we changed position on the back seat of the car some worrying noises could be heard as the jacks moved. To be honest by that time I would not have cared if the car had fallen off a cliff face, let alone the jacks!

This was the first time I discovered the delights of the 69 position, a truly unforgettable experience, in the back seat of a 1939 Flying 9 and up on jacks!

My mate Paddy Hargan helped me to sand down and repaint the car over the Easter holiday. I now had a colour choice and settled for a two-tone finish, red on the bottom, cream on top. We worked really hard on the car and although it was hand-painted rather than sprayed, it looked really smart when finished.

To celebrate the finish of the repairs we agreed to take her out for a trial run, and decided we would go to Whitstable. We had a full load on board, Derek alongside me in the front and Mum, sister Chris and baby Mark in the back seat. All went well; the car was running nicely, and there was no sign of problems until we got a few miles along the Thanet Way and were stopped by a police motorcyclist. My (applied for) road tax disc had not come back from the issuing body, so I would be prosecuted, a good start to my motoring career!

As he had stopped us the copper decided to check over the car, and proceeded to each corner, pushing down hard on the wings to test the suspension. Mark started crying, so the policeman stopped and asked what was wrong. My sister had the presence of mind to say 'It's the uniform, officer, it frightens him, I'm sorry'. The policeman showed his caring side and discontinued the car's examination, told me that I would be prosecuted for not displaying a tax disc and left.

Further down the road, a little puzzled, I asked Chris 'How long has the baby been like that, with a thing about uniforms?'

'He hasn't' she replied. 'But when the policeman was rocking the suspension, something was pushing the seat and him up and down from beneath and that's what frightened him!'

I needed a qualified driver to accompany me until I passed my test. As John Wicks lived near me it was agreed that he would call for me in the mornings, leave his pushbike at my house and come to work with me in my 'new' car. This was great in theory; the only trouble was that John was almost as bad as I was at getting up in the mornings. If I wasn't late he was, and vice versa. In the end the pair of us were late so often that we were both on prompt muster. The rest of the gang thought this was hilarious, and probably the first time in the dockyard's history that a skipper and his apprentice were put on prompt muster together. What fame!

However, this seemed to sort us out, and from that time on both of us mended our ways and achieved normal attendance records.

I think Johnny Wicks was nearly as fond of the little Standard as I was. His favourite expression was that the car had 'semi elliptic laminated transverse leaf springing' - it took me some time to work out that this meant that it had bloody great springs at the back. It also had cable brakes, six-volt ignition, no radio, no heater and a three-speed gearbox. It made a pronounced squeak when you went around a corner as the suspension was so worn that the tyres would rub against the body, a different sound if you turned left or right! It also had a tendency to slide down a camber if you braked hard on certain roads, so you had to turn the wheel to compensate. It certainly wasn't fast. We would often chase rabbits when driving home from the country pubs we used to frequent, and the rabbits invariably won.

What it did have was a starting handle (thank god), and character - bags and bags of character. I had that car for six months, and then sold it to one of the other apprentices.

At work things were progressing very well. The fitter's afloat gang were in the main a decent gang, so much so that we would occasionally meet up, usually on a Friday night, at the Dewdrop pub for a game of darts. Bob Webb and I used to play a lot of darts at this time and on one of these Fridays we were both playing very well. The convention was that the winners stayed on the board and played the next challengers. This Friday we started at about 8.30 and beat all comers until just before closing time, when we both got bored and fatigue overtook us. The landlord was very impressed with our darts display and almost begged us to join his darts team. We declined, as we had no intention of being tied into this routine. The next time we went to the pub we played really badly, our games were rubbish and the landlord ignored us. Heroes to zeros in two weeks!

The major task for our fitter's gang was the refit of HMS *Rame Head*, and it was here that I first encountered asbestos. In the machinery spaces on board ship it was commonplace, and we thought it hilarious to throw large quantities of asbestos at each other, like a snowball fight. Another party piece, usually by a visiting tradesman, was to give the asbestos pipe covers a hefty blow, which showered the immediate area with a blanket of asbestos dust - what fun!

The exposure to this dust was aggravated by the encouragement to work 'time in lieu', which basically meant that you took half an hour for your lunch and left work half an hour earlier in the evening. The idea was to increase production; the workforce would not go back to 'shore' for their lunch but eat it on board, mostly where they worked, to reduce stoppage time. This meant that many workmen ate their sandwiches in an obnoxious environment, full of asbestos dust!

Another amazing (to me at the time) was the number of toilets required at the side of the dockyard basins to satisfy convention. The Navy had separate 'heads' (as the toilets are termed) for ratings, POs/CPOs and officers, while the dockyard requirement was for separate toilets for workmen, chargemen, inspectors and foremen – four more types, making seven in all. This seemed like severe overkill, but when you visited some of the workmen's toilets and saw what sort of state that they were left in, the picture became a little clearer.

When we finished the refit of the *Rame Head* (a submarine depot ship), a team was selected to go out with her on sea trials, and I was one of them. This in itself was a compliment, as only those who were considered to have contributed significantly to the refit were considered.

The sea trial started for me on a Sunday morning. The trials party had to assemble at Chatham's Bull's Nose (the locks entrance), and we would be taken by trot boat to Sheerness, where the *Rame Head* had anchored, having left Chatham Dockyard on Friday previously.

When she left on Friday most of us were a little jealous that an advance party, which included some of the workmen who lived furthest away, would be going with her and would therefore be entitled to two days' extra pay. In the event the fitters' team on board earned their extra money, as a minor problem arose on an important piece of equipment (the manoeuvring valve), and a considerable effort was required in the short time available to ensure that the ship was ready to start her sea trials proper on Monday.

The first day on board was one of familiarization. Although I knew the ship from the period I had spent working on her, it seemed very different now with almost all the machinery running. Another difference was that all the ship's crew were aboard now, running the ship's machinery, discussing the trials programme details and taking readings from all the active equipment.

Most of the compartments were fairly crowded at this time as the Navy and civilians were working in tandem running, checking, adjusting and handing over equipment. It was noisy, hot and crowded. The apprentices were told to make themselves scarce for a while until the initial activities were all set in place, as generally space was at a premium and we were going to get in the way. We headed for the Mess area and enjoyed ourselves playing cards and darts.

Charlie Carpenter, our chargeman, came around to check on us later in the afternoon, and I took the opportunity to plead with him to let me join the refit party in the main engine room. He was a little hesitant, but I finally persuaded him with the argument that this was a one-off opportunity for me to gain some first-hand experience on this variety of operational equipment, and that I was keen as mustard to help. Persuaded by my enthusiasm, he instructed me to report to him in the engine room, after the initial early morning checks, not before 10 o'clock.

At 10 o' clock I entered the engine room at deck level and made my way down the first two vertical ladders, working my way down the interim levels to approach the engine room landing. As I got halfway down the final ladder, about five feet from the grating, a fuel oil pipe above my head burst. It was not a major burst, a joint had failed, but it was enough to frighten the life out of me and soak me through with warm oil with the consistency of treacle. I stood there shocked, doing an impression of Nat King Cole and wondering quite what to do next.

That problem was solved for me. Charlie came storming over from the opposite side of the platform, looked at me in disgust, and said 'You, you must be a Jonah, fuck off!'

I could not believe my bad luck. I was distraught beyond words, but could do nothing except sneak off for a shower and change of clothes. I thought it best not to pester Charlie for another job too much for the rest of that day, but next morning I felt sufficiently confident to try again.

Charlie had a sympathetic smile on his face next morning, and asked how I was. I decided that this was a good time to ask for another job and was surprised when he said that he had just the thing for me. He said one of the main shaft plumber blocks was showing a tendency to overheat, so my job would be to monitor it.

The good news was that I had been given another job to do; but the bad news was, what were these plumber blocks, and where were they?

It all became clear very soon. Charlie took me right down to the shaft tunnel at the bottom of the ship. The shaft tunnel is the very long compartment which carries the main drive shaft along the bottom of the ship and out through the stern gland into the water. There it is connected to the propeller which drives the ship.

At frequent intervals, about twenty feet apart, are large bearings which support the shaft, housed in casings called plumber blocks. My job was to monitor the temperature of these bearings by placing my hand on to the top of the blocks, feeling for any sharp increase in temperature: not very scientific, but I was told that if I checked these bearings in this way at intervals of say fifteen minutes, it would be an effective and vital check.

The shaft tunnel was, in common with most other ships' compartments, very poorly lit. The headroom was such that I could not stand upright, so in making frequent journeys along the tunnel to check these bearings I must have looked like Quasimodo on a bad day. Worse still, I was not wearing my watch (it was still covered with oil residue), and had no idea of the time. I came out of the tunnel a couple of times and made my way up to the engine room to check the time, convinced that I had been down there for at least three hours, only to find out that it was only an hour and a quarter since I had started my checks. Time certainly dragged, and it was easy for my imagination to run riot.

After a few forward and back checks I decided to have a look at the stern gland, where the propeller shaft exited the ship. It was leaking! I decided that this needed to be reported immediately, before we all sank, and trying to disguise my panic I went back to report the revelation to Charlie Carpenter. He did me the courtesy of coming back with me to investigate, and then explained that the water leaking passed the gland which had caused me such alarm was in fact the means of cooling the bearing, and perfectly normal. I just wished someone had told me earlier.

When I returned to my place of duty back inside the shaft tunnel, I had another quick look at the stern gland, just to make sure. It was then that it occurred to me that the spot where I was working was about fifteen feet below the water line. Bloody hell! What if we hit an iceberg? I would be the last one out. By the time I had got halfway up all the ladders to get to the deck, I would be in Davy Jones' locker. I controlled my panic and resumed my routine checks as instructed, but it just shows how the imagination can cause havoc in a confined, dark space when you are on your own.

After two days doing the checks in the shaft tunnel, Charlie decided that the bearings no longer presented a threat and that I could come up from my isolation and join the others. Looking back I'm not sure if this job was as urgent as it was supposed to be, or if it was a convenient means of keeping me out of the way, just in case I was a Jonah!

The rest of the trial went really well. The Navy were very happy to accept the ship, as all equipment had been tested and operated well within the required limits. We got back into Chatham mid-afternoon on Friday.

A couple of weeks later the eagerly-awaited 'trials pay' was in our pay packets, and it was by far the biggest sum that I had received in wages since starting work. I don't remember the amount, but I do remember that it included overtime and several trials allowances, and at that time I believe it was comparable to over three weeks' normal pay.

That was the good news. Unfortunately, shortly afterwards, my girlfriend Larry decided that she and I were finished. She was already seeing someone else. She didn't even tell me - it was just that each time I called for her she was late getting home, or not there, so it just petered out.

The last time I called to take her out was a little frightening, but looking back it was probably one of my biggest opportunities lost. I called as usual to find Larry out, so her mum let me in. She said she thought her daughter would not be long and that she would make us a cup of tea while I waited for her.

When she came back with the tea she came and sat down beside me on the settee; looking back, that was unusual. After we had drunk our tea, with still no sign of Larry, I asked her mum if she knew where she had gone. She talked vaguely about a place I had never heard of in Gillingham, but as I asked her where it was she suddenly put her hand on my thigh. She then proceeded to draw a map of the location, travelling up, down and inside my tensed thigh, while I squirmed and did my utmost to disguise the onset of a serious stiffy.

I confess that I chickened out, mumbled farewell and left. Her actions did not seem quite blatant enough for me to be 100% sure that we were replaying that scene from *The Graduate*

- but who am I kidding, of course we were. I rather regret that I did not have the balls to take her up on it. If she was anything like her daughter it would have been a fantastic experience! Sadly, I will never know.

The sea trials were almost at the end of my period of training on the afloat section, where I learned how all the support functions for the ship's refit came together and saw how things worked at the sharp end. It also marked the end of my fourth year of apprentice training.

FINAL YEAR

When my apprentice entry finished our fourth year of training, we were all sent into the factory to compensate for the acute shortage of skilled machinists.

The foreman interviewed each of us individually to explain this unusual occurrence, and to discuss any preference we had concerning which section we would like to work on.

The interview was quite short, as he had about thirty lads to see, but it could be paraphrased in my case as:

Foreman: 'OK Mr Smith, tell me where you would like to work, and I'll see if I can match your choice to my requirements.'

Me: 'Thank you sir. I would like to work on the diesels section.'

Foreman: 'Sorry, report to the heavy turning section.'

Most of the apprentices told a similar story. There was a desperate need for machinists, so that was where we were going. *Fait accompli*.

The heavy turning section was where large, heavy-duty capstan lathes were operated. The capstan lathe had a turret pre-loaded with the required tools for a specific job. It was fairly quick in operation and generally used to produce high numbers in batch work.

The chargeman of the section showed me to my allocated lathe and left me with instructions to familiarize myself with the operation of it and practise on a few dummy workpieces, as I would not be given a job proper until the following day. The next day I practised some more on the lathe and had a chance to scrutinize the other workmen on the section. This worried me a great deal. Because the work was almost entirely on the bonus scheme, the men worked their socks off to earn the big bucks. That in itself was OK, but because of the repetitive nature of the jobs the men were like zombies, jumping up to start work as soon as the hooter (start of work signal) went, then watching a machine do a repeat operation for perhaps a thousand cycles, stopping only for dinner and the odd toilet break before starting again. No wonder they looked like lost and depressed souls.

Around mid morning the chargeman came to see me, and asked how I was getting on. He didn't seem impressed when I could not display the enthusiasm he was looking for. He told me that my first job had been delayed, but would be delivered before dinnertime. He also said that it would be a good job for me to start on - it was five thousand flanges for HMS Forth.

I thought that at least he had a sense of humour. Five thousand flanges, that's a good one!

Guess what happened, just before dinner? A Lister truck arrived at my lathe, complete with a trailer behind, both loaded to overflowing with blank flanges - all for me.

The work required on these flanges was to face, drill, bore and cut a welding radius. The flanges had been flame-cut in the boiler shop, which had the effect of hardening the material around the cuts. This meant that hardened (tipped) tools had to be used to cut them, and a lubricant/coolant cutting fluid needed to be sprayed continuously while cutting was being done.

I mention the above details to give an insight into the working environment. You had to start work as soon as the hooter went. Every time the lathe cutting tool hit the flange it produced a high-pitched screaming noise while cutting the hardened flanges, and the lubricant/coolant splashed back on to your face and hands. To say I wasn't keen would be something of an understatement.

The chargeman came back in the afternoon and tried to cheer me up by telling me that if I worked hard and did well I might be considered for overtime. Bloody hell! I didn't like the idea of eight hours a day doing this work, and no way was I going to ask for overtime.

I looked at one of the 'top men' on the section, a ginger-haired guy aged about thirty. His job was to manufacture catapult breaking rings, which were (a) manufactured to very exact requirements, and (b) required on a continuous basis. This guy looked ancient before his time, at least ten years older than his actual age, suffered permanent styes around his eyes and had a grey, defeated appearance. Any interest and enthusiasm he might once have had for anything other than work had been drowned by the necessity to work continuously for up to 60 hours a week on a repetitive task.

Later in the week I had a visit from Paul 'the mad' Kenyon,

who was now working in the factory as well. I was having a supermoan about hating the section I was working on and the fact that the need to regularly change the chuck (a heavy drive component on the lathe) was causing me considerable grief, as I had a back problem.

It was then that we hatched our cunning plan. Paul persuaded me that if I went to my doctors and complained about my back, I would be put on sick leave. I didn't need much persuading, especially as he said that he intended to go sick himself next week, and I really hated operating that lathe. He then explained that to make this ruse plausible it would be wise to do a little play-acting. I would need to be seen changing the heavy chuck, and halfway through the operation, I should give a shout of pain and drop the chuck. We did a mini rehearsal, and then, feeling that the moment was right, I went for it.

Bugger me, at the critical time when the nearest spectator should have seen this masterpiece enacted, he was distracted and missed it! I had to repeat the exercise, after a little rest, a short time later. I felt a little guilty about going sick in this way, but in fairness I did have a back problem at this time which certainly was made worse by the heavy lifting on this section, so I exaggerated rather than invented the problem.

I managed to escape from the heavy turning section after continued pleas, and only limited success in my work output; I just could not settle on that section at all. I was transferred to Section 31, Turbines and Auxiliaries, where I would complete my apprenticeship.

The Turbines section comprised about ten fitters and usually a couple of apprentices. When I first joined I thought it would be sensible to get a good understanding of what went on, as I was due to complete my apprenticeship there, and usually you could expect to stay on the section where you completed your time - finished your apprenticeship.

The section was typical of most of those in the factory at that time. The majority of the fitters seemed to be very old. Some actually were, while others were simply old before their time. In common with all the other sections, mine had its own hierarchy; obviously apprentices were at the bottom of the food chain and we were soon made aware of these facts of life, or ignored altogether depending on the prevailing mood. The senior fitters had the pick of the work and input into any of the day-to-day decisions and jealously guarded their seniority. Scattered around the work area were hat pegs, and woe betide any interloper who inadvertently used one of the seniors' pegs. They each had their own little station comprising hat peg, toolbox storage and bench space.

Everyone wore hats. The 'cheesecutter' was the most popular, but others preferred the trilby. A lot of the men had two hats, one they wore on the way to work and an old one they changed into once they got there.

We apprentices used to marvel at one of the old boys in particular. He was almost completely bald and obviously very self-conscious about this, so his hat changing ritual was smooth and professional. Shortly after arriving at work he would place himself facing his hat peg with his work cap in his right hand. He would take a quick look round, and then as the left hand snatched the trilby from his head it was replaced immediately by the work cap in his right hand. A very polished manoeuvre, repeated in reverse at going-home time.

Many of the workmen who changed their clothes before going home were those transferred from Sheerness when that dockyard closed. Transport on special buses was made available, free of charge, for three years after the transfer, in an attempt to soften the impact of the redundancy and other problems that this major shutdown caused.

On section 31 the two lead fitters were Bob Weeks and Bob Nicholls, and they specialized in feed pumps, the pumps which supply water to ships' boilers. These two were definitely first in the pecking order, but perhaps this was quite natural as they had been there the longest, and the chargeman knew that when he gave them a job it would always be done well and in time. No problems. The other fitters on the section included Roy Beard, Norman Stanley, John Jarret and several more elderly fitters whose names I never knew, who would not mix with upstart apprentices.

We worked in pairs, and my first pairing was with Norman Stanley. He was a cheerful ex-Navy man, shortish and fattish. I think we worked very well together, most of the time refitting forced lubrication pumps and other miscellaneous equipment as and when. One job I was given at this time which I really enjoyed was the static balancing of (mainly) large pump impellers. This involved rotating the impeller, its shaft supported on knife edges, to identify the areas of imbalance, so that weights could be added or material removed as appropriate to achieve the balance necessary. We also had a dynamic balancing machine available in the factory at this time, but only one operator was fully trained in the operation of it. This caused continual holdups, as his attendance was unreliable due to sick leave. As I was very interested in this work I applied to go on a course and be trained as a deputy for the balancing machine operator, but of course this did not happen; whether it was a lack of training funds or lack of interest by managers I do not know.

One special forced lubrication pump which Norman and I were working on was urgently required, so we were asked to work overtime on a Saturday to speed the refit. Norman – ex-Navy, remember - liked a pint and decided that we should go for a quick one in the lunch break. I would drive, as at this time he did not have a car.

Going for a drink in the dinner hour presented two problems. First we were not really allowed to leave the dockyard, as we only had half an hour for our break. Second, we needed to have an excuse as to where we had been when we came back to work after the liquid lunch. We thought we would probably get away with stretching the half an hour slightly, and Norman solved the second problem by taking one of the large pump bearings we were refurbishing over to the coppersmiths for remetalling, obtaining an assurance that we could collect it straight after dinner.

So we went for our pint or three, and Norman, being either

a diplomat or a firm believer in insurance, took a bottle of beer back with us for the chargeman, just in case. When we got back we parked up, collected the bearing from the coppersmith's workshop and returned to the side entrance to the factory. As we entered we saw at once that the chargeman had spotted us from the other side of the bay and was making his way towards us. Shit! Had he been looking for us?

We tried to appear ultra casual, with just the expected sense of urgency while making our way back to our workbench. Unfortunately Norman, in his panic, his eyes fixed on the approaching chargeman, did not see a wire hawser stretched across the workshop gangway and tripped.

Bollocks! The bearing, newly remetalled and quite valuable, leapt into the air and did three or four somersaults in slow motion. But Norman redeemed himself. Somehow he regained his balance and caught the bearing with all the aplomb of a test cricketer. It took an unbelievable effort to stop myself laughing.

The chargeman did allow himself a little smile and asked where we had been, but he appeared to be reasonably happy with Norman's explanation that we had gone for a quick pint to celebrate something or other; I kept my mouth shut. I heard the chargeman say later that we couldn't really have been drinking or we would not have juggled so well. Norman presented him with his bottle of beer, so everyone was happy.

Norman had started taking driving lessons, and one day, after much hesitation, he asked me if I would take him out, as the competent driver, to supplement his driving school lessons.

Like a fool I said yes. Norman was the worst would-be driver I had ever met. I used to dread the sessions we had together as he would frighten the life out of me. The most difficult bit was to stop trembling at the end of the lesson, and say 'well that wasn't too bad Norman, you're getting there!' without him noticing the teeth marks on the dashboard and the fact that all colour had been drained from me. During those weeks I gained a complete understanding of a *kamikaze* pilot trainer's mindset. I'm not sure that I had anything to do with it, but when the time came for his test he passed! I do not know to this day whether the examiner was drunk, on drugs or insane. Possibly all three.

As was the custom, I was next moved on to work with another of the fitters, Roy Beard. Roy was a dapper little guy, quite mouthy to the apprentices and sometimes sarcastic to the other fitters on the section. He came from Sheerness, and was a piss-taker extraordinaire. The other thing you would notice about Roy was that he had a glass eye. When I first worked with him I felt a little self-conscious looking at it, but by the end of the first week I felt comfortable enough to ask him how he had lost it.

He explained that he used to work afloat with his mate Stan, who was also at Chatham but on a different section, in the dockyard at Sheerness. Stan and Roy were great mates. One day while chipping off nuts (breaking up nuts which had become impossible to undo due to exposure to extreme temperature) Stan had a splinter fly into his eye, which damaged it beyond treatment. When Stan returned to work complete with glass eye,

Roy suggested that the gang should adopt the usual approach and take the piss, as this would actually help Stan come to terms with his misfortune much more quickly.

So Roy took the piss, and he was good at it. But six months later he suffered an almost identical accident, and lost an eye in the same way. This type of accident was fairly commonplace in the dockyards at that time. Roy was quite happy about his disability, and it affected him very little except that he obviously had no peripheral vision on one side. He said that one of the most embarrassing moments of the whole episode was when he had to go into hospital for an 'eye fitting'. This meant he had to sit on a stool facing a very attractive young female doctor who was looking deeply into his eye for an extended period. This was the medical person whose job it was to match the false eye, colour and pattern, to the existing one!

Although Roy was not top dog on the section, he was sufficiently up the pecking order to get a good selection and variety of jobs. This was good news for me, as working with him I was earning a little bonus pay and expanding my experience on these types of equipment in particular and fitting in general. I got on well with Roy and even used to meet up with him on some Friday nights when with a few mates we ventured into Sheerness. There were some good pubs on the island of Sheppey at that time, and it was always a good night out.

One Friday night we had visited a few pubs in the High Street and the Conservative Club, and decided on fish and chips before we headed home. We scoffed them walking back to the car, and one of the guys with me, inspired by the football on the TV, screwed his wrapper up and threw it at me, calling 'Go on Nige, score with this one.'

I duly obliged, swung my leg to give the 'ball' a hefty swipe - and watched in horror as my winklepicker shot into the air and landed on the first floor windowsill above a shop. It had started to rain and the pavement was wet. I had to knock several times before the door to the flat above the shop was answered, and then had difficulty explaining how my shoe had ended up on this guy's windowsill. In the end he made some comment like 'bloody nutters' and disappeared inside. Seconds later he opened the window, with difficulty, and threw down my shoe. He was not a happy teddy.

The social scene was pretty good at this time. I had recently got myself another car, a beautiful 1957 Wolseley Model 15/50. This cost me £315 from Russell's garage in Rochester, and for that I got gleaming black bodywork, a walnut dash, red leather upholstery and a great chance to impress the birds.

One of our favourite haunts when my mates were home on leave was the Crescendo Club in Chatham, a strip club. It would be very tame by today's standards, but back then it was the dog's bollocks. I'm sure some of the acts were students just earning a few extra pounds in their holidays, although some of the acts mixed in with them were very professional. It was all good clean fun really, as the girls never went completely nude, and the atmosphere was always jovial and friendly.

Except for one night. John 'Stacy' Workman and Jeff Tassell were a couple of regulars; they used to have a good drink at Rochester Rugby Club and breeze into the Crescendo just before the acts started. When they came in they lit up the place. Always ready with a massive repertoire of jokes, they were noisy and exuberant but never over the top. On this particular Saturday night the boys came in as usual, and sat a few feet away from where me and my mates were sitting. The stripper was doing her act to the strains of *Please don't tease me* by Cliff Richard; the idea was that she would do half of her act while the record played once, then they would play the record again and she would finish it.

All went well until she finished the first part of the act and stopped, bent over and with her bum only just covered with the tiniest pair of knickers, about a foot from Jeff Tassell's nose. He obviously quite enjoyed the scenery, but I believe he was slightly embarrassed, and being always ready with a quip he said 'Charmin', bloody charmin!'

Those of us who knew Jeff realized that this was just a bit of fun, but when several people in the audience started to laugh the girl took it personally. She spun around and snarled at Jeff 'One more remark like that sonny and I'm off'. To which Jeff replied 'Never mind, bring on the dancing girls'.

More laughter, girl storms off. Nothing much happened for several minutes, and no one imagined there was a problem. To cut a long story short, although the boys offered to apologise through the manager, the girl had taken offence and refused to finish her act until they were made to leave. They left, apologizing to the assembled audience but still in high spirits.

The girl came back and finished her act, and when she had finished there was a deathly hush. Not one person clapped. She glowered at us all and stormed off. I don't think she was booked again.

Usually when we left the Crescendo we would have to walk back home to Rainham, so we would often make a slight detour to a coffee stall near the viaduct in Railway Street. This was one of the 'places to be' around midnight on a Friday or Saturday night, as all the local 'celebrities' would call in. Peter Sharp was one of these; a self-proclaimed hard man with a huge mop of fair hair, complete with a DA (duck's arse) haircut of course, and shirt unbuttoned to the waist whatever the weather, he was hard to miss. I must say that I never saw him cause any trouble and he seemed to be a reasonable sort who was just keen on a bit of notoriety.

The major interest at the coffee stall was the motorbikes. I would estimate that there could be over a hundred of them on show on some nights, and what bikes they were!

The main display was in two lines, and they were immaculately-kept models of almost every make. At the top of the range were the Triumph Bonnevilles, Trophies, Model 110s, 100s, Speed Twins etc, Norton Dominators, Model 99s and 88s, BSA Super Rockets, Road Rockets and Gold Stars. Other makes would include Velocette, AJS, Matchless, Triumph Nortons, BSA Nortons and Ariels, while even the odd Vincent Black Shadow or Lightning would appear periodically. One thing most of them had in common was that they were polished to perfection, and were their owners' pride and joy. Many of the owners would admit to taking their bikes into their kitchens to polish up the aluminium engine parts until they gleamed like chromium.

Although I always enjoyed the motorbike show at the coffee stall, it often left me with a nightmare vision of something that I dreamed had happened on one of my occasional visits. I had parked my motorbike on its centre stand and turned away when I heard a crash. My bike had fallen over on to the bike next to it, damaging it and knocking it over. That bike in turn knocked over the one next to it, which resulted in a cascade of damaged motorbikes along the entire line in front of the coffee stall. Shit! I was confronted by 50 snarling bike boys. They were not amused. I was lucky to escape alive.

My preferred fare at the stall was a steak and kidney pie smothered in brown sauce and a cup of tea. Actually, I was not quite sure if it was tea, but it was hot and wet anyway. Thus fortified we could start the trek back to Rainham.

The walk home could be quite eventful. Naturally the task was invariably trying to find somewhere open for more beer, and seek out some women. It was a tall order for young men who were nearly skint, after midnight in the Medway Towns. One plan we would adopt was to head down to Leysdown - there was bound to be some crumpet down there, wasn't there? Fat chance of course, but at the time it always seemed quite feasible. Two occasions when we made attempts spring to mind, but for the time being, as I don't want to chance ending up in jail, they will remain untold!

My next and last move on the Turbines section was to work with one of the senior hands, Bob Nicholls. Promotion? Perhaps my real potential had been recognized at last! Or it may have been that Bob had lost his regular fitter partner, Bob Weeks, who had been made chargeman when George Allen retired. Anyway, I was now to work with Bob and that suited both of us just fine. Bob was in his sixties, of average build, not much hair left and usually cheerful and chatty.

He was also very nosey. I don't mean that in a nasty way, but he really enjoyed going around the shop floor, mainly on his own section, talking to people and finding out all their business. If you wanted to know anything about anybody, you asked Bob.

The other thing about Bob was that he always LOOKED busy. He always had a small component in one hand, and would polish this intermittently with either a file or a piece of emery paper while he extracted the latest lurid details from all and sundry. You could never say that he was not actually working. He had this game off to a fine art. Having said that, Bob was a nice old guy, harmless and inoffensive. He was also a very good fitter, and would gladly pass on his experience and expertise to anyone who was experiencing technical problems.

When the turbine-driven pumps we were refitting had been completed, they had to be tested. Across the road from the factory was the test house, which had a high pressure steam supply specifically for these tests. We were testing a new to service pump, which meant we would be in the test house for several days. At this time my car was overdue for an oil change, so after agreeing it with Bob I decided that I would do this in one of my dinner-hour breaks while we were working in the test house, a little bit 'out of the way'. The big advantage here was that the car could be driven inside the test house for this work, so even if it was raining it would not present a problem. I had a contact who could get me some high quality oil, so I was all set.

On the day involved we were having problems getting the necessary steam supplies for our test runs, so we started late. In consequence we were a little late taking our dinner break. I started the oil change as soon as I had finished my hurried sandwiches. I had all the old oil drained out and the new oil filter fitted loosely in position, and topped the engine up with the fresh oil.

Of course this was where it all went wrong. Bob, who was keeping watch, suddenly shouted, 'Chargeman's coming Nige, get the car out quick!'

Sure enough the chargeman was on his way over, probably to check if we were having any more problems with the steam supply. Bob went over and operated the roller shutter door, ready for my quick exit. I quickly replaced the oil filler cap, put the tools to one side and reversed the car out. Unfortunately, where the oil filter was not fully tightened, oil was pissing out all over the place. When I checked it later, I found that most of the fresh oil had been wasted. Shit! Still at least we passed inspection by the chargeman and after I had mopped up the oil mess, there were no repercussions. I think I learned several lessons that day.

The time passed quite quickly on this section, and was very

interesting, thanks to the variety of jobs that came in. The fitters here were also in the main helpful, and did their best to help us improve and acquire new skills.

I finished my apprenticeship while I was working on this section, and continued there for about another six months. I would probably have been happy to stay there if the work had been more regular, but it was becoming increasingly more patchy with frequent long periods of waiting time with no work to do, as more and more work was being placed with contractors.

At this time a vacancy notice was put on the notice board in the main workshop, asking for applicants for a planning assistant (technical progressman) in the Weapons section. The pay was not great, an allowance of twenty-one shillings a week, but the job sounded interesting and I saw it as an exciting new challenge. I explained to Bob Nicholls that I was thinking of applying for the job, and asked his advice. It was as usual simple and to the point. 'Why not?' he said. 'Go for it old son, there's nothing for you here.'

I applied for the job and got it, so I left the factory and started my new job at the very bottom of the management stream.

And the rest, as they say, is history.

NOTE 1

September 1958 Fitter Apprentice Entry

Clive Akers

Pete Appleby (Ace)

Jim Apps (BO Apps)

John Arnold

Malcolm Boorman

Dave Campbell (Panda)

Derek Chambers

Alan Clatworthy

Len Crowhurst

Bert Daniels

Bob Foreman

Mick Pearce

Dave Riley

Vic Salmon

Dick Seamark

Brian Simpson

Robert Smith (Nige)

Roy Smith

Bob Webb

Chris Woods

Clive Walters

My apologies to any others who I may have omitted.

NOTE 2
Spring entry 1958 Fitter Apprentice Entry
(Advanced entry next door in ATC)

Mick Beer

Johnny Blezzard

Pete Brooks

Vinny Cottingham

Paul Gurney (Spike)

Bernard Hargan (Paddy)

Len Harris

Geoff. Hayward

Ernie Hockney

Mick Moad

Cyril Moffat

Bruce Naylor

'Spud' Taylor

Ron. Walters

Dave Wolf

John Workman (Stacy)

Dudley Young

Again, apologies to those I have forgotten.

PART 2

THE TECHNICAL
PROGRESSMAN'

CONTENTS

NOTE 3. "The Cast", Weapons Section,
HM Dockyard Chatham, Circa 1966

DECISIONS, DECISIONS

So this is it then? The apprenticeship is over at last. Five years of training and poor money, and now I am a fully qualified fitter and turner. The bee's knees.

Wrong. I was qualified, but I soon realized that only now would I start to learn, and a lot of experience was needed before I could consider myself a tradesman proper.

On completion of my apprenticeship I remained on Section 31 (Turbine Auxiliaries and Pumps) in the engineering factory for about 6 months. The major problem with this was that the work was drying up and patchy, and consisted mainly of refitting (overhauling) pumps for store (to be held in the Naval Stores until required for use by another ship or dockyard). This made it difficult to learn and improve my skills, and time hangs so heavily when there is little to keep you occupied. Worst of all was the need to look busy when visitors or managers came into the section, and the frustration at spending such a long time training and then finding no apparent end result. At this time I looked at leaving the Dockyard, as many of my contemporaries had, but I hesitated, as I was not sure that an engineering fitter was to be my long-term chosen career.

This feeling was probably prompted by working in a section consisting almost entirely of old men. The majority were 55-plus and most were over 60. To a 21-year-old this was almost antique!

For all sorts of reasons, including the hard times many had experienced during the war etc, they were not a happy lot, very rarely smiling, and had little or no conversation, personality, drive or enthusiasm. They seemed just grey automatons waiting for their retirement, or death. It was not the place to nurture future plans and ambitions.

The second most important reason why I was reluctant to seek other in-trade employment was that the majority of 'external' engineering works were mainly employing machinists. This usually meant 'minding' an automatic lathe or milling machine and succumbing to the daily grind of 'knocking out' millions of widgets (components), often working overtime to achieve decent wages, invariably on piecework (bonus), and in a dirty, noisy, and unpleasant environment. This did absolutely nothing to inspire me.

However, to change my life's direction and enter into a completely different vocation without any relevant qualifications was not going to be easy, so I stayed on section 31 and waited until something that promised a little more optimism for the future came along.

The life-changing event for me was a Vacancy Notice (VN), which appeared on the section's notice board. (This was the means of promulgating internal job vacancies.)

A vacancy had arisen in the Weapons (ships' armaments) Section Planning Office as a Technical Progressman (planning assistant) at the enhanced pay rate of 21 shillings per week.

CHAPTER 1

I sought advice from my ex-skipper, Bob Nicholls, about applying for this job. His succinct advice was – 'Well, what have you got to lose?' That said it all really; nothing. So I applied for this job, went for the interview, and was successful.

LEARNING THE ROPES

I reported for work at my new section on the appointed day and was directed to the Trade Office on the top floor of a new brick-built extension at the front of the weapons shop, where I was introduced to the Chargeman, Peter Lowry. We made our introductions, and Pete explained a few of the domestic arrangements - location of the toilets, clocking-on station etc. He said he would take me into the main office to make the introductions, but he stopped when he noticed that I was still wearing my normal work boots. He remarked 'You won't need those any more old son, we always wear shoes around the office.' I felt a little embarrassed, but grateful for the advice.

We went into the main office, known at that time as 'TO8' (Trade Office number 8), and Peter requested quiet. Then he announced: 'Can I have your attention please? We have a new starter, Bob Smith, and he will be working with Jack Payne.' Everyone in the office turned, nodded and said 'Welcome Bob'. A good start, and I felt at home.

The office was divided into two halves. On the left hand side were John Pattman, Jim Greenaway and Norman Shipley, who were the Estimators, supported by Ken Hancock and Fred Murr, the Technical Progressmen. On the other side of the office were Estimators Ron Hill and Jack Payne supported by two more Technical Progressmen, Bob Butler and now myself. Another Technical Progressman, without portfolio (although allegedly concerned with the introduction of the new Stage III Weapons Workshop), Keith Harris, completed the technical complement, and two Non-Technical Progressmen (Bill Allen and Ted Broadie) completed the staffing.

Outside the planning office a corridor led to the Inspector's office (Frank Stevens), the Library, run by Fred Ludlow, and a small room containing a wash basin and a toilet cubicle. At the end of the corridor was the Stock Control Office, run by Jack Taylor and two female assistants. This office held details of all major weapons equipments and major sub-assemblies, their location and their state of repair: serviceable, repairable, or currently being repaired.

The ground floor housed the Inspector's office (three staff) and the two Foremen's offices. One was for the shops (Main Shop, Annexe, and the Preservation and Packaging shop or PIP); the other Foreman was responsible for the 'Afloat' work (work that was carried out on board the ships). The main toilet block completed the ground floor accommodation.

Over the next few weeks I gradually got to explore the other parts of the section. These included the Weapons Annexe run by the Chargeman, Eric Carter, where compressors and hydraulic pumps were overhauled and tested. An old school-pal, Bob

Webb, worked here, along with the other fitters, Bob Moncur, Lenny Price, Lenny Harris and a few others.

Next door was the PIP shop (Preservation and Industrial Packaging), run by the Chargeman, Phil Hobling, where large tanks of various steam-heated chemicals were used to clean components and assemblies, some to be returned to a refitting section, others fully preserved and packed for dispatch to the Naval Stores.

Phil Hobling was a lively character. He had been transferred from the Optical Shop near the Dockyard's Bull Nose when the work repairing ships' binoculars and sights had dwindled. Although he was near to retirement age he was very active, and always ready with a plethora of the latest jokes he had heard at his favourite watering hole, the Falcon Pub in Marlborough Road.

The main weapons shop itself was split into various sections. The main area was where the very large ships' main armament (4.5 inch guns) were refitted, along with various other smaller assemblies and equipments. This area was run by the Chargeman, Ned Foster.

At the end of the main shop were the dust-proof room and the section's small machine shop. The dust-proof room was where the more sensitive assemblies could be worked on in a clean and controlled area. Items such as the tachometric boxes were refitted here. These were a type of very simple mechanical computer which were used to control the gun mountings' movement and positioning. The machine shop had a small selection of machine tools, including a lathe, milling machine, a shaper and a drill, and was used to provide urgent and specialized machining support to the workshops; it was run by Harry Barnett.

To one side of the workshop was a small discrete area used by a couple of boilermakers who were attached to the section. They would manufacture or repair small to medium-sized items such as handrails, covers, machinery seatings and brackets and take details of any larger items which would then be manufactured in the main boilershop. At the head of the workshop were the naval stores (which stocked jointing, fastenings, and consumables, replacement overalls, and other day-to-day requirements) and with it was the loan tool store area. Next came the clocking station, the Trade Union representative's office (Fred Foster), a cloakroom and drying room area, and stairs which led to a mezzanine floor where the weapons equipment stores (spare parts and assemblies) were located (run by Len Parfitt).

Stairs at the far end of the workshop led to the Sight Gallery. This was primarily where the afloat gangs resided. Usually only one or two would be in the shop working on an assembly which had been removed from the ship. John 'Ginger' Peters was often to be found in this area, and he was known to be a very good contact if any engraving was required. John was highly skilled at engraving, and could provide work at least equal in quality to that provided by local sources; he was already engraving cups and trophies presented by the various dockyard sports sections. The Chargeman was a largish outgoing type called Ken 'Brockie' Brockwell.

CHAPTER 2

Just outside the main workshop on the south side, a long single-storey building housed the diagnosticians. These were senior and highly-trained staff recruited from the workforce to undertake the various testing activities climaxing at the 'set to work' stage of the refits. Any major equipment was reliant on these teams to ensure that the equipment was fully operational and fit for purpose in every respect. They had their own special test equipment, and considerable technical literature complementing the section's Technical Library.

The workshop had a steady flow of work, and there was an upbeat feeling to the place. Most of the staff and workforce usually had a smile on their faces; it was a good place to work.

The section also ran a very active social club, so that's what Keith Harris did? I went on a couple of coach trips organized by the club, the first of which was to the Talk of the Town, where we saw the singer Frank Ifield. Some of the girls, including my girlfriend Joy, were devastated when they heard that Cliff Richard had been the headline act the week previously - poor old Frank didn't have the same appeal! However, he put on a good show, and it would have been a good night if our group hadn't been sitting close to an air conditioning unit which pumped out cold air all night. The food was fairly average too, and only just about warm by the time we were served.

The other main show I went to with the Social Club was at the Circus Tavern, just over the Thames in Essex. I can recall that we were all impressed by the size and décor of the venue, but again getting the meals out to the tables while the food was still hot proved to be impossible for the limited staff available. I can't remember who was playing at the show, so it can't have been very memorable.

Other events were organized by the Social Club committee, and these included 'Pitch and Putt' at the Mote Park in Maidstone and 'Bat and Trap' at the Five Bells in Church Street, Gillingham. These nights were usually good fun. Most of the managers would come along at some time or another and join in. Sometimes they even offered to buy us a pint!

The Social Club also ran a Premium Bonds club where all these members contributed five shillings (25p) each week, and were allocated bonds in return, about once a month. I've still got all my bonds, and I'm still waiting for them to present me with a decent prize!

Other trips organized by the Social Club were to the Theatre and the Shepherd Neame brewery in Faversham, which was for some unknown reason very popular!

The job itself, as a Technical Progressman, was obviously completely different to anything I had been used to up to that time. All of a sudden all my recently-used hands-on skills as a fitter were to be tucked away into the memory bank, while other attributes which had been dormant for so long had to be recalled. Much later on I was to look back at some of the earliest work I had done in my new job as a Progressman, and was amazed at my handwriting. It had not been used to any great degree for perhaps ten years, and not surprisingly it looked just like a schoolboy's.

At first everything was strange. Working in a new section, I soon discovered that a lot of the equipment we dealt with was referred to by acronyms; a close range blind fire director was known as a CRBFD, for instance. Then the myriad of forms, much loved by the MoD, and referred to by their numbers (rather than what they were for) had to be learned and remembered. For example S145a was a Stores Requisition, D83 a Stores Return Note, D387 a Special Demand Form, D1045 a Works Requisition Form, etc etc.

The next part of my education was to get to know where the work that was to be undertaken in the other (external) workshops would be done, and how to request it. Once the works request had been made, the requested completion date would be logged, to enable progress checks to be made. This would constitute a major part of my new job as a Progressman.

Sometimes, work completion updates would be arranged by telephone, backed up by written authority. These checks could be supplemented by workshop visits, which were often very interesting, and made the jobs come to life.

The major workshops visited for work progress updates were the Engineering Factory, the Boilershop and the Electrical Repair Workshops, while others included the Joiners/Patternmakers, Hose Shop, Coppersmiths and the Smithery/Chain Test areas.

In the Engineering Factory almost any machining operation could be carried out. The machine tools in this workshop included lathes (various types and sizes), milling machines, slotters, drilling machines, shapers and grinders, some of which were computer controlled. Workpieces could be shaped/manufactured to almost infinite combinations.

CHAPTER 2

Various refitting sections overhauled all but the very largest shipborne equipment and water pressure testing, static/dynamic balancing, dimensional inspections, testing machines, both destructive and non-destructive, and a Tool Room were part of this comprehensive engineering facility.

Managers' offices (Inspectors and Foremen), Dimensional Inspection and the Trade Planning Offices were located at the North-East of the building. First line supervisors (the chargemen) had their offices co-located on their sections.

The Boilershop was a massive factory, second only in size to the engineering factory, with a large clock tower at its western end. It manufactured a wide variety of items from plate or bar steel (including some smaller boilers) and prefabricated sections/compartments for installation on board ships (funnels, lockers, racks, shelves, benches, trunking etc). Specialized brackets were made to drawings or in accordance with simple sketches as appropriate.

Various heat treatments (hardening, tempering etc) could be done using one of the several forges located in the workshop. The forges were mainly used to heat the workpieces to a 'soft' condition (red/white hot) which could then be hammered into the required shape.

Later on a massive hammer, previously located in the Smithery and powered by steam, was installed in the Boilershop and converted to a pneumatic supply, to enable the forming of red-hot workpieces into large basic forgings.

The Electrical Repair Workshop specialized in the testing of new electric motors (prior to installation) and the overhaul and testing of in-service electric motors of all types and sizes, both AC and DC. Additionally all electrical components (control boxes, starters, solenoids, lighting and heating equipment and a diverse variety of associated items) could be refitted and tested in this workshop.

Other workshops included the Hose Shop, which would manufacture and test any hoses required for water, hydraulics, pneumatic, or steam services, as well as canvas and leather items, while coppersmiths would provide new and reconditioned pipework if required.

The Smithery and Chain Test houses had provision to test chains, shackles, hawsers, metal and rope strops etc after manufacture or as part of a periodic test/inspection procedure.

The Joiners/Patternmakers workshop provided repair capability for wooden furniture/fittings on board ship, and could manufacture new items from provided drawings. High quality and professional standard or bespoke furniture was manufactured in this workshop for use in the officers' quarters and wardrooms on board the ships. Top quality timber or occasionally veneered woods were crafted into intricate items and polished up to a mirror finish. Ships' and boats' badges were also manufactured as required in this workshop.

Finally, the Hydraulic Shop played a major role in the repair work in overhauling and testing of components and assemblies fitted in the ships' hydraulic systems, eg steering pumps and hydroplane equipment.

Another significant and important task of mine was to

arrange work or materials from outside sources, known as 'direct local purchases' or 'special demands'. This would include things such as repairs or spares for specialist equipment not supplied through the Naval Stores system.

A walk through the Weapons sections was different each time as the refitting work was progressed and completed, and new and different equipment was brought in to take its place.

Walking through the main shop, you could always see one of the main ships' armaments (mountings, these are called), a massive 4.5 inch twin-barrelled gun, which always reminded me of an iceberg, as most of the working parts were under the gun itself, and on board ship would be located below deck. It would take many months to refit these mammoth pieces because of their complexity and the requirement to test each sub-assembly before and after installation.

Fred Whale was the leading light on this equipment, with his mate Les Taylor. Fred was quite a character. One of his unusual habits used to manifest itself whilst he was talking to one of the other workmen in the shop. While he was talking very rapidly and enthusiastically he would undo all the buttons on the front of this person's overalls and then do them up again, without apparently realizing he was doing it!

The other large items in the main shop were the ships' directors. This is the equipment which controls the guns and positions them onto their targets. At this time mechanically-operated directors were still being used, the common one for the main armaments being the Mk 6M; these were usually refitted by Peter Castle.

This was the main equipment of my concern. I found the work very interesting, especially as I got on well with Pete, and I felt we made a good team. I also established a good working relationship with the Drawing Office, and over a short period of time was able to secure a complete set of the latest issue of working drawings (I estimate about 1000 in the set).

Routine day-to-day tasks would comprise arranging overhauls or testing of the sub equipments (often in the Hydraulic Shop), the manufacture of components (usually in the Engineering Factory), arranging plating (or other protective coatings such as painting or anodizing) and purchase of 'special' equipment.

I was also allocated the task of compiling the 'Monthly Letter', which was the list of all the equipments being worked on in the section, showing their state of progress. This was used as the basis for the routine planning review meetings.

The Technical Library was an essential asset to the section. It held updated copies of the Navy's 'bibles' (Books of Reference or BRs as they were known). These contained all the technical and administrative information required in the operation of a naval establishment.

Held additionally were technical reference books covering all the topics necessary, including such information as specifications for materials, bearings, fastenings, protective coatings, oils and lubricants, heat treatments etc. A major and vital part of the technical library service was to ensure that all the information was kept up to date with the latest amendments.

This was critical to ensuring that when the equipment left the section it was always updated to the latest specification, and all the literature held in the Library was referred to and treated as 'controlled' for this reason.

Other equipment being refitted would normally include 40mm Bofors guns, which could be battery (Mk 8), electrical (Mk 9) or more usually the hydraulically-operated (Mk 7) version. There were also 20mm Oerlikon guns, which were mainly used in anti-aircraft or close-range defence roles.

Like most offices, the work would at times be hectic, sometimes boring. One particular Friday lunchtime will, I'm sure, stay in all of our memory banks forever.

It had been a very busy morning, with all of the chargemen wanting urgent stores or materials (which they had mostly forgotten) for the weekend overtime working. The panic over, things went quiet about ten to twelve, and we all puffed out our cheeks and took a deep breath. After a few minutes Freddie Murr on the other side of the office was absent-mindedly 'pinging' his rule on his desk in time to a subconscious melody. After a few seconds, someone on our side of the office picked up the beat by gently banging their knee against the side panel of their desk.

Next to enter this orchestral treat were two guys humming and one da-da-da-ing, each tapping out a rhythm with their knuckles on their desks. The icing on this particular cake was when the chargeman (Pete Lowry) started to prance down the central aisle in the office playing an imaginary trombone with enormous gusto. Pete was a big fella and was carrying more than a little too much weight, and he invariably had a comical air about him. This looked like a scene straight out of the Jungle Book. The whole office was now really rocking. I don't know what the tune was, but it was of a good generous tempo and progressively increasing in volume!

At the height of this orchestral masterpiece, the Inspector (Frank Stevens) walked in and was hit by a wall of sound. He stopped a yard inside the door, rooted to the spot, mouth open and a look of monumental surprise on his face. The 'music' tapered off quite quickly and Frank recovered his composure (just). He glared at Pete Lowry and said 'What the hell's going on in here? It sounds like a bloody bear garden!' With that, he spun on his heel and left, slamming the door on the way out. Complete silence. Then Pete Lowry started to giggle, and the whole office collapsed into uncontrollable mirth. We were all concerned that Pete would be in trouble and be reprimanded, but he later assured us all that there were no (apparent) repercussions. I consider myself lucky that I was transferred into the Weapons section at this time, as the Management, and in particular the Trade Office Inspector (Frank Stevens, my Line Manager), were very progressive (certainly ahead of the game) in terms of staff development. In two key areas they led the way compared to all the other sections in the Dockyard at this time.

Firstly, almost all of the equipment we worked on was covered by excellent training courses at one of the Navy's 'schools' at Portsmouth, HMS *Sultan*, HMS *Excellent*, HMS *Dolphin* etc, and we were strongly encouraged to attend these.

Secondly, Frank Stevens ran lectures and classes to prepare any staff interested in advancement by taking the MOD Navy sponsored examination papers. This was in preparation to sit the 'Inspector of Trades' Examination which was held every two years, sponsored by the Navy Department. This examination was the normal and preferred promotion route into middle and senior management. At that time people would not only be sitting the exam from the Home Dockyards (Chatham, Devonport, Portsmouth and Rosyth) but also from naval bases/establishments worldwide (we still had some then!) including Malta, Gibraltar, Singapore and many others.

Frank held classes after work one night a week when we were set homework and could discuss last week's topics and problems on a group basis and pool information.

The essential requirement to enter these study sessions was to obtain a copy of the naval engineering 'Bible', BR (Book of Reference) 3003 Part 2. This was not a restricted publication, and could be purchased at places like W H Smiths. I obtained my copy second hand from my pal Bob Webb.

The bottom line was that the Management on this section gave every encouragement to any staff who showed an interest in promotion or advancement, and most of us went on and got at least one or two promotions. These results could be traced back directly to the encouragement and assistance given to us by our forward-looking line managers.

CHAPTER 3

BACK TO SCHOOL

The 'Pompey' courses were legendary, not so much for the technical expertise acquired, which was considerable as most of the course Tutors were ex Chief WEAs (Weapons Engineering Artificer), or similar, therefore highly experienced and knowledgeable, but because of the students. Usually at least two students would attend from the same dockyard on each course, and several courses could be running simultaneously. Therefore four, five or six men from Chatham would often be attending courses at the same time.

The preferred lodgings were with Mrs Simmonds in Salisbury Road, Southsea. This was not only because the food was excellent but also, importantly, these "digs" were cheaper than elsewhere. At this time course attendees were given a daily allowance, and if you found really cheap digs, it left you with more beer money! I even know of people (not from Chatham) who slept in their cars (and were moved on several times by police during the night) so that they could save the money they had claimed for lodgings! Incidentally, by about mid-week these people had started to look more than a little frayed at the edges!

Mrs Simmonds would usually start the week giving her guests enormous food portions and gradually reduce these over the week until by going home time the portion sizes were just about right. The sleeping accommodation was, let's say, adequate, usually two or three beds in a room, and very basic. These sleeping arrangements were never a problem though, as it was only a place to 'crash down' after a night out, usually involving drinking.

Another incentive for staying with Mrs Simmonds was that she was rumoured to have two very attractive daughters, so there was always the possibility that you might get lucky! All in all Mrs Simmonds was the place to lodge, and you had to get your booking in early, as the word soon got out and the guys from the other dockyards would try to book in there as well.

The Portsmouth weapons courses, as previously explained, were very professionally run. The instructors were usually senior NCOs (Chief Petty Officer or equivalent) and they had many years experience working with and maintaining the equipment they taught. They knew the kit backwards.

The courses themselves supplemented the theoretical lectures with the opportunity to get 'hands-on', stripping the equipment, re-assembling it and doing any tests that were required. Special emphasis was given to fault finding and modifications. Practical and written tests were included during and at the end of all courses. If you wanted to learn and had even the slightest intelligence, you would find these courses invaluable.

The various training establishments, HMS *Sultan*, *Excellent*, *Vernon*, *Dolphin* and others, had excellent facilities, decent classrooms, test/training rigs and video and projection equipment, and all courses provided stationery items and comprehensive 'hand out' notes to be taken away and retained for future reference.

I attended most of the courses on offer, but one in particular I shall never forget. The course was in the winter 1965/66 at HMS *Excellent*, to be instructed on a gun directional system. Two other guys from Chatham, Bob Moncur and Trevor Sargent, went with me. I would take the other two with me in my car, a trusty Wolseley model 15/50, registration VEL 797, a number plate I find easy to remember. I was nominated to drive as Bob had a two-seater, and Trevor didn't drive.

The journey down to Portsmouth and the first two days of the course were fairly routine - course, pub, bed, course, pub, bed - but Wednesday nights were always a bit special and something to look forward to - the 'Widows' Hop' at the Mecca.

On this particular Wednesday we met up with two of the other Chatham guys, Ted Coward and Brian Turner, who were in Portsmouth on different courses and staying at different 'digs'. While Ted and Brian decided to display their dancing skills (sensible chaps), Bob and I decided to display our drinking prowess (Bob was ex-Merchant Navy, and loved a drink or three!)

We were quite happy drinking our chosen poison for the evening (pints of Double Diamond with Pernod chasers), and about 9.30 we bumped into the chief who was our course instructor (Chief O. A. Fair). He said we were obviously having a good night and asked us what we were drinking. Double Diamond with Pernod chasers, we told him.

'Bloody hell, you'll be ill in the morning', he said. 'Whadya mean?' we replied (far too stupid and drunk to take advice). 'We're roughie-toughies, not soft like you wimpy sailors.' He was right; we did suffer for it next morning, and how!

In the meantime we carried on drinking, and shortly afterwards when I came back from another trip to the toilet, Bob had company. I don't mean to be rude, but this woman was *ugly*. That's not very nice I know, but her face was dominated by an enormous nose, hooked like a witch's but so wide it looked as if someone had thrown a bunch of sausages at her face and they had stuck!

I feared for Bob, because I was convinced that if she turned her head sharply this enormous conk would decapitate him. However, shortly after I returned she decided to leave and I had the opportunity to quiz Bob on what had happened. Apparently as soon as I got up to go to the toilet she had targeted Bob and sat down at our table. With very little preamble she had asked him if he wanted a 'good time' (They could go to a hotel she knew of not far off). When Bob politely declined, she then offered a 'knee-trembler' quickie in the alley alongside the dance hall, which would cost thirty bob (£1.50). Again Bob said thanks but no thanks, so her parting shot was 'OK then, how's about I give you a quick wank under the table for ten bob?' By this time I was on my way back to the table, and she had spotted more likely prospects elsewhere.

At the evening's end we made our way back to Salisbury Road unmolested, but drunk as skunks. Next morning was a nightmare. I had the grandfather of a hangover and suicide seemed the only sensible option. At breakfast Mrs Simmonds produced the usual full English before I could stop her, sausage, bacon, eggs, mushrooms and tomatoes glaring at me from the plate and daring me to try them. The smell that wafted up around my greenish face induced almost uncontrollable waves of nausea. If I hadn't known Mrs Simmonds better I would have sworn that she was a sadist.

On her return to the breakfast room she saw the breakfast untouched, and I had to explain that I didn't feel too well. The breakfast disappeared in a flash (boy, was I grateful) but almost immediately (or so it seemed) it was replaced by a large plate of scrambled eggs. Oh dear! I sat there. This was indeed a test of wills. Could I outstare the scrambled eggs?

They remained in place, untouched, and perhaps ten minutes later Mrs Simmonds removed them, to my utmost relief! I don't think my mumbled apologies were fully understood.

On to 'class' then, and to try to get through the day without (a) vomiting over all and sundry, or (b) dying from acute alcoholic poisoning and its best friend the hangover from hell.

The morning passed agonizingly slowly. The Chief Instructor thought our condition was most amusing, and made a big play of slamming down desk lids at every opportunity, and an even bigger play of offering us headache cures, which we accepted. He said, quite rightly, that we had been warned that our drinking exploits would come back to haunt us, and how right he was. Somehow I made it through the morning session, and by lunchtime I was feeling much better; I thought I might live, and started to feel hungry. The other classmates said they were off to a local fish and chip shop which they knew to be very good, and this sounded fine to me.

We got to the 'chippy' and placed our orders. Mine was a large cod and chips (by this time I was starving) and I waited, salivating. My enormous fish and chips were eventually placed in front of me, and boy did it look good! Was I going to enjoy this!

Well no, I wasn't. As soon as I lifted the batter off my lovely piece of fish and the smell wafted up around my nose, a violent feeling of imminent nausea attacked me and I had to bolt for the door. I wasn't sick, but there was no way that I was going to be able to eat just yet. That would teach me, I wouldn't be drinking any more. Well, not until the evening!

During the afternoon session we had to change classrooms to work on some training equipment across the site. As we walked through the 'school' along by the water the Chief looked at the sky (which was a strange colour) and said ' Just look at that sky, we'll have some snow tomorrow'. We all laughed, as it wasn't that cold. We should have known better; he was right.

We decided, Bob Moncur, Trev and I, that we ought to have a quiet night out on Thursday. We had been told by one of the lads who was on a different course (Freddy Kimmings) that the place to go for a good night out and the chance to meet some attractive women was the Joker Club. This was a small nightclub in the centre of town which offered various types of gambling.

When we went out for the evening we didn't intend to visit the club, but as the evening wore on, a few beers later it seemed like a good idea. In fact, a very good idea.

Incidentally quite a few of the Portsmouth/Southsea pubs

were tied to the Brickwoods Brewery at this time, and this was a brew to avoid at all costs as far as most of the Chatham lads were concerned. Quite early on in our visits to Portsmouth we had found Brickwoods ales to be disgusting. In fact we had a contest to see who could drink the most. We lined up a pint each along the bar of this pub, and the winner would be the one who could drink their pint first, or drink the most out of their pint. Bear in mind that amongst us were the notorious 'Beer-Pigs' from Chatham, and they would drink anything. Well not on that night. I think the winner in this particular contest drunk less than three quarters of his pint, and we were amazed at his fortitude in being able to do this! That beer was horrible. The nearest anyone came to explaining its taste was that it was like lukewarm cat's sick and coffee. Not even the King of the Beer Pigs, Ted Robinson, could swallow this Brickwoods' beer, so it must have been really bad.

Incidentally, Ted was another of the amazing characters about at that time. When we went on a course with him he would invariably chase us all up after our evening meal, which we usually had together, so that we could get out on our drinking session with him in good time. It was usually a bit of a struggle getting out in a hurry, as we were full to the gunnels with Mrs Simmonds' evening meal and felt completely bloated. This never seemed to deter Ted however, and we would all be chased out to the pub selected to start our evening's pleasures. This was when the first problem started, because as the landlord pulled up the pints Ted would invariably take one of the first ones, and before the last was pulled he would have drunk his and would say: 'come on then, gee up, who's for another?' We would look woundedly at each other and try to keep up. After about four pints at this pace some of us (me included) would go on to 'halves' but we still couldn't keep up!

One incident, often recalled, was classic Ted. A group of us were walking 'home' (back to Southsea) from a good night out in town, and as we made our way along the seafront we were passing the boating lake when a completely rubbish drunken discussion reached its high point. Ted said 'It's a matter of willpower, mind over matter, and I'll prove it to you.'

With that he sat down, removed his socks and shoes, rolled up his trouser legs and clambered over a dwarf wall into the (shallow) end of the boating lake. 'I'll show you what I mean' he said, and prepared to walk into the lake. 'What's he doing?' someone asked.

It appeared that Ted was going to walk ON the water across the lake as a demonstration of his willpower! One of the guys, I believe it was Jim O'Kane, was trying to reason with him, but of course by now it was a matter of pride.

Ted got about four feet into the lake (on the bottom, not on top of the water) when a passing police patrol car happened by. When they had been appraised of the situation, they looked at us, rather sympathetically I thought, and told us to 'bugger off home'. Good advice. We did.

So on this Thursday night we had our 'few beers' (not Brickwoods) and headed off towards the Joker night club. The night itself was strictly routine. We had a couple of drinks (half pint bottles and quite expensive), and spent a couple of pounds each at the card tables, without really having a clue as what to do. Trev was quite smitten by one of the croupiers, but then again Trev was convinced that most of the female population were in love with him anyway. Bob and I had decided by about 11 pm that we were not going to 'pull', as we thought the girls in the club were not likely to be very interested in a couple of almost skint dockyard mateys.

Trev, however, had other thoughts. He had somehow persuaded a croupier that he fancied to let him walk her home. He told us that she finished work in about 15 minutes, lived quite near, and her 'pad' was on our route walking home. Would we wait for him and we could all walk that way together?

A reasonable request, so that's what we did. When the girl finished her shift we all left together and walked back towards Southsea. We arrived at the place where the girl lived, said goodnight, left Trev to see the girl to her door and made our way back to Salisbury Road and our most welcome beds.

Next morning at breakfast we asked Trev if everything was all right (by this time he was usually deeply in love and talking about getting engaged, or some other rubbish) but he was not over-enthusiastic in his replies. So she hadn't found her one true love overnight?

We did ask Trev 'How did you get to take such a gorgeous dolly bird like that home? Did you resort to your usual bullshit and tell her you were a wealthy playboy or something?'

He gave us his best little-boy-lost look and said he might possibly have exaggerated a little on one or two comments he had made to her.

'Like what?' we asked.

'Well, I may have let slip that I have a new sports car, that my mum and dad are very wealthy and I'm an only child.'

We had to smile. We knew Trev could spin a good yarn (as with most of us on a good day), but no harm done. Or so we thought.

At mid morning the Navy has a tea/coffee/cigarette break, known as a 'stand easy'. Just prior to stand easy on this Friday morning a naval rating knocked on the door of our lecture room and told the Chief (Instructor) that Chief Petty Officer Smith was to report to the Lieutenant (known in naval parlance as Jimmie the One) at stand easy. Our instructor told the rating that this class was all civilians, so he should try elsewhere. We had our stand easy, and forgot about the incident.

Shortly after stand easy the rating appeared again, and told the Chief that 'Mr Smith' was required to report to the Lieutenant immediately. Uproar amongst the class members, and I left to seek out 'Jimmy the One'. I was escorted to the Lieutenants' Office by the rating. I knocked and entered.

The lieutenant introduced himself, we shook hands, and he asked me to sit down. He then explained that he found himself in a very awkward situation, and would like my help. I had no idea what he was talking about, but said that I would certainly help if I could.

He then asked me if I had been to the Joker Club last night with some friends. When I answered 'Yes', he dropped the bombshell. He explained: 'I know that you are not directly involved, but we have received a telephone call this morning accusing one of the party you were with last night of attempted rape.'

Rape? I couldn't believe it. Apparently the girl could remember my name, and was accusing one of the group I was with.

The Lieutenant asked if I knew who the person in question might be, and if so would I get them to contact him immediately. The girl had threatened to go to the (civil) police if she had not heard from the lieutenant, and received an apology, by twelve o'clock (noon). The lieutenant also asked if any of 'my party' was injured as the girl had stated that when she tried to ward off her attacker she had hit him with a large piece of timber!

To say that I was livid was probably the understatement of the year. I got Trev out of the classroom and told him sort it out with the Lieutenant NOW. I didn't even think to ask him what had happened, although I was almost certain that there was no complaint to answer; explanations could come later.

It was all sorted before lunch. The lieutenant didn't give us chapter and verse, but piecing together what we did know, and what we were told, it seems likely that the girl had decided to try her luck with a spot of blackmail.

Trev had tried to impress the girl and had told her that he had very wealthy parents who had just brought him a nice new sports car for his birthday and that they lived in a great big house on the coast in Kent, etc etc. It was thought that this was most likely the trigger for the blackmail attempt. During the course of the discussion with the Lieutenant, the girl said several times that she wished to keep this news from the papers and his parents, but that would depend upon circumstances.

It transpired that when investigations were made this was not the first time that this sort of incident had occurred with the same girl involved. Trev was told there was no case to answer and he was free to go. Whew! Lessons learnt there!

It had started snowing on Friday morning (just as the Chief had said), soon after eight o'clock, and by ten o'clock there was four inches of snow everywhere. The Establishment had been monitoring the worsening weather reports, and decided that all courses would finish by noon at the latest. By this time another two inches of snow had fallen, so now it was six inches deep and still falling!

We left HMS *Excellent* at 12 noon, and immediately hit the kerb outside the 'School' gate, as the snow was already so deep that we could not distinguish the path from the road. The first job was to find a filling station and top up with petrol. This was when we realized just how cold it was. I could not open the flap above the petrol filler cap as the lock had frozen solid. I used my cigarette lighter to heat up the key, and after several attempts the key went in, unlocked the cap, and I could fill up.

The next problem was seeing through the windscreen. Our breath was condensing on the inside of the glass and immediately freezing up! (The car heater was fairly primitive, and could not cope.) Luckily, or perhaps by planning, I had a gallon can of anti-freeze in the boot when I managed to get it unlocked, and we used this to cover the outside and inside of the windscreen, and even used a duster soaked in anti-freeze to keep my glasses clear!

We also took advantage of this stop to take extra (dirty) clothes out of our cases and put them on over the top of those that we were wearing, to try to keep ourselves warm.

So we started the torturous route back home. There was no A3(M) or M27 then, and EVERYBODY was trying to get home. We, like everybody else, could not make any speed because the roads were so congested and still covered in ice and snow - bloody dangerous. We crawled along the A27 at a snail's pace. It was still very cold, and the only good news was that it wasn't snowing quite as hard. Every time we came to a standstill, usually after just a few yards, it was difficult to start again, as the car just slipped on the ice and slid down the camber into the kerb. When the tyre came up against the kerb it would find sufficient traction to move on a few more yards, provided it was just a gentle tweak on the throttle.

By about 10 pm it seemed we had been travelling forever, but we had only reached the outskirts of Brighton. We could see a large roundabout up ahead, which was causing the latest hold-up. It looked like a scene from an old war film! All the cars had ground to a halt, and people had got out of their cars to exchange experiences.

In the car behind us was a young woman with two children. When we got out of the car to investigate this latest hold up, she did the same. She told us that she was very concerned that her husband would be worrying where she was as she had left Portsmouth at one o'clock. No mobile 'phones in those days.

We told her that we had left before her, so she had done very well; also we tried to reassure her about her husband's concerns, as all the radio news stations had told people what was happening.

After we had been at this spot for about ten minutes the traffic still showed no signs of moving. We were all so hungry that Trev decided he would try to find a nearby pub, before they closed, to get something to eat; crisps or chocolate perhaps? We were starving.

Trev disappeared with our caution in his ears not to be too long, as Murphy's Law dictated that as soon as he went the traffic would start to move again and we would have to go without him! Our luck held for once and he made it back to the car, armed with chocolate and crisps, just before the traffic started moving again. We shared our chocolate and crisps with the woman and children in the car behind. She was delighted, and you should have seen the kids' faces.

The rest of the journey home from Brighton, once we were clear of this wretched roundabout, was slow, but after what we had experienced all day it was almost a treat. There had not been the same extremely heavy snowfalls we had had in Hampshire, and by now a lot of travellers had managed to make it home safely, so the roads were not so crowded. We arrived back in Medway exhausted, really cold, and really, really fed up, at about half past one on Saturday morning.

Trev lived in Whitstable, so there was no way he would be able to get home that night (or to be correct, morning as it was now). Bob offered to put him up at his place in Gillingham, and the offer was gratefully accepted. Trev's real complaint, and one which he had been wittering on about for practically the whole journey home, was that he would not be home in time for his mate's stag party on Friday night. Some chance! We had been enjoying the pleasures of being stuck in a snow-bound A27 somewhere near Brighton when all the frivolities were taking place.

I dropped Trev and Bob off in Gillingham and hurried home to my rented house in Ingle Road, Chatham. I was in a hurry to get home, not only because I was knackered, hungry, and thirsty after the nightmare journey back but because for the last hour I had been really desperate for a poop!

Home at last, I dashed through the house to our outside privy, and sat down feeling grateful, relieved, and content with the world! Heaven! No light in this toilet, of course, and suddenly I felt rather cold and wet. Looking upwards, I could see the stars! As my eyes adjusted to the gloom I could see that a big hole had appeared in the toilet roof; obviously several tiles had gone missing, and the toilet floor now had a nice new carpet - of snow. I didn't linger, having completed the job.

This trip did have a happy ending though, as the Dockyard finance department ultimately paid us the 14 hours travelling time it took us to get back! Almost unheard of, as they were usually really mean bastards.

That course was the most memorable for all sorts of reasons, but almost all the courses seemed to provide at least one incident which was memorable in its own right, and usually hilarious, at least at the time. Another incident quickly comes to mind, again involving Ted Robinson, beer-drinker extraordinaire. I was staying at Mrs Simmons', as usual, and sharing a bedroom with Keith 'Porky' Harris. We had all had our evening meal, had our wash and scrub-up and changed into our 'fanny-trapping suits', and stinking of Old Spice aftershave we were in the downstairs lounge watching TV, while waiting for Ted to finish his ablutions and join us.

We were making polite conversation with Mrs Simmons and more importantly her two very tasty daughters, while sussing out any remote chance with either/both of them, when suddenly all hell let loose. An anguished shout was quickly followed by some very heavy crash-bangs, and very colourful swearing. It was BANG, SCRAPE, CRASH, then 'Fuck it!' and 'Bollocks!'

We all rushed out into the hallway and there before us was a truly wonderful sight to behold. Ted, rushing from the bathroom in just his bathrobe, had slipped at the top of the stairs and fallen down the lot. Our first concern was that he might have badly injured himself, as it was a long way to fall, top to bottom, but our concern was short lived as we saw the spectacle before us.

Ted was lying at the bottom of the stairs in a sort of star shape, his legs pointing upstairs. His hair was all over his face, and his gingerish beard was wet and straggly, 'Jesus Christ!' he shouted, although to us he looked more like Rasputin, on a very bad day. His white bathrobe had been pulled open, and as he laid there his 'tackle and two' (which was indeed a frightening spectacle) was exposed to all and sundry.

We (the boys) all giggled. They (the girls) went sort of wide-eyed, rushed to his aid, and sought his reassurance that nothing was broken. I noticed that their eyes did flick down several times to check on the 'family jewels', and remained there just too long before Ted had adjusted his dress.

Was it me, or did I afterwards notice that Mrs Simmons could sometimes be seen with a fond smile on her face when looking at Ted, and he also seemed to get even bigger dinner portions after this occurrence?

It may sound as if the courses at Portsmouth were all play, and not much attention was given to our studies, but nothing could be further from the truth. The fact is that a group of young lads away from home will usually find entertainment of some sort to keep themselves amused, and this usually involves drinking and women. However, we were all very grateful for the opportunity to attend these excellent instructional courses; we studied hard and gained the maximum benefit from them. I can't remember anyone failing the end of course exams and tests. We took this expertise back to our parent shipyards, and were the better skilled because of it.

CHAPTER 4

PROGRESSMAN'S PROGRESS

After about eighteen months in the new job I felt I had mastered most of the new skills required as Technical Progressman, and was really enjoying the work. Most of my colleagues were young (of a similar age to myself) or at least had a young outlook. A lot of the time I was given the autonomy to improve the technical assistance I could provide by obtaining excellent technical publications such as the 'Adspec 1110' which catalogued all ball and roller bearings held within the naval Stores (this was thousands), with a brief description of their recommended application (how and where they should be used).

I soon became the Section's 'expert' and could advise on the application and quality of the bearings, usually by interpretation of the dot-marking system. The Adspec also cross-referenced to the Army and RAF supply chains, so we were able to obtain items from those if necessary.

Another excellent guide was BR1336/68; this was the reference which covered the multitude of oils and greases which were held, or could be supplied through the stores system, and the use for which they were designed. Very handy when oil types were superseded or changed.

The time passed very quickly, due in no small part to the job satisfaction which I felt, as I was able to see that partly by the results of my efforts the tasks in the workshops had been progressed or completed. I enjoyed the work, and because I enjoyed it, I was good at it. I did not realize at the time that this was being noticed. However, I did make the odd mistake, and one in particular led to a serious 'piss-take' from my colleagues. I was asked to order 30 pairs of pipe-clips for the 40mm gun mounting, from the Pattern Shop. Somehow in the 'denomination' box (the type of number required, eg single, dozen or hundred) I managed to put SET instead of PAIR. A set in this case was 24 pairs, so I had ordered 24 times the quantity required!

Christ, when they arrived there were pipe-clips everywhere, and didn't my mates let me know it. 'How's the Pattern Shop Nige, still on night-shift knocking out your pipe-clips?'

Well, I certainly learnt a lesson on that one, and was very careful with the 'denomination' box on demands after that.

At about this time, eighteen months into the job, Bob Butler retired. He sat on the next desk to me, and was the very experienced Submarine Technical Progressman. I was asked if I would like to assist and provide cover for these duties for the Submarine Section, or more correctly the Submarine Weapons Section. This was a very good sign, as this was one of the most demanding and important jobs in the office. It was a sure sign that I was considered to be competent in my duties, and to have the potential for advancement.

I jumped at the chance to take on this new high-profile challenge as I looked forward to learning the new equipment and managerial skills which I would require, albeit on a relief-cover basis. I was certain that I would do a good job in this area, which would provide the platform for future promotion.

I had a week's familiarization with Bob, so that he could explain the distinct skills and contacts that would be required in these duties. Bob was a serious sort of individual, ex Navy, but very knowledgeable and conscientious. He helped me all that he could in the handover period.

The Submarine Section equipment was different for lots of reasons. For example:

- Most of the equipment was in direct contact with salt water, so different materials were often used (phosphor-bronze, aluminium-bronze, gunmetal and naval brasses etc.), all with varying degrees of anti-corrosion qualities.

- One of the first major tasks was to replace some of the major assemblies with the latest specification of bronze, as a result of extensive trials and problems encountered.

- Some of the equipment would need to be subjected to high test pressures, pressures which would be encountered when the submarine was submerged and at depth.

- As the torpedo tubes were the main armament of the submarine, they were considered to be 'critical equipment'.

- The equipment was more often affected by modifications and was updated constantly.

- Torpedo tube equipment usually had a bearing on the 'integrity of the hull'; therefore it was seen as key equipment and subject to special testing and safety requirements.

- Most planned work done on the torpedo equipment was undertaken using material lists.

This was an excellent document, used mainly when major refits or complicated modifications were to be carried out, produced by the Drawing Office. They usually accompanied a set of engineering drawings, and tabulated the item number, drawing reference, item description, number required and source of supply. This would be shown as the NATO Stock Number (NSN) or if not a 'patternised' item (an item supplied through the naval stores system). It would also be the authority to purchase from local suppliers.

The work would require regular inspection/progress visits to the submarine being refitted, which I always found to be extremely interesting. This is not to say that I would have liked to go to sea in a submarine, or even to work as an engineer on board for an extended period, as the extremely cramped conditions had to be seen to be believed!

I always found that in general the ships' and boats' crews (surface and submarine), got on extremely well with the dockyard repair teams, although this was obviously in both parties' main interests; it was more than this. I believe it was a relationship brought about by mutual respect, and I feel that this bond was the strongest with the dockyard repair teams and the submarine crews.

Time seemed to pass very quickly, and soon we had a visit by one of our old colleagues, Bob Moncur, who had been transferred on promotion to RNAD (an armament depot) at Coulport in

Scotland, about three months earlier. Bob was always the one with a biting wit, and the way he told a story, with a deadpan expression and not the hint of a smile, would have us all in stitches.

We asked him how he got on with his posting, and as near as I can remember this was his reply. He said that the first major difference he noticed was the weather. If we thought the weather was bad 'down south', we should think again (Bob had been transferred in late September, so it was winter weather he was experiencing). He said that it felt as if it had not stopped raining since he had arrived in Scotland, and usually the rain was accompanied by a biting cold wind. This situation was made even worse by time of year, which meant that the days were so short and it barely seemed to get light most days. He thought Coulport was a dark and depressing town, so not much to cheer you up really.

His first day at work was a revelation. After the routine 'signing-in', issuing of a gate pass and the other usual domestic/administrative arrangements, he was introduced to his new boss and they embarked on a workshop tour. They entered a large workshop with two rows of benches running along the whole length, with workmen working on opposite sides. The workshop was obviously quite old and the first thing that struck Bob was that the lighting should be improved. Then the noise; not machinery but the unmistakable sound of hammering on metallic objects.

As they approached the first bench Bob could see, to his horror, that a workman was hitting a very large brass-cased ammunition shell with a big lead hammer. Boy, was he giving it some stick! Bob stiffened, backed away and very nearly shat himself. He looked at the supervisor wide-eyed and open mouthed, and was met with a paternal smile. 'It's perfectly safe', he was told. 'All necessary safety measures are taken, and at this stage the ammunition is not in an active state.' Yeah? Well, it still took some getting used to!

As time went by Bob became more comfortable in his new working environment, and lost the background feeling that Armageddon was just around the corner. His principal task was to produce a time estimate to complete the various activities in the Armament Depot. This was work he enjoyed, having been doing similar work in the naval Base at Chatham, and he was fully experienced in time and motion procedures and the many other skills and practices required in the management of bonus payment schemes.

The other thing that helped Bob was that he felt that the work practices at Chatham were far more advanced than those at Coulport, which he considered to be somewhat behind in the way they conducted their business.

The social life in this part of Scotland at that time did not impress Bob. The pubs were men-only, dingy establishments where the natives were far from friendly. If spoken to they tended to scowl back and reply in an often incomprehensible broad Scots dialect. Up until that time he had not encountered any attempts to make friends, or even friendly conversation, by the locals.

Bob's 'digs' were not the best either. The Personnel Department had arranged his accommodation, so that when he reported for duty the first time he would have a pre-arranged place to stay. He was booked in to stay with an elderly widow-lady in the older part of the town. Bob described her as at least eighty years old, but very sprightly. She looked (unfair to say, but perfectly true) exactly like the wicked witch in *The Wizard of Oz*, dressed always in black from head to foot. She rarely spoke except to complain.

She provided an evening meal as part of the arrangement, but the food was impossible to identify, and although the colour varied very slightly the taste (or lack of it) did not.

He occupied the 'box' bedroom. This he was told, had previously been occupied by the landlady's son when he had lived at home, and as he had probably left home some fifty years earlier, at least, the room didn't look as if it had been decorated since. You get the picture, don't you?

All of the above paled into insignificance however, by comparison with the cold. The lodgings were a Victorian two-up, two-down terraced house, which was small and had no heat retention at all. It was dark and damp and had no central heating or double-glazing. After the evening meal, a couple of hours could be spent in the 'living room' where the tiny black and white television would be showing the soaps and programmes of the landlady's choice. This was the only room in the place that had a fire lit on a regular basis.

If you can picture this scene: a small dark room, the centrepiece a tiny coal fire which seemed to produce little more heat that a torch bulb. In pride of place, directly in front of the fire was the landlady's cat, always. The landlady sat in her chair directly in front of the fire, and Bob would be sneaking a view from the side! He could often see the fire, although he never actually felt it. It was about this time that Bob realized just how frugal the landlady was in her spending habits.

Bob did not stay in these digs for very long, and his reason for leaving was a little unusual. One night things were as always: small fire flickering away, cat curled up in front of it, landlady dozing fitfully. Another night filled with fun and frivolity was in store. Suddenly a commotion was heard in the street outside, with a bell ringing and lots of shouting. Neither Bob nor the landlady made any quick move to investigate, as of course if you moved you would surrender your place in the pecking order near the fire.

Suddenly: disaster. There was a sound of rushing water and almost immediately the whole room was enveloped in a massive cloud of soot. Bob, shocked, looked across the room, but could only just make out a pair of eyes, wide open and startled, through the billowing soot clouds. He heard, rather than saw, the cat dashing around the room in panic, trying to locate the door. It eventually found its way out, and was believed to be last seen streaking towards Glasgow.

Apparently a fire in next door's chimney had been reported to the fire brigade, and these guys had turned up looking like an excerpt from an old black and white movie with an antique fire tender and part-time volunteer firemen. When they arrived it was obviously very dark, although several neighbours had braved the cold, made it into the street and were now milling around panicking.

The lead fireman had made the roof-top, but in his excitement he had placed the water hose down the wrong chimney – Bob's lodgings. It took some little while before the mistake was recognized, by which time the hose had flooded the wrong house, and the original chimney fire had put itself out.

We were all helpless with laughter when Bob recounted this story to us in his inimitable and hilarious fashion, and tongue-in-cheek we accused him of starting the fire so that he would have a good excuse to change his digs. Anyway, he did change his digs, and ended up in far more civilized accommodation.

Bob settled down in the new job, and now that he had nice accommodation, things were looking up. After a while he (almost) got used to the wretched weather. He used to say that in Coulport it had just stopped raining, it was raining, or it was about to rain; usually the middle one.

He did come back to Chatham to visit friends and relatives still in the area, and usually made a point of calling in to the Dockyard to see us on the Weapons Section. We always enjoyed his visits, his hilarious story-telling and the news from north of the border.

CHAPTER 5

DOWN THE PUB

The social scene at this time was great, although of course at the time we did not appreciate it. Mainly our social lives centred on pubs, but what pubs they were! In your early twenties, the world is your oyster. If only we could have realized it!

One of my best friends at this time was Ted Arnold, who lived in Upchurch, and his local was the Brown Jug. He used to "force" me to go there with him, and we had some great Friday and Saturday nights there. This pub was something else, you really should have been there, for you would have enjoyed it as much as we did.

Several things combine to make a good pub, but the main one in the case of the Jug was that the Landlord, Eric Funnel, who was fairly young but very experienced, and really did know how to run a pub. He had a very outgoing personality, fully supported his darts and euchre (a card game) teams, and was always looking for ways to improve the entertainment value of his pub. He and his wife Pat made an excellent team. No wonder that eventually they were among the longest serving publicans in Kent, if not the longest.

The other main ingredient of a successful pub is the customers. What a load of characters this lot were. We won't see the likes of them again.

One of the most notable of these characters was 'Schubert', so called because of his penchant for playing classical music on the old piano in the back bar. Schubert was a Scot, obviously well educated, and it was strongly rumoured that he came from a very wealthy and well-connected family in Scotland, who gave him a regular 'allowance' as long as he (the black sheep of the family) promised to stay away.

His piano playing was a bit of a problem. Early evening, 6.30-7 pm, he would play quite nicely, but he would then start his drinking. This was usually a 'Final Selection' (a very strong bottled beer), followed by a large scotch whisky chaser. After a few of these, usually by about nine o'clock, the piano playing was loud and awful. Les Dawson wasn't in it. Eric would normally appear at this stage and tell him it was time to go home, often with the inducement of one for the road.

One night when Schubert was in especially fine form and roaring drunk, most of the pub turned out to see him leave. He used to drive a large old black Vauxhall, and on this night it wouldn't start. One of the lads offered to help and opened up the bonnet of the car. 'You'd better come and look at this' he suggested to the interested group that had gathered, me included. Underneath the bonnet there was a gallon jerry can wired in place above the carburettor. This was Schubert's petrol tank, and it was empty. To cut a long story short, when he realized he had run out of petrol, Schubert fell out of the car, staggered to the boot, retrieved another gallon can and filled up. We all stood well back, in case the whole lot exploded.

Back in the car, he started up and lurched off up the road, leaving clouds of dense smoke in his wake. Fifty yards up the road he nudged the bank on the nearside of the road and veered violently across to the opposite side, glancing a telegraph pole and putting (another) dent in his front wing. Completely undeterred, he continued on his way the short distance to the houseboat which was his home. Luckily this was only about half a mile from the pub, but heaven help anyone who met him coming from the other direction.

Quite often at weekends some of the locals would get together in an impromptu music session. George Chaney was one of the leading lights in this, and he would bring his guitar or banjo to entertain us. One of the other locals used to keep time with a 'kerdonker'. This was a large weighted boot with a long broom handle secured inside and sticking upwards. All around the handle were nails loosely holding metal beer-bottle tops so that they were allowed to move against each other and make a jingling sound. This was accompanied by the rhythmic thumping of the boot onto the pub floor, keeping in time with the music.

The principal in these singsong sessions was usually Freddie Kimmings, often supported by his brother and/or sister. I had known Fred ever since our primary school days, and he had always been the life and soul of the party. He had a vast repertoire of drinking songs, and knew most of the current pop stuff as well, and would break into song at the drop of a hat. He loved to sing, and he *really* loved his beer. Often when the pub closed, Fred would dash out to his car and return with a couple of empty five-litre plastic containers which he would get Eric the landlord to fill up with 'Master Brew' beer to take home for supper.

Freddie was a character in his own right, and it used to amaze us lads how he got away with running two long-term girlfriends, each knowing about and apparently accepting the other. This was not even a short-term situation, but one which lasted for years. He had set nights which were allocated to his girls, and they normally shared weekends!

Phoebe was Eric's mum, usually known as Fag Ash Lil. She lived with Pat and Eric at the pub, and loved to play in the card schools, especially euchre, at which she excelled. Sunday night was usually the big cards night, and often five or six tables would be busy all evening.

I have cause to remember one Sunday night euchre session very well because it was highly embarrassing for me (afterwards).

One of the couples that used to visit the pub regularly on a Sunday for the cards was Pete and Margaret from Maidstone. On this particular night Ted and I were partners playing euchre against Phoebe and Margaret. After about ten minutes into the session I was struck by an acute case of wind. This was bad enough, but I had been drinking Guinness the previous evening, and had had a massive curry for dinner. Well, the inevitable happened and I farted. Not the honest-to-goodness type, which says 'here I am'; no, this was the carpet slipper type, the very spiteful kind. I had had a couple of pints during the course of the evening anyway, and was feeling pleasantly at peace with the world. Well, it swelled up around us, an unseen cloak of pernicious fart. I couldn't help myself; I had this delicious feeling that my fart would at any second strike with enormous effect.

The first one came and went unnoticed. I searched for clues - any signs of distress/panic amongst the others? Nothing. Well, maybe a slight reaction. I thought I had seen Phoebe blink, and Ted's nose twitch.

All this time I was fighting like buggery to stop myself giggling and standing up, arms aloft, and shouting 'It's mine, It's mine, all mine!'

The second one was a real beauty, even if I say so myself. It crept out with such panache that I knew it was in a class of its own. Suddenly Phoebe stood up and glared at all of us around the table.

'Jesus Christ, who's is that?' she demanded 'Someone's arsehole's on fire!'

The game was up. My faraway look of extreme pride and pleasure was replaced by uncontrollable giggles. Tears down cheeks. A memory to savour!

It's funny how one's attitude to farts can change. My pal Ted used to say that when he was first married and his wife farted he would say 'Never mind, darling, naughty pooper!'

After about a year or so of being married, if she did it again he would go all wrinkly-lipped and snarl: 'Stop that you dirty cow, before you shit yourself!' Perhaps an indication that romance was dead?

Landlord Eric was always ready to organize; often on a Saturday night at about ten o'clock he would ask if anyone wanted fish and chips. If there were sufficient takers, and there usually were, he would head off to the chippy in Newington with a shipping order. When he got back the pub would 'shut down' for twenty minutes or so while all and sundry scoffed their fish and chips.

One episode which happened about this time concerned a trip to the coast to go cockling (collect cockles). This was organized after a chance remark late on a Saturday night; not always a good idea. The tide was out early next morning, so it meant an early start from the pub.

A Mini Van was made available, loaded with the necessary crates of beer and off they went. At lunchtime Eric produced rolls, and proceeded to fill them with cheese which he had provided. Everybody tucked in except one of the lads, who steadfastly refused anything to eat at all. They all thought that perhaps he felt a little queasy after last night's boozing; it wasn't until much later that he explained that immediately prior to Eric doing the cheese rolls, he had been spotted having a shit, and no one saw him wash his hands! Anyway, no-one seemed to have any ill effects, either from the cockles or from the landlord's lack of hygiene.

One Friday night as we were leaving the pub, Ted's neighbour Whispering Reg Smith, who I had not met before, asked if we would give him a lift home. I had no problem with this as I was taking Ted there anyway. When we got to Ted's a

very unsteady Reg got out of the car and asked what he owed
me for the lift home. I said that I did not want any money as I
was going that way anyway. Reg then turned very abusive and
loud (hence the name, probably). He put his hand in his pocket,
threw a handful of money into the car, told me to fuck off several
times, slammed the car door and wandered off. This apparently,
was his party piece. Ted later explained that Reg was well known
in the road for his exploits.

For example, on one occasion Lyn (Ted's wife) was woken
up about five o'clock in the morning by the reflection of a
roaring fire in the bedroom window. Worried in case the house
was on fire, Lyn jumped out of bed and stared out of the window.
Looking across into Reg's garden next door she could see Reg's
wife doing the washing in a galvanized tin bath over an open
fire. This was the fire Lyn had seen. When Lyn talked to her
neighbour some time later, she explained that Reg had spent all
their housekeeping money on drink, and as a result their gas had
been disconnected, so this was the only way she was able to do
their washing. She was doing it at night as she was too
embarrassed to let neighbours see her doing this during the day.

It certainly wasn't easy for Lyn's neighbour. She had a
particular dread of Christmas as Reg liked to celebrate (even
more than usual) at this time of year, and last year had been a
disaster. He had been out at lunchtime on Christmas Eve, and
had a skinful. When he got home after lunch he started drinking
again, and by early evening he was with the fairies.

At about 8.30 there was a knock on the door. It was a

Salvation Army soldier collecting for the charity and preaching the message concerning the demon drink. Reg was so impressed with the Salvation Army guy that he invited him in and listened intently. Suddenly Reg saw the light, realized the error of his ways and was determined to do something about it. With the Salvation Army man's encouragement and help, all of Reg's Christmas (and other) drinks were emptied down the drain-Halleluiah! Halleluiah!

Next morning when Reg went to get his 'livener', he discovered that every single drop of booze that had been in the house last night had gone down the drain. He could not remember anything about this. To say that he was not amused doesn't even come near. His wife got all the blame and a good pasting for not stopping him from destroying his booze.

Another local at the Jug was Old Jack; in fact he lived in. He was another character, dry humour, shortish, tubby, usually wearing a waistcoat and a trilby hat. He was believed to be Phoebe's boyfriend. One night Eric served Phoebe a Cherry B, as she had expressed a wish to try a different drink. Eric said, as a throwaway line, 'You had better watch those Mum, they are pretty potent'. Jack, standing at the end of the bar, looked over the top of his glasses and sneered 'Be careful? Those Cherry B's are gnat's piss, they won't hurt you, unless you drink a pint of them'.

Eric took the bait. 'Gnat's piss, are they? Well I bet you can't drink a pint of them. If you drink it, I'll pay for it.'

So the challenge was on. Eric got a pint glass, poured four Cherry Bs into it and gave it to Jack. 'There you go then' he said, 'get that down your neck - if you're man enough!'

Red rag to a bull. Jack knocked back over half of the glass's contents in one go, paused and smacked his lips. 'Go on then, get on with it', was Eric's instruction.

Jack emptied the glass, banged it on the counter and surveyed the watching on-lookers with a barely concealed sense of pride. 'Told you, gnat's piss' he volunteered.

Several minutes later Jack went quiet, and his face went a funny colour. It wasn't red, more of a deep plum colour. He looked around the bar with a slightly confused look on his face, then gently slid down the bar and collapsed into a heap in the corner, unconscious.

Eric was the first to react. 'Gnat's piss eh?' he asked. 'Will some of you old boys give me a hand to put this twat to bed?' They did, and Jack was quiet for a couple of days.

Another great pub was the Three Tuns. This was my local more than the Jug really, in terms of being at the bottom of the road in which I lived, and it took over as our place to go for a drink once the drink and drive regulations started to bite. I used the 'Tuns' intermittently over quite a few years, and this pub also had its crazy characters and several landlords during this time.

The first landlord I remember was Old Charlie, a larger-than-life character who loved his darts team. Several weeks after I moved into the village (Lower Halstow) we visited the pub for the first time. Everyone seemed reasonably friendly and it looked as if it was going to be a normal evening until about 10.30, when Charlie burst through the door carrying a very large darts trophy which they had just won. Obviously flushed with the momentous achievement by his darts team (and a good few Scotch whiskies I guess), he lit the place up. Everyone was told to refill their glasses to toast the magnificent success of the darts team, and the place was instantly buzzing.

At around 11.15 we were about to leave when we were challenged by Charlie. 'What's up, don't you like my beer?' he asked, engaging the top bolt on the front door. A little sheepish, I replied that I thought eleven o'clock was closing time, and we were expected to leave. 'Don't upset yourself, old son, we don't worry too much about that sort of thing down here', he explained patiently. So we had another, actually a few more, and got home about half past one. I thought – I could get to like this place!

Friday night was always a busy night in the Tuns. Sometimes forty guys would be packed into the public bar. A dozen or so were jobbing builders, and loads of work was discussed, offered and arranged in between joke-telling sessions and lots of heavy drinking.

One of the regulars was a legend for his success with the ladies. He would often arrange to meet one of his special 'girlfriends' half way through the evening, when he would go missing for about an hour or so. On at least two occasions his wife telephoned the pub and demanded to speak to him, as she had a pretty good idea what was going on. When this happened the landlady would get one of his mates to answer the phone and tell his wife he had just gone to the toilet. This didn't really convince the wife, and she insisted that they got him to phone back in the next ten minutes. One of his mates would then dash up to the lay-by alongside a nearby orchard, and when the violent rocking of the car stopped, he would tap on the window and explain the emergency. The stud would re-enter the bar, make a wonderfully imaginative call to his wife, and all would be well - until the next time.

This guy was not overly discreet and his stories would entertain and fill us with jealousy in equal measures, on a regular basis. Initially we thought most of the escapades were products of his very fertile imagination. However, many of us would bump into him, usually in an out-of-the-way pub with different women, none of them his wife, and all of them good lookers. Mind you he did have the necessary requirements for his 'hobby'. He had the time, the inclination (oh yes!) and the money, as he ran his own company.

He was of course, not the only playboy in the village. In fact it seemed that at this time about 90% of the Friday night drinking school were having a bit on the side - or at least they said they did, or were working on it.

Not all the extra-marital escapades were confined to the customer's side of the bar. The old landlord, Charlie, had retired and one of several younger couples who had subsequently taken over were running the pub. Of course the landlord heard most of the tales from the opposite side of the bar, and he decided that he ought to take advantage of any opportunities that might come his way. I know he made up a foursome on several occasions with the aforementioned village stud, and no doubt a good time was had by all, but I remember one night was quite extraordinary, and far more memorable to me than all the others put together.

On this particular night the landlord had been out with some of his mates to a party, having left his wife and the barmaid in charge for the evening. He got back to the pub after midnight, drunk as a skunk. The landlady had excused herself about half an hour earlier, probably anticipating her husband's condition, and left the barmaid to see the few regulars off the property and to lock up. When the landlord got back he did not appear to want his customers to rush off home - in fact he served more drinks to those who asked and had one himself. He had obviously had a very good evening, was full of himself, and started flirting with the barmaid.

At this point it should be explained that she was a little on the plain side, but quite well built and a good sport. Well, one thing led to another, and it was easy to see what was on the landlord's mind. After making a blanket enquiry if anyone wanted another drink, he asked the barmaid if she would help him to find a brewery invoice in the back room. Off they went.

Between the public bar and the back room there was a small glass partition or serving hatch which was never used, and with large cordial and mixer bottles in front of it was never cleaned and largely forgotten about. Certainly the landlord had forgotten about it! One of the drinking party crept around the bar and peeped through. 'Christ, you'd better have a look at this' he whispered, waving us around the bar to spy through the hatch.

What a picture! The landlord had his trousers and pants

down around his ankles and the barmaid was bent over the table, skirt up around her waist. The landlord had his cock in hand and was manoeuvring, grunting and pushing and trying to get John Thomas home.

At last, success. She whimpered 'That's it, that's great, now fuck me to a standstill!' Like he needed any more encouragement! He might have been pissed, but Christ wasn't he randy! She obviously knew what she wanted, and now the opportunity had presented itself.

I must admit the sex scene being played out before us was quite a turn on (for me) but I had sensed the others moving away and when I looked round I saw why.

While the landlord was playing his little cameo role saying 'I warned you what would happen if I caught you serving late drinks', and thrusting like there was no tomorrow, the barmaid in turn was whimpering 'Yes, I know I'm naughty, I deserve it, punish me with that big hard cock!' Dear oh dear! Very theatrical.

I then realized that there was further movement alongside me and that two of the other customers were pumping the spirit optics for all they were worth. Several glasses were filled up with at least trebles, and either drunk down in one go or passed onto the bar for their mates. I would estimate that in the next ten minutes, half a bottle of rum and at least the same of brandy was swallowed without touching the sides.

The barmaid reappeared first, rather chirpy I thought, and started to make 'Don't you have homes to go to?' noises. The landlord did 'surface' before we left, looking a little sheepish, but with a significant smile on his face. It looked like a job well done.

A regular at the pub at this time, and a long term village resident, was Les Jones. Les was a larger-than-life character who lit the place up when he entered the bar.

During this period Les was mostly working at the Bowater paper works in Gillingham as a maintenance fitter, and this meant that all week he would be visiting the many different sections in the factory, picking up new jokes for his impressive repertoire. On Friday nights in particular Les would keep us entertained for hours, without repeating a joke once.

Les and I were also regulars at the Lower Halstow Working Man's Club, which was originally built for the recreation of the Eastwoods brickfield workers and located in an oast house-style building at the end of Westfield cottages.

There were again, so many characters that frequented this club, including Ray Cheyney, the Singing Shepherd (he usually gave us 'Old Shep' — bloody depressing); Bernie the Bolt, whose blue song repertoire included Bollocking Bill the Sailor etc, and Karen, the Beer Queen. She was immaculately dressed and turned out, but usually pissed by closing time.

Some of Les' relatives were also regulars (the village was almost incestuous at this time) and one of his sisters-in-law would occasionally come out with a greeting which intrigued us all. Apparently when Les was first married, he lived in a tiny, damp cottage in the centre of the village, which has long since been demolished. He was an enthusiastic and very competent sportsman, and played rugby, football and cricket at a high level. One Sunday morning he was late changing into his cricket gear, and the top drawer of his chest of drawers (where his sports kit was kept) was stuck due to the damp. He wrenched the drawer open and removed his kit, then tried to push the drawer closed with his hip. The drawer didn't move, so in frustration he gave it another full-on shove with his pelvis. This time the drawer slammed shut, trapping his cock inside!

He said he could not begin to describe the pain, and his anguished shouts could probably be heard in Upchurch, the next village! Picture him, eyes watering, standing on tip-toe. He had released himself by the time that his wife (Emmy) had reached the bedroom, coming up the stairs two at a time, but his cock had taken an awful battering. It was black, blue and throbbing!

No long-term damage was done; Les even got to the cricket match, but said that he was walking like a saddle-sore cowboy for a couple of days. He also volunteered that he was a little cautious when he put the 'old man' back to work for the first time shortly after his accident. Emmy was sworn to secrecy regarding the mishap, but of course she subsequently revealed all the sordid details to her sister.

Some months later, Les's sister-in-law had an accident involving the sash-cord windows in the back bedroom of her cottage. She was trying to open the window, which had jammed, by pushing upwards with both hands and with her body close in to the bottom half. Suddenly the sash cord broke and the top half of the window came down like a portcullis, trapping her dress and pinching her left breast into the frame. Her distressed shouts were heard, and she was quickly released by her shocked husband, luckily sustaining only nasty bruising, grazing and soreness. Subsequent offers and attempts to massage the affected area, and anywhere else for that matter, were supposedly refused.

Having been made aware of the background as above, it was now simple to recognize the reasoning behind the 'party-piece' greetings:

'Hello there, cock-in-the-drawer, how's things?'

'Fine, tit-in-the-window, how are you?'

Les was a smashing fella, and we became good friends.

Most of the social scene at this time was centred on the pubs. The most memorable nights happened when my mates were home on leave, and we could meet up for a Saturday night out on the town. Pete Barnes was in the RAF, Derek Hawkes was in the Navy, Richard (Dood) Hicks (my nephew) was at University (London School of Economics), and I (the 'fourth musketeer') was a dockyard matey. A diverse collection, we probably hadn't seen each other for several weeks, so there was plenty to talk about.

We were young, good looking and had a few bob in our pockets, so it was look out Medway, here we come! We could almost taste the anticipation of a good night out. Usually we would catch the bus from Rainham to Luton Arches in Chatham. The plan was to have a pint in all the pubs we liked (which was most of them) along the high street, going into Rochester High Street and along to Star Hill. Some chance! It must have been about two miles, and at this time I would guess that there were about thirty pubs along this route. Most are gone now unfortunately, but the ones I remember as our favourites were (starting from Luton Arches end) the East

End Hotel, the Coachmakers' Arms, the White Lion, the Fountain, the Duchess of Edinburgh, the Red Lion, the Sun Hotel (the Sunshades), the Von Alton, the Royal Exchange, the Rose and Crown, the Ship Inn, the North Foreland and the Hare and Hounds, although we never got that far without cheating and missing out a few! (Apologies to the other pubs I have missed out, if they are still there!)

The Duchess of Edinburgh and the Fountain always struck me as being quite lively, and here it was even more of an incentive to behave, as fighting often broke out and usually some of the working girls would be present (not fighting, offering their services).

Looking back it was all fairly tame stuff by today's standards. Most of the pubs were quiet early on, and we could hop from pub to pub, have our pints (most of which were pretty ordinary as I recall) and on to the next boozer. It was going home that sobered us up.

We didn't have money for taxis, so if we missed the last bus, which we invariably did, it was the long walk home. Rainham was only about four miles, but that can be a long way if it starts to rain, or the weather decides to deteriorate, and of course we didn't wear anything on top of our suits. If we had any money left we would sometimes visit the coffee stall in Railway Street for a steak and kidney pie (with plenty of brown sauce) and a cup of tea, plenty of sugar. Oh yes, we knew how to live!

The other main activity walking home (where we always expected to meet up with four gorgeous girls who were looking to meet up with the men of their dreams (us), and seduce us repeatedly, in spite of pleas for mercy) was 'hedge hopping'. For the uninitiated, this basically means running alongside a hedge (plenty of these along Watling Street) until you have built up enough speed to enable you to jump into the top of the hedge, which cushions your fall (hopefully). My problem with this was that the other guys had more than one suit, whereas I didn't. After a couple of jumps into the hedge I realized what was happening to my suit (how would I attract the crumpet without it?) and decided that hedge–hopping was not for me.

Chatham and Rochester were the places to go for the best entertainment. Most of the pubs were lively at the weekend, and there were so many in those days that we were spoilt for choice!

One of my favourite pubs at this time was the Rose and Crown opposite Grays' motorbike showroom at the Rochester end of the High Street. Usually on Saturday nights the pub would be full of darts players, several of whom were Irish lads who were building the M2 motorway, and Saturday nights they were out for a good drink, to let off steam, and an evening of darts. This pub was also a good base for an evening tour (pub crawl) and an ideal meeting place if a night at Victor Silvester's Dance Hall above the Gaumont Cinema at Star Hill was planned. This was where Dood would try to persuade us to go, as he had always fancied himself as a good ballroom dancer, and the answer to many a maiden's prayer to boot!

One such evening amuses me when I think back. Dood was on a summer break from university and was working at the Metal

Box Factory in Strood to raise some funds. This provided the bonus opportunity to meet a lot of the girls that worked on the factory shop-floor, and at this time he was courting one called Joyce. Joyce was a good looker, blond bouffant hair, nice make up, and legs which ran all the way up to her bum before they got cheeky (the old jokes are the best...)

This particular night Joyce was sitting opposite me, wearing a very mini mini-skirt, and I was joke telling, as usual. She had by this time sunk several Cherry Bs. The joke involved was the old chestnut about "If you cut a flea's legs off it goes stone deaf", and I was explaining this with appropriate hand actions. Unfortunately, as I acted out the joke, the cigarette I was smoking brushed against Joyce's knee and laddered her tights.

'You silly bugger!' she announced. 'Look what you've done to my tights!' She pulled up her mini-skirt to show us the extent of the damage, not realizing (or perhaps she did?) that she was giving half the pub a splendid view of her wonderful assets. Dood blushed, and wished that she hadn't explained quite so well; we were amazed and delighted. She became a firm favourite of all the pub from that day on. Boy, what a view!

On the dancing theme, another haunt of ours was the 'Pav', the Pavilion Ballroom, Gillingham. I don't really know why we went there except that there probably wasn't anywhere else to go. I think the Pav was really a training centre for the Samaritans. You could go out on a Saturday night, have a few beers with the lads and end up in the Pav, and that's when depression would set in - in a big way. I had been to lots of dance halls around the country, but never had I seen such a collection of ugly women assembled together at the same time. Not all of them of course, but a significant number, and certainly enough to terrify a young man. Not only that, but they invariably seemed to take great pleasure in refusing to dance when politely asked (I think this was probably one of the few thrills they got).

Dood, of course, loved the Pav, as it gave him the opportunity to demonstrate his dancing prowess, and of course he took his own 'bird', who happened to be Joyce. After persistent pleading from all the lads to bring some of her friends from the Metal Box factory as blind dates for us lads, he came up trumps; well sort of. He got Joyce to bring one of her friends with her.

That was the good news. The bad news was that she made most of the women at the Pav seem almost average. This one was never going to be called a looker. Of course, she latched onto me, and as the evening wore on she became less ugly, passable even - in the dark. To cut a long story short, she pestered me all evening to take her home. As a throwaway line I said I had left my motorbike at home as I would be drinking, so if she would like to walk home to Rainham with me to collect my bike I would give her a lift home! Ha ha, that should stop her persistent requests.

Well, no. Of course she said yes – in fact she jumped at the chance. (I thought afterwards that it was only marginally less distance to walk to Rainham than for her to walk home to Strood). At the evening's end I walked home and she tagged along. As we made our way alongside the Orchards in Lower

Gillingham I did consider suggesting that we hop over the fence and stop for a monumental roger, but by this time I had sobered up somewhat, and although I was drunk, I wasn't that drunk. (This was a major failing on my part, I was always too fussy.)

We eventually got to the bottom of my road in Rainham and I suddenly realized that I wasn't keen on this girl knowing exactly where I lived. I explained that I would need a while to get the bike out and start it up, so I was going to go on ahead. I dashed off. Bloody hell, I couldn't half run when I had to. I got the bike out and met the girl half way down the road. I took her home to Strood (still in the suit, no helmet etc) and dropped her off, refusing the offer of coffee, as this would have been dangerous. Also by now it was gone two o'clock and I was knackered. It was bloody cold going home on the bike, but at least I had escaped relatively unscathed!

I must admit that I did see her a couple of times afterwards, to make up a foursome with Dood and Joyce, but only when it was very dark. It was never going to be a long term thing.

My first motorbike – a 125cc Royal Enfield. No "Ton up" machine
this one. More like £18 worth of trouble!

My pride & joy – my BSA Model B31. A great bike, this picture was
taken after the accident and rebuild.

A naval frigate entering the North Lock

A nuclear submarine undocking, No 7 Dock Chatham

A nuclear submarine leaving the ships' basin, Chatham Dockyard

Weapons Table Tennis Club, 1966: L-R Geoff Hancock, Bill Hayward,
Dave Randall, Peter Broughton, Dave Riley, Ray Packham, Bert Newborough,
Bob Smith and Martin Strike.

The Civil Service Sports & Social Club, Lawn Tennis Section.
Bob Smith is second left, back row.

The Medway Towns Table Tennis League Annual Presentation 1970/71 in St Mary's Canteen, Chatham Dockyard. Bert Newborough receives his Sportsman of the Year Trophy from the European Table Tennis Champion, Jill Hammersley, asking her: "Have you got any old table tennis bats you don't want?" Dave Randall wishes he wasn't there!

Mr R J Smith
TSG

23 January 1992

Dear Bob

I am delighted to inform you that you have been granted a Special Bonus Award of £400.

This award is made in recognition of your dedication and outstanding performance throughout the period of the Gulf War.

Authorisation for payment has been sent to CPRO(B) and should appear in your account in the near future. A copy of this letter will be placed on your Personal File.

Thank you for all your hard work and support during an exceptionally busy and demanding period.

Yours Sincerely

Keith Steel

Letter from Keith Steel

Quality work at Ashford

ABRO Ashford has won an accolade for the quality of its work and procedures. Both workforce and management are extremely proud of this achievement, but the British Standards Institute award ISO 9002 is tinged with irony and sadness because the certificate has been earned just six months before the ABRO workshop closes. Even so, it reflects great credit and loyalty of the workforce.

The workshop and workforce, now down to 156, are casualties of the "peace dividend" rundown in the MOD and also the Channel high-speed rail link route which will go across the site.

Andrew Hunter, Director of BSI, said: "This is a significant achievement for any organisation, even more so for one which faces the kind of challenge that ABRO does. It demonstrates there is a very clear commitment right through the organisation and a high level of teamwork. These things don't happen by accident."

The proud staff watch as Andrew Hunter, Director of BSI,
hands the diploma to Carl Floyd, Workshop Director.

Featured in the Abro News

Tedworth House - not bad 'digs'!

REME Regimental Dinner, Officers' Mess (Foley Arms) Malvern, March 2000. Author is third from left, bottom row.

Dear Mr Smith,

On your retirement, I should like to convey to you on behalf of the Permanent Under-Secretary of State his warm thanks for your valued work in the Ministry of Defence and his appreciation of the many years of service you have given.

From my personal standpoint, I would like to express my gratitude for your more recent contribution to ATSA and its forerunners, as well as our sister agency ABRO, in support of Army Equipment.

I should also like to express on behalf of all your colleagues best wishes for a long and happy retirement.

Yours Ever,

Tony Benn

Retirement letter from Tony Benn, Chief Executive of the ATSA

ONWARDS AND UPWARDS

I had by now settled in to my new duties on the section, and was enjoying it. The fact that the target dates we were working to were realistic and important, especially regarding the overhaul of the submarines, provided a high degree of job satisfaction. The people I was working with, the production team, the Design Division (drawing office), the contractors, and the support trades which manufactured or supplied the enormous amount of sub assemblies and equipments, were without exception, keen and dedicated to their work.

The other major bonus of working on the submarines was that due to its importance, correct and updated information was usually available. All equipment fitted on board was scrupulously monitored for defects (pre-installation testing), and updated to the latest specification, and complete and updated records were mandatory.

Configuration control (the 'standard' use of equipment and its location in a batch of ships or submarines) was a system which was preferred on surface ships, but was much more stringently controlled on submarines. The important reasons for this were:

- If a submarine on patrol experienced a failure on any of its equipment, and the necessary spares were not available on board, it was essential that the correct spares were supplied and that they would fit exactly into the space vacated by the defective items. This was to minimize downtime and ensure the correct performance of the replacement item.

- This system enabled the supply system, the Naval Stores, to ensure that it purchased only the correct spares required, and that they were to the latest specification and modification state.

- Configuration control could play an important role in reducing 'noise shorts'. This is basically ensuring that all equipment is fitted with the proper resilient mountings, and that it is not located close enough to vibrate against other equipment or a bulkhead. Noise shorts are a critical factor in silent running for submarines, and the British subs at this time had an excellent and well-deserved reputation in this procedure.

An important element in the submarine overhauls was ensuring that the latest issue of engineering drawings were supplied and used for the refit. These would show any modifications necessary to improve the efficiency and reliability of the boat, or would reflect some other essential change required. At least two sets of drawings would be issued to the planning office prior to the boat's refit starting; one set for the production team, as working copies, and one set to be kept in the Technical Library for replacements or for perusal by Production Management.

Both sets of drawings would usually be accompanied by a material list, which as previously explained would list any associated drawings required; items to be manufactured locally (in the Dockyard); items to be sourced from contractor supply; any protective finish that was required to the components, eg heat treatments, chrome plating or galvanizing; and any other information considered to be relevant which would be required during the refit.

I believed I had established a good rapport with the guys in the drawing office, and found that if approached properly, they were more than happy to provide additional drawings, quite often very quickly, and would obtain additional technical data if this was required. I think that at this stage of my working life, my enthusiastic attitude and determination to do a good job was recognized and appreciated by colleagues and work contacts alike, and helped me become recognized as an asset to the section, and one to watch for the future.

On-board visits to the submarines were sometimes requested by the Production Inspectors. These were always very interesting, as you could see exactly where the equipment was installed, and get a real feel for how your efforts in the refit fitted into the grand scheme of things. Additionally, you could get an insight into the difficulty the production boys had squeezing all this equipment into the space provided - and of course it had to work, after it had been installed! It is quite impressive to see the compartments on board the submarines packed with all the equipment necessary for its self-contained patrols.

Apart from the main and secondary propulsion systems - engines, usually diesel or electric - systems included fresh and salt water, refrigeration, air conditioning, hydraulics, HP and LP air systems, electrical power and lighting, navigational, weapons, galley equipment, officers and crew's quarters, and much more which had to be cramped in somewhere. Bearing in mind that British submarines are much smaller than surface craft, you begin to see what an achievement this is.

The on-board visits were always very interesting, but at the same time it was always good to get back to the office environment, to get warm and to escape the feeling of claustrophobia.

The submarines tended to be docked where the specialist shore supplies were available; this was in No 3 or 4 Dock, in the South Yard area, or more likely 6 or 7 dock (south of Basin 1). Progress update visits were also made to the main production workshops before the regular monthly Planning and Progress review meetings. This was a good opportunity to establish working contacts with my 'opposite numbers', the Progressmen, and also the line managers at these production centres, which were providing the required support effort for the equipment being refitted.

The Engineering Factory was probably the biggest support centre for our refit programmes. Almost any metal object could be manufactured in this massive workshop. The usual output was pipework flanges, pump shafts and impellors, special nuts and bolts and engine parts, along with practically anything else that was required.

Almost all the normal materials were machined in this workshop, including the ferrous irons and steels and the non-ferrous materials more commonly used in the submarines, including naval brasses, phosphor bronze, gunmetal, copper, aluminium, and even the more exotic materials such as lignum vitae (an extremely dense wood).

The variety of machine tools was equally surprising. There were various types of lathe, including a massive long-bed type which was used to machine ships' main shafting. Sometimes ships' shafts would become heavily scored at the bearing landings. A reclamation could often be carried out by coating the damaged area of the shaft with an Araldite mix and then using this specialized lathe to machine the repaired area back to the standard dimensions. Other lathe types included precision, capstan and numerical-controlled variations. Grinding machines, milling machines, shaping and slotting machines and drills were among the other specialist machine tools available.

None of this equipment would have been much use if skilled men had not been available to operate them. Some of the machine operators had worked in this factory for ten, twenty or even thirty years, sometimes many years on the same machine, and were really top-grade machinists. Engineering drawings were usually supplied for them to work from, but they were equally happy with a thumbline sketch on the back of a fag packet, and would produce a beautifully finished end product. These old guys could make their machines work wonders.

Another major support area was the Electrical Repair

Workshops. They overhauled all the electrical motors (AC and DC) which had been removed from the boat, and had the necessary facilities to rewire and test them before they were returned and re-installed back on board. All control gear, starters and any associated equipment could be returned to an as-new condition in these workshops.

The main Boilershop did not only manufacture and repair boilers. The main services to us were to provide brackets, cabinets or cupboards, handrails, floor-decking and welding tasks. They also carried out various heat treatments, and manufactured forgings (with the Smithery). Associated with the boilermakers, the laggers would remove lagging to enable equipment to be removed to the workshops for overhaul, and re-lag it on completion of the repairs and the reinstatement of the equipment into the vessel.

By now the dangers of working in an asbestos dust contaminated area had been recognized, and appropriate precautions were taken to protect the workforce from this extreme hazard. This would usually mean closing any compartment where removal or replacement of asbestos was necessary, and only the authorized and prepared workforce could enter, until checks had been made to ensure that it was safe to re-enter.

A very important input into the repair programme was the service provided by the Coppersmiths' Centre, manufacturing new or replacement pipes to connect the various engineering systems. 'Wires' (rod templates to the same shape and length of the required pipes) would be taken on board and returned to the shop, where the new pipe would be made, flanges fitted (one end fixed and one end loose for final length adjustment on board) by welding or brazing (with the holes pre-drilled), and returned to the boat for installation. The boat's systems could not usually be flushed and tested until the last pipe was delivered and installed.

Various other support was required, depending upon the type of boat and the 'depth' of refit; but this would usually include:

- The Hose Shop, which as the name implies would provide hoses for the various services found on board the boat: steam, water, hydraulic. oil etc.

- The Fridge Shop. The main refrigeration plants would normally be overhauled in situ (on board the boat), with any smaller domestic-type units sent to the Fridge Shop for overhaul and testing.

- The Pattern Shop/Joiners. Any furniture type repairs, patterns for the production of castings, wooden partitions, shelving, and bespoke cupboards would be arranged by this centre.

The Dockyard Laboratory was available when there was a need for unusually detailed technical support, or if scientific analysis or testing was required.

The other dockyard centres would provide support as required, and contractors provided goods and services as requested.

All in all these visits helped to give me the necessary insight to the Dockyard's structure and workings, and an understanding of who did what, and where.

CHAPTER 6

One of the more interesting aspects of working on the submarine equipment was that I would now be working for John (Sarge) Pattman, who had in the meantime been promoted to Inspector, and was mad. When I say mad, I don't really mean that in a derogatory way, as Sarge was a really nice bloke; he had a heart of gold (although did his best to hide it), and was conscientious to a fault. Yes, a good bloke, but mad as a box of badgers!

I'll give you a couple of examples. One morning as I got to work and was parking up, I noticed a very agitated Sarge in the car park pacing around his car and talking to himself. I went into the office building, clocked on and made my way into my place of work. After a few minutes the door flew open and Sarge stormed in. 'Get your coat on mate' he said, 'We're going up to Hale Hamilton's.' These were the West London contractors who supplied most of the High Pressure Air Controls for the weapons equipment.

'Hang on John,' I said, 'We'll need an order form and demand number, and it would be a good idea to tell them we're coming to visit.'

'No time for that old crap mate, I know what we want, come on!' Typical John.

'Well, I've got to clock off if we are leaving the Dockyard,' I explained.

'No time for that either mate, we're leaving now!' John answered, agitated, and proceeded to jostle me down towards his car. So off we shot (the phrase 'like a bat out of hell' comes to mind).

John was not a good driver. By that I mean that if he was annoyed, and that happened all the time, he would go a nice plum colour from the neck upwards, his hair would flop down over his eyes, and he would glare at his passenger while berating whoever had upset him, in a barely controlled fury. All this would happen as he was staring at his passenger, with little reference to the road ahead. He certainly frightened me; it was just like a ride at the circus on the Wall of Death.

When we got to the outskirts of London, John became unsure of his route and looked to me for inspiration. I thought it best to admit that I didn't know the way, and this did not go down well at all. For the next few miles John scowled and muttered, with the occasional barbed glance in my direction.

We eventually got to the factory and after some detailed explanations we collected the required items. Job done. But now I had the nightmare journey back to look forward to!

John also had trouble accepting delays on his store demands. On one occasion he had ordered a major assembly for the torpedo tubes with (against my advice) a very short and unrealistic delivery date. When the requested items didn't show, John asked for them to be 'chased' and the expected delivery date obtained. It transpired that there was only one of these items in store and that was earmarked for a submarine with a higher priority. Demands had been placed with the manufacturer for additional items, and they would be available in the normal expected timeframe.

Not good enough for John. Although 'his' submarine was in

refit and a lower priority, he wanted to obtain the item held in store for the other sub. John told me to contact the stores and request that the item be diverted for us at Chatham. Of course the Stores Officer refused and referred me to his boss, who also said no.

Still not good enough for John, who was by this time getting really wound up and frustrated. 'Phone his boss, mate, keep going till someone will give us the go-ahead' he said. So I phoned his boss, who said no and referred me up the chain of command.

Eventually, I was speaking to a very posh voice at the other end, and I was insisting that this item must be released to us at Chatham to prevent jeopardizing our refit programme. The person at the other end listened quite patiently, and then asked me my name and rank. I explained that I was the Technical Progressman for the Weapons Section at Chatham. Silence at the other end, and then he asked 'What is a Technical Progressman?'

I felt a bit silly by now, as it was obvious that this guy had never before heard of someone so far down the food-chain. I subsequently discovered that he was in fact a Naval Commander, and he gave John P. a massive bollocking for trying to circumnavigate the stores delivery system. John behaved himself for almost two weeks!

When John Pattman was promoted to Inspector and left the Planning Office, his replacement, Dennis Osborne, arrived. Dennis was a really nice chap, a big guy, ex RAF, always cheerful and an old-fashioned gent. He hadn't been on the section long when he was involved in an incident which had us all in hysterics for weeks.

Kathy, our tea lady was in the habit of emptying the large tea-pot that she used for the office down the toilet bowl in the cubicle next door. On this particular day Dennis was halfway through a wee inside the cubicle with the door only half closed, very large Mr Cocky in hand. Kathy, in a massive hurry as usual, entered the room and threw open the toilet door while swinging the upturned teapot (half full of cold tea) towards the toilet pan, muttering to herself as usual.

Bugger! The cold tea fountain was over Dennis's cock before he had time to dodge.

Apparently he stood there open mouthed, cock in hand (now nicely mottled with the tea-leaves) in a state of shock and embarrassment, unable to move or react. Kathy was heard to say, 'Bloody hell, you silly bastard, why don't you close the door?'

In fact she lingered far too long to stare at the 'one-eyed Python', which was a thing of beauty even camouflaged with caffeine. Eventually she forced her gaze away, and dashed out of the door giggling in a highly nervous state! Dennis always got the chocolate biscuits after that.

CHAPTER 7

SPORT AND RECREATION

It wasn't all work and no play. I love to play my sports, always did. I had played table tennis since my youth club days, and still fancied myself as a good player, so when I heard that several of the workforce used to go to the No. 9 Weapons Store on St Mary's Island to play in the lunch hour, I was very interested and decided to take a look. They used to set up two tables in the stores building, and take it in turns to play each other.

I was surprised to find that the standard of play varied considerably, and that some of the players there could beat me. The guy who organized the practice sessions was Dave Randall, and he explained that they had several teams from the Weapons club which played competitive games in the league. To cut a long story short, I joined the club and we started the Weapons IV team, in Medway Table Tennis League, Division 6.

Some of the original club players at that time included Jeff Hancock, Bill Hayward, Dave Randall, Peter Broughton, Dave Riley, Ray Packham, Bert Newborough and Martin Strike.

I played for many years, mainly in Division 2, as we won several promotions through the Divisions. I usually played with Bert

Newborough, one of the real characters in the local table tennis world. I believe that when I started playing league table tennis he was over fifty years old, but very fit for his age and a very good player. We shared some great memories, not least of all of the Medway Towns Table Tennis League annual trophy presentation evenings.

The first one I went to was held in Rochester, and the guest of honour presenting the trophies was John Simpson, the Gillingham goalkeeper and a local hero at the time. I remember his words as he presented me with my trophy: 'Take good care of it, I don't give much away!'

Another of the presentation evenings provided a hilarious interlude. The event was held in the St Mary's Island Canteen in the Chatham Dockyard, and the guest of honour presenting the trophies was Jill Hammersley, the European champion at the time. By the time we were going up to collect our trophies, Bert had already received a (surprise) award, Rochester and District Table Tennis League Sportsman of the Year, and was up on the stage again for Jill to present us with the divisional winner's trophy. Jill was obviously pleased to see the old boy receive his trophy and was making the usual polite noises. Bert was in his element, accepted his trophy with a flourish and then in a conspiratorial tone, but just loud enough for us to hear said 'Thanks very much, I expect to do even better next year. By the way, you haven't got any of your old bats you don't want, have you?'

I played in the same team as Bert for many years, and I had cause to regret it one evening when we (Weapons) were playing the Elliot's team away. It is convention that the opposition assists the home team and helps to do some of the match scoring. I volunteered to score a match, not realising that Bert would be playing against his son Malcolm for the opposition. Neither Bert nor his son played an attacking shot in the first leg, just pushing the ball back to each other for 25 minutes! This was before the 'Expedite' rule, which prevents this kind of thing happening. Come to think of it, it is probably why the Expedite rule came in! Towards the end of this match, we were all praying for a quick death. To finish my reminiscing on table tennis matters, just prior to my finishing playing in the league, after nearly fifty years, I played for the Riverside team and one of our new team members was Paul Newborough, Bert's grandson. Boy, did that make me feel old!

I think it would have made Bert very proud to see his son and grandson playing league table tennis, and both good players. From my point of view it was interesting to see Bert's grandson playing a very attacking game, playing smash shots at every opportunity, while Bert himself only played an attacking shot once, and that was by accident! (joke.)

Bert Newborough was also a very keen tennis player, and played for many years for the Civil Service Club. He found out that I used to play for my school team (Chatham Technical High School), and encouraged me to join the Civil Service Club, located opposite the Central Hotel on Watling Street. There were four grass courts, which were kept in good condition, and usually at weekends when I went along, there was a good friendly group to give you a game. Some of my table tennis group were also tennis players, including Derek Harris and Fred Best.

Again, for his age Bert was a wonderful player, and used his head and experience rather than his legs. One thing he couldn't do of course was run, so if he started to get too far in front of me in any game, I would play my trump card. When he played the ball to me I would cut it back to him with very heavy slice so that when it bounced on the other side of the net it died. Bert couldn't get in quick enough to retrieve the ball. 'You blighter!' he would say, very nearly blaspheming for Bert. I spent many happy weekend afternoons at the tennis club. Table tennis in the winter months, and lawn tennis in the summer. Happy days!

Football was my real love. England had just won the World Cup, and how I wished that I had had the talent to match the effort I was prepared to put in. However, I joined the team I was to represent (Red Star) for many years after the skipper, Barry 'Jock' Nicol, invited me along to one of their pre-season training sessions at Luton Rec (Recreation Ground). I discovered that I had as much talent as most of the team!

Thus I was signed on, and my illustrious football career with Red Star had begun. I played for them for many years, dragging them down through the football divisions.

Red Star was run by Jim Silver, who was quite a character. A heavy smoker (who wasn't in those days?), Jim was fairly laid back and unfortunately had a very bad stutter, so it was extremely difficult for him to give us all a thundering good bollocking when we lost heavily (which wasn't too unusual). I was a very keen player, and I'm sure I was often picked to play because I would always turn up, play anywhere on the field, and didn't complain, rather than being blessed with any outstanding ability. I would take all my football kit to work when I was working overtime on a Saturday, clock off at two o'clock and rush up to the Civil Service sports ground in time for the kick off.

The Civil Service Sports Club facilities were by this time looking decidedly tatty. The groundsman, Bill Wragg, wasn't exactly a ball of fire, and although he looked after the bowls (top priority) and to a lesser extent the tennis courts, both of which were mainly used in the summer, and therefore could be worked upon in nicer conditions, the football pitches always seemed to be too much trouble for him. If he could persuade the referees that the grounds were unfit to play on, that suited him just fine, and he would invariably try to get the matches called off, as it seemed that it was too much of an effort for him to mark out the pitches etc.

There was never any hot water available in the showers. Although the changing rooms were supposed to be kept locked when the matches were being played, several times money and valuables went missing, and it was often rumoured that Bill had not bothered to lock up. On a personal note, I used to get on quite well with Bill, and he always seemed to be friendly with me. I don't know how much of this was because my girlfriend Joy lived just up the road from Bill, so I knew where he lived!

One of the frequent away venues was the Black Lion playing fields in Gillingham (not the present day building and facilities - in the late 60s things were much more primitive). The original changing rooms had no showers; instead a large bath which could accommodate about ten men was the post-match washing facility. This was OK, but there were several pitches, and as the games were played simultaneously, after matches it was first come, first served. Needless to say the water was not changed until the matches had finished and all the players had bathed and changed. In consequence, if you were the last team to finish your match and get into the bath, it looked just like mulligatawny soup!

We were usually late kicking off, for as I often said at the time we were the only team I knew that could get tired out just getting changed for a match!

We kicked off late, so we finished our matches late, and were left with the mulligatawny soup option, if you were that desperate.

Some memories of matches stay with you forever. I remember one when we played 'Strand' (Athletic I believe), at the Black Lion playing fields. The Strand were known at this time to be a bit 'basic' (they would kick you rather than the ball if they got the chance).

On this day they had the two Simmons brothers playing, and both were obviously pissed at kick-off. We scored twice in a very untidy first half, so the Simmons boys decided to try a little intimidation. They kicked us off the pitch in the second half, and after being verbally cautioned (but not booked) they started to abuse the referee. I hadn't seen that degree of blatant abuse of a referee before, and haven't since; effing and blinding wasn't in it, it was right in the ref's face. He seemed completely out of his depth, and I doubt if he ever refereed another match in his life! We lost the match, by the way.

Another match I remember well, was when I scored TWO goals in one match. (Not own goals, although I was pretty good at those.) I had given up smoking (again) about three weeks before, and really felt that the benefits were starting to show. My breathing seemed much easier, and I felt as if I could run all day (mostly psychological of course). Anyway, the first goal was a 20-yard lob over the keeper's head and the second was a left-foot shot (yes, left foot, the one I don't kick with) all along the ground when we were pressurizing at a corner. I still have the newspaper cutting! We won 3-2. I was that excited I went to the pub that night to celebrate with my mate Ted Arnold, and after a few pints I decided that a celebratory cigar wouldn't affect my no smoking situation. Wrong. After three cigars that night I was back on the smoking again. A bad move.

A show-stopping episode never seen on 'Match of the Day' happened when we (the defence) complained to the forwards that they were not holding onto the ball when it was cleared from the defence. This meant it was continually coming back to us, until eventually the opposition scored, through constant pressure.

'For Christ's sake keep hold of the ball and give us a break at the back!' pleaded our centre-half, Barry Harris.

'Huh! Think you can do any better?' was the response from our centre-forward.

'Yes, I bloody well can, and I'll show you, we'll swap positions for the second half and I'll go up front', replied Barry. And so the die was set.

Barry was a stocky centre-half, and all our football kit was medium size. I mention this because his shorts in particular didn't fit him too well. They were far too small. This didn't matter too much when he was playing at centre-half, as his running was mainly restricted to ten-yard blocking runs and heading out high balls. Playing at centre-forward was altogether different.

About 10 minutes into the second half, one of us defenders sent a long ball to our (new) centre-forward Barry. He caught the ball on his chest and started on a determined run towards the opposition's goal, brushing aside one or two defenders as he went. As he got to the opposition's penalty area, we noticed that their keeper was laughing - not just a giggle but a full-bloodied rib-hugging guffaw. With their keeper temporarily and mysteriously incapacitated, now was our big chance to score. Go on Barry, hammer it in!

He did. It missed, and the ball flew way over their bar.

Now we had the time to check on the strange behaviour of the opposition's keeper.

What had made him laugh so much, we enquired?

'Look at his shorts!' the keeper replied, pointing at Barry and still hooting. We all looked at Barry's shorts and saw that because they were so inadequate, during his extended run they had allowed his cock to escape, and it was protruding from the bottom of his shorts. Bloody hell! Quite frightening, even for us, and we had seen it all before in the showers.

The keeper, still giggling, managed to explain. 'When I saw you steaming in at me in goal, I wasn't sure if you were going to have a shot or try to put a good fuck into me' he said.

Enough said, how do you follow that?

I also used to play on Sunday mornings, friendly matches for

Wigmore. These were all away matches, as we had no home venue, and we mostly played pub teams in villages around Maidstone. Bob Webb, a pal from schooldays, and another friend, Brian Jackson, a diver in the Dockyard, were two of the regulars in the Sunday team. Two of the teams we played on a regular basis were the Duke of Wellington at Ryarsh and a team from Hadlow, where it always seemed to take forever to get there. These matches were great fun. They were not taken too seriously, but were more of a good workout and a pleasant way to get rid of last night's beer.

CHAPTER 8

PART OF THE TEAM

I had now been doing the Technical Progressman job for a couple of years and I felt I was really contributing to the section's output. I now understood how the naval Stores system worked (where items were held, which forms were used to demand and return items etc) and where to source the items which were to be made locally. I had worked hard, even if I say so myself, to learn and to improve my working skills, and it was paying off. The difficult problems and tensions of my earlier days were a thing of the past. I had settled in, was doing a good job, and I was well liked and popular. Not to say modest, of course!

The production officers recognized that I had now acquired the necessary skills, and could be relied upon to provide the assistance they required. It was still a learning process, which was as it should be, but I now felt that I was fully trained. Having said that, we still looked to extend our knowledge and have a bit of fun at the same time. One of the other Progressmen (Harry Rogers, or HT as he was known), had joined the Planning Office recently. The two of us used to quiz each other on knowledge of the Naval Stores class/group references. All equipment held in the Naval Stores has a unique reference number which comprises a four-figure class/group, eg 0269 would be a bearing (Ball or Roller), and it would be followed by the pattern number, eg 914-0627. So the conversation would go something like:

Me: 'OK Harry, what is Naval Stores Class/Group 0269?'

HT: 'Ball and Roller bearings. OK Smithy, What is Naval Stores Class/Group 0212?'

Me: 'Nuts, Bolts, and Fastenings.'

HT: 'OK - What is Naval Stores Class/Group 0413?'

Me: 'Ebonite Quills and Rubber Goods.'

We always found this one highly amusing. (What do they say about little things pleasing little minds?)

At about this time several vacancies occurred for Chargeman (Technical Supervisor), which later evolved into the Professional and Technology Officer Grade IV, the first line management role. The Dockyard Personnel Department decided to invite interested volunteers to attend a selection interview, and I was encouraged to go. I attended the interview and remember that Johnny Bubb and Ron Barnes were two of the three Board members on the interview panel.

I can still remember that one of the interview questions was 'What material is EN57?' (Answer: it's a corrosion-resisting steel, a type of stainless.)

I passed the interview, and while I waited for a permanent vacancy to occur, was invited to do Deputy Chargeman duties in the Weapons Section. This was to cover for annual leave and sick leave, and other periods of absence by the permanent chargemen, and would provide me with invaluable experience for when I took up my permanent post on promotion.

CHAPTER 8

My first period of 'cover' was for Eric Carter, the Chargeman in the Weapons Annexe section. Eric was a nice old boy; he must have been well over 60 years old at this time (which seemed ancient to me), slightly built and quietly spoken.

Harry Barnett had taken over from Peter Lowry as the Chargeman in the Planning Office, not, we were told, anything to do with Pete's band-playing antics, but more due to the fact that Harry had suffered heart trouble, and it was thought that the Planning Office would provide a less stressful working environment. Anyway, Harry had a word in my 'shell like' when he knew I was going to do deputy for Eric Carter. He explained that Eric was not really very interested in the planning returns that were required weekly by the Planning Office, and preferred to continue with his own system. As he was so near to retirement, no one wanted to harass him, so his planning returns were 'guesstimated' by the Planning Office. Harry said he wanted me to get the proper returns done, without upsetting Eric too much, while I was deputising.

Before he went on leave, I asked Eric if I could change things a little to make it easier for me, and he readily agreed. Then I did as I was told, and rearranged the work cards into the (previously unused) loading boxes, which showed which work each man on the section was working on, and of course from this you could work out how much work was still to be done - the principle of work loading. This made the completion of the section workload reports that the Planning Office needed easy to complete.

The receipt of these long-awaited report forms delighted Harry in the Planning Office; however his joy was short-lived. When Eric returned from his leave, I explained in great detail what I had done and how easy it was to fill in the required forms. He listened very patiently and nodded sagely from time to time. He seemed quite impressed, and thanked me for taking care of the section in his absence. 'Do you think that you will be all right to do these returns now Eric?' I asked. 'No problems, young man,' was his reassuring reply.

I felt quite pleased that my first period in substitution had gone so well. The paperwork side of the job was in place and up to date, and the supervisory duties had proved very interesting. This may have been helped by the fact that I knew two of the fitters very well, Bob Webb and Len Harris, who were usually employed refitting the Reavall TC4 air compressors used in the subs.

About four weeks later Eric took some more leave and I was asked to deputise again. When I went down to the section for the handover, I found that he had reverted to his old 'system'. There were workcards everywhere, no apparent system or logic (to me anyway), and only he knew how he worked it. But perhaps that was the object of the exercise? Oh well, c'est la vie!

My next period of substitution cover was for Ned Foster, the Chargeman of the Main Shop. The most high profile task in the Main Shop was the refit of the ships' main armament, the 4.5" Mk 6 gun mountings. These massive assemblies can be quite an awe-inspiring sight, not only for their size and complexity, but because they are just like an iceberg - most of the mounting cannot be seen as it is usually underground, being mounted over large purpose-designed pits. The two fitters who refitted most of these mountings were Les Taylor and Freddy Whale; they had worked on these assemblies over many years and become expert. This was probably the only piece of kit that could equal the submarine equipment in terms of priority and importance, which was reflected when stores were demanded or materials ordered. A higher than normal delivery code could be used and would usually be accepted and achieved.

Freddy and Les initially seemed to me to be quite aloof and reluctant to join in with the day-to-day happenings in the workshop, but when I did the chargehand duties it soon became clear that they were always helpful and ready to advise if asked. It was just that they preferred to get on with their work in hand and were happy to concentrate on that. That was probably what made them so reliable and efficient.

The 4.5" Gun mounting is a very complex piece of kit, and extensive test equipment is required, especially for the gun's hydraulic system. Purpose-built hydraulic system filtration packs are used to flush the warmed hydraulic oil continually until the acceptable degree of purity is achieved.

At the east end of the main workshop was a discrete area known as the dustproof room. This area contained a back projection microscope which was used to view the size of any contamination particles found in the hydraulic oil, taken regularly from test points during the flushing process. A clean examination area was essential for these and other tests. Other critical tests checked for backlash and gear engagement loads in the guns' gearboxes.

Other guns were refitted in the workshop as well. The main 'bread and butter' gun was the 40mm Mk 7, a twin Bofors gun used for anti-aircraft and close range defence roles. The Mk 7 was a hydraulically-operated unit; other variants in service at this time being the Mk 8, a battery-operated version, and the Mk 9, electrically operated. These two variants however were rarer and tended to be used in specialist roles.

The other gun mounting we overhauled in the workshop on a regular basis at this time was the Oerlikon 20mm, a very simple twin-barrelled gun. Although quite dated, they were found to be very useful to the Navy for close range protection, particularly when the larger armaments could not depress sufficiently to fire at very close range targets, eg to deter small, usually fast craft from attacking.

Several of the support trades were usually in attendance in the workshop, and a significant part of my duties was to ensure that they were not held up in doing their tasks, that they knew which tasks we required of them, when they were required, and that they had been requisitioned to do this work. This was where I would learn my basic liaison and communication skills.

The main assist trades included the boilermakers, who had a small workshop area dedicated to them. They would supply us with brackets, handrails, machine seatings, any steel or aluminium platework that was required, and welding tasks if necessary.

Electricians, although not in constant attendance, would be removing original equipment for transport to the Electrical Workshop for repairs and reinstalling and testing these items as they were returned. This would chiefly be electric motors, starters, control gear lighting and instrument panels.

Coppersmiths also played an important part in the refits. Old pipework was removed and taken to their workshop (or the PIP shop) for cleaning and test; any damaged or broken pipework or that failing testing would be replaced. New and refurbished pipes were annealed (stress removed and softened) if required, prior to replacement within the gun mounting. The majority of the pipework was for the hydraulic, lubricating oil, air and cooling water systems.

At the west end of the main workshop were the Limited Working Stock Store ('The Stores') and the Loan Tool Store. The stores held, among other items, all the consumable supplies which would be required during the refit process. These included nuts, bolts, washers, various jointing materials (Permanite and oil and water jointing, insertion rubber and cork sheets etc), 'O' seals, sprays, polishes, oils greases, grease guns, liquid measures, labels, string, cleaning rags, emery papers and consumable tools such as files, knives and hacksaw blades.

The Loan Tool Store situated next door held the large, expensive, specialized or unusual equipment (including some test sets, general purpose and specialised) which would be used intermittently during the refit. These items were 'drawn out' for a specific task and returned to the Loan Tool Store on completion.

A card showing all the equipment details and serial numbers would be signed by the workman, who would also give his works number when he drew and returned the kit. This system also ensured that the items when returned into the store were checked and/or tested to ensure that they were always in a serviceable condition and ready for re-issue.

These stores were known as 'controlled items'. These special items, or controlled stores, would vary depending upon which equipment was being refitted, but would usually include such items as special spanners (usually in boxed sets), torque wrenches, unusual taps and dies, extractors and test-pumps and gauges.

Completing the store setup was the Weapons Equipment Store. This was located on a mezzanine floor adjacent to the Afloat Chargeman's office. This store held the weapons-specific store items (spare parts). Full details of these items would be held within the Stock Control Office.

Located below the mezzanine floor was the drying room, a heated room where clothes and overalls could be dried out, for workmen coming to work, returning from working outside or on board the ship or submarine.

Last but not least, opposite the clocking-in station was the office of the Trade Union Convener, Fred Foster. Fred was a very popular member of the team. This was mainly because of his very friendly and cheerful personality, his 'go the extra mile' efforts to champion his members' causes and perhaps most importantly, his common-sense approach. He was well respected by the management team, and very popular with his Trade Union members.

One of the real characters I now came across was Pete

Rowlands. Pete was a labourer in the workshop, and was unfortunate enough to be cursed with learning difficulties. When he got excited he used to bark: it was a very good impression of a large dog. He would be walking through the main shop and suddenly burst into a loud 'WOOF, WOOF, WOOF'! This took a bit of getting used to, but after a while the regular workforce hardly noticed it any more. However it was quite amusing to see the look on visitors' faces when it happened. Incidentally Pete was as strong as an ox, and a very good worker.

I found my first period as Chargehand in the main shop without problems, very interesting and enjoyable, and not at all as daunting as I had first imagined, due in no small part to the willingness and helpful attitude of the workforce in the section.

I returned to the Planning Office to resume my normal duties and to tidy up the problems that had been carried over during my absence. It was at about this time that Don Rousell joined the Planning Office as a colleague doing progressman duties and taking over the submarine work. Don lived in Faversham and came up on the train every morning, which meant a very early start and probably explained why he always looked shagged out. He did however have a wicked sense of humour, which would explain in part why we got on so well. Don liked to go fishing, usually on the coast near his home (Faversham or Whitstable), and as I was very keen at this time also, we always had a few fishermen's tales to relate.

Don's real love of his life was his sailing. He owned a

catamaran which he raced, and was very successful locally. If he had had a good weekend's racing, and sometimes even if not, he would relate in humorous terms the weekend's boating activities. He always made it sound very interesting, with tales of meeting loads of new and existing friends, and it was obviously very exciting out on the water seeing the local coastline from another perspective.

On several occasions he had suggested I might like to crew for him, and as he made it sound so exciting and out of the usual, I was almost at the point of accepting; I was only reluctant because I was not a strong swimmer. Then he brought the photos in. Shit! The crew member was on the hull, which was way out of the water, about four or five feet I would guess, and judging by the wake the boat was creating they were doing a considerable speed.

I noticed also that the crewman seemed to have rather a strange look on his face, as if he was trying to decide if he had just shit himself, and if he was ever going to get to the shore in one piece! I declined the offer to go crewing.

We did organize the occasional office nights out between ourselves. This wasn't easy because of the geographical spread of our homes. The one night that comes most easily to mind was when Don organized a trip to his local (well almost local), the Shipwright's Arms at Oare.

What Don forgot to tell us was that the landlady, Mrs Tester, used to like a drink or three, and when she had had a drink she would often come around into the bar and get *very* friendly with the customers. This night when she came to the other side of the bar she made a beeline for Ron Hill. Ron was one of the Estimators in our office, probably in his mid forties, very quietly spoken, inoffensive and appeared almost shy. Mrs Tester pounced. She sat on Ron's lap and proceeded to twirl his non-existent curls (Ron was very bald). She appeared to be whispering sweet nothings in his ear, and was obviously in a state of near delirium. Ron wasn't. I don't think he quite knew what to do. Should he push her off his lap and chance being rude? No - that wouldn't do. Should he let her 'get on with it'? No, that wouldn't do either.

He was by this stage fully embarrassed, and glowing a beautiful pink. Don, on the other hand - he had organized the night out remember - was giggling fit to burst. He had spilt half of his pint laughing —served him right!

Ron was eventually saved by the arrival of the landlord. Initially his arrival looked as if it might be a mixed blessing; how would he, the landlord, react to the interesting spectacle before him? No problem, he had obviously seen it all before. He instructed his wife to 'stop pestering the customers' and see who needed serving in the saloon bar. Surprisingly, Mrs Tester prised herself off Ron, gave him a 'thank you very much' smile and headed off to the saloon.

Phew! Ron breathed a big sigh of relief, and so did we - she might have pounced on any of us! The rest of the evening was quiet. Well, how do you follow that?

Only a couple of weeks later, I was asked to do the Deputy

Chargeman duties in the PIP Shop. The 'top man' in the shop was Norman Peters. Norman was over six feet tall, perhaps in his mid-forties, with lots of black hair swept back and Brylcreemed into place and a lively demeanour. He was very keen on sport (I believe he could have been ex Army), and kept himself very fit by cycling to work. He effectively ran the place. Second-in-command was Percy Wheeler, a few years older than Norman; he had worked in the shop for many years, knew the place inside out, and despite having a very bad club foot was highly mobile. The other guys were fairly anonymous; didn't say too much, just got on with their jobs.

The PIP shop stank. The de-greasing, de-painting and de-rusting processes required industrial strength cleaners. Although normally the large double doors, the main entry and exit were left open, this was insufficient to vent the acrid stench created by the huge tanks of powerful cleaning chemicals. A couple of small extraction fans paid lip-service to fume extraction, but to deal adequately with this environment a dedicated and powerful fume extraction system would have been required.

I suspect that in the early days of the workshop when the cleaning systems were different, and probably also the layout of the shop and the chemicals used, it had been OK, but now it certainly was not. Over the years the chemical cleaning tanks had been enlarged (to accommodate larger assemblies), steam heating coils had been fitted into most of the tanks (to heat the chemicals and make them more effective, and at the same time soften the contamination to be removed), and much more powerful chemicals were now being used. This is not intended as a direct criticism of the management team, as this situation (like so many others) evolved gradually, with small changes one at a time, until the present unsatisfactory situation was arrived at. No one had the time or inclination to look back to the original concept. The present setup worked very well, the cleaning process being to a very high standard, and no one complained about the conditions (too much) - what, and lose the overtime?

So conditions were largely ignored. The present layout housed the large steam-heated tanks, usually one containing Ardrox, and the other Tricoethylene. As an attempt to minimize the generation of fumes into the atmosphere these tanks were topped with what looked like large table-tennis balls completely covering and floating on top of the liquid cleaner. They helped, but not much.

Two more large tanks were sited almost alongside. The first was a hot water bath, which finished the cleaning process, removing the odd particles of grease, paint flakes or whatever. The last tank was empty, but was used with a powerful water lance to flush all the remaining cleaning chemicals from the cleaned assemblies. This tank could also be used with paraffin to brush off small items which were lightly contaminated, and then to use the water jets to rinse them clean.

Benches located around the work areas held the materials for their specific tasks. Along one side was an area which held all the large rolls of 'mouldable wrap' (a heavy duty type of synthetic cloth impregnated with an oily substance), with which items were wrapped before additional layers of preservation/packaging were added. Next was an area storing large rolls of polythene sheets used to manufacture heavy duty packing bags, and with them were a couple (one large, one small) of heat-sealing machines.

Along the opposite side of the workshop, large quantities of corrugated cardboard sheets were stacked. These were used for the manufacture of cardboard packing boxes of all shapes and sizes. A folding machine used for the manufacture of the boxes was positioned nearby.

At the end were two printing machines, one a printing machine proper which was used to manufacture the identification labels secured to the packaged item, and also on the box or package that it came in. The other was really an embosser, used to create metal printed labels used on packing cases etc.

Stored on shelves along both sides were various other materials used in the packaging process. These included nylon twine, string, brown sticky paper reels, pre-printed labels and bags of desiccant (silica gel), a substance put in with a packaged item to absorb moisture, thereby keeping the packaged item 'dry' and preventing corrosion and deterioration.

The layout was completed by a tiny office for the Chargeman (desk, chair, cupboard, and phone) and a small 'rest room' where the workforce could eat their sandwiches, with access to a small oven for heating tins of soup, pies etc.

Saturdays (overtime) were a special day. Norman would offer to cook a bacon-and-egg breakfast for anyone who wanted it. I was flattered to be asked, and very grateful, but somehow I could not face eating bacon and egg (even if it was my favourite) in that place, in those conditions. No, the smell put me right off; not for me. However, most of the others enjoyed it, so good luck to them.

Saturday overtime was usually to cope with the work demand; in other words not all the work that had to be done could be completed in the normal working week. Bear in mind that most of the work in the PIP shop was process related, and had to be completed in a finite time. For example large items might require eight hours soaking in the cleaning agent tanks to soften and remove the paint/grease/rust so they could be returned to as-new and clean condition.

So Saturday overtime was used to catch-up with the backlog. Approximately every six weeks however, the cleaning tanks had to be drained, cleaned and replenished with new chemicals. The interval would obviously depend upon the usage in that period. On these Saturdays the shop would be closed for normal production work, and this and other maintenance tasks would take precedence. Stock levels, ordering of materials and servicing of the equipment were organized to be synchronized to these 'down days'. The Yard Services 'gang' would be requested to attend, and do their servicing to the steam traps on the heating system and the cleaning tanks and any other maintenance or testing that was due. The electrical items were treated in the same way, checks and maintenance being done on the electric motors and the lighting.

One of the problems I experienced as the Deputy Chargeman in the PIP shop was how to respond to the frequent requests for 'rabbits'. A 'rabbit' is the Dockyard term for private jobs intended for home, sometimes called 'homers'. Unfortunately the PIP shop was a gold mine for items and services that were in great demand, and I hadn't been told what to expect in the way of the frequent requests.

It soon became clear that the cleaning tanks were very popular with motor and motorbike enthusiasts, to get their components all new and shiny, as well as gardening types with their mowers, guys who had boats and scores of other people who wanted some item or other properly cleaned.

Other requests were for supplies of the nylon line (ideal for fishing I was told), polythene sheets (greenhouses?) and various printing requests. The PIP shop had supplies of various coloured papers and excellent printing facilities. It could even professionally scroll or provide 'teeth-edge' surrounds on tickets and invitation cards - very handy!

My personal thoughts were that it was all a matter of degree. If someone wanted a small job done for themselves, there was no profit motive, and he did not keep coming back, I thought it was probably OK. However some of the request were just taking the piss.

I had a quiet word with Norman, for advice really, and told him how I felt about the situation. His reaction was commonsense and to the point. He explained that most of the unofficial requests didn't come through me (I didn't see them, as the requester went direct to the workman, often when I was out of the workshop) and the workforce had enough sense and experience to keep these enterprises under control by refusing most of them. He suggested that I should refuse all except a few 'genuine' requests. Good advice, I thought. The thin end of the wedge is the one you usually miss!

I really enjoyed the time I spent as the Deputy Chargeman in the PIP shop, in spite of the obnoxious working environment, which always left me with a sense of unease. What were all these acrid fumes doing to our insides, on a day-by-day basis? However, I was only on duty in this section for short deputizing periods, so hopefully any damage would be minimal. With that reservation, the job was great. The team were motivated and conscientious, and accepted me without reservation; I believe they recognised that it was my intention to help them maintain the excellent support they provided, and they responded accordingly.

I had now attended courses on Network Scheduling and Planning Tools, including PERT (Programme Evaluation and Review Technique), pie charts, ghant (bar) charts and simple logic diagrams. These systems were invaluable for complex activities, eg a nuclear submarine refit, where literally hundreds of activities would be happening either simultaneously or in quick succession to each other, and it was vitally important to identify problems and delays to ensure early and quick remedial actions.

With the simpler activities commonplace in the Dockyard, less complex and easier systems to manage were better suited to the normal tasks. The basic tool of the overall planning system was the 'Section Workload Report'. This simple system listed the work packages in an approximate priority, and showed the total number of hours allocated to complete the work.

The number of operators (fitters/labourers/others) was multiplied by the net hours in the working week. If 40 hours were worked (gross) in the week, an allowance had to be made for 'diversions' (things such as union meetings, first aid lectures etc), so a figure of 35 would probably be used. Therefore, the work package hours would be divided by 35 and loaded in successive weeks until the project was completed. As the section capacity was known (number of men x 35), each week could be loaded to the known figure. The main advantages of this scheme of course, were that it could demonstrate the need for additional staff or overtime to complete jobs, or conversely identify periods when extra work would be required to keep the section fully employed.

I personally had no problems at all working with the system, and found it to be an extremely valuable management tool. Having said that, I must confess that I was already a convert to the need for a simple but effective planning system, almost from day one. However, some of my peers, and certainly a significant percentage of the older first line managers, viewed the inception of planning systems with major reservations. This, I believe, was primarily for three reasons:

Firstly, I think a lot of the older supervisors saw the introduction of a planning system as an erosion of their control over the work done in their section, and the requirement for them to make weekly formal reports worried them.

Secondly, the philosophy behind the introduction of the planning requirement was not adequately explained, before the systems were implemented.

The last reason was that financial control was now dramatically changing the way the dockyards operated. Financial returns were now a way of life, and caused considerable headaches for the production boys, who had to change their ways, making cases for funding, and showing value for money. Now that planning feedback was to be required, it seemed to be another needless task required by departments detached from the 'sharp end'. In other words, the planners were seen to be tarred with the same brush as the (perceived) useless Finance Branch. (No help, just a hindrance to the production staff.)

As I said, this was not my understanding at all; I found that by effective planning, vital assistance could be offered to the production teams. This fostered real teamwork, and together we got the boats out in time. This achievement should not be underestimated, as Chatham Dockyard was invariably proven to be able to refit the warships put in its charge not only to time, but to cost and to quality. This, I would suggest, made life a lot easier for the Royal Navy, and made a significant contribution to the defence of the realm.

About six months after my successful Chargeman's interview, my name had reached the top of the 'awaiting promotion' list, and I was offered a permanent post as the

Technical Supervisor (the new name for the Chargemen) on the Outstations section of the Yard Services Department. I was sorry to leave the Weapons Section and all the friends I had made there, but I knew it was time for a move, and this promotion was a good opportunity for me to pursue my ambitions and secure my future.

So, heavy hearted, I left the Weapons Section in October 1968 and took up my new post with the Yard Services Department. But that's another story…

THE CAST

Weapons Section, HM Dockyard, Chatham, circa 1966

Commander 'G' - Cmdr (RN) Harding.

Foremen: Vic Bennett, Ken Lovell, Foreman Weapons Afloat (FWA) and Shops (FWS).

Inspectors: Ted Baker, Ron Collins, Arthur Regan, Frank Stevens. Peter Biddle, Fred Kimmings, Bill Carden, John Patman were all later.

Chargemen: Charlie Adams, Harry Barnett, Alec Bond, Ken Brockwell, Eric Carter, Ned Foster, Pete Lowry, Phil Hobling, Bill Stevens (also Trade Union Official).

Fitters: Bob Webb, Lenny Price, Len Harris, Bob Moncur, Fred Whale, Les Taylor, John Peters, Rod Berwick, Peter Castle, Roy Beard, Ernie Holden, Barry Harris, Brian Turner, Ted Robinson,

Ken Oliver and Trevor Sergeant.

PIP Shop: Norman Peters and Percy Wheeler.

Planning Office: Estimators; Jim Greenaway, Norman Shipley, Dennis Osborne, Jack Payne, Ron Hill, John Pattman (before promotion) Horry Wood (later).

Progressmen (Technical): Ken Hancock, Fred Murr, Keith Harris, Bob Butler and Bob Smith; Don Rousell and Harry Rogers (both later).

Progressmen (Non-Technical): Ted Broady and Bill Allen.

Stock Control Office: Jack Taylor + 2 clerical assistants.

Stores Officer: Len Parfitt.

Trade Union (AUEW) Convener: Fred Foster.

Technical Library: Fred Ludlow.

Diagnosticians: Ted Coward, Wally Mason, Charlie Swan.

And most importantly: The Tea Lady, Kathy Cook.

Apologies to all those not mentioned above.

PART 3

THE APPRENTICE, THE PROGRESSMAN, AND NOW THE REST OF IT

CONTENTS

CHATHAM DOCKYARD: YSM OUTSTATIONS

'The working class can kiss my ass, I've got a
chargeman's job at last'

(Dockyard ditty, usually sung (in jest) at the time of your first promotion)

21 October 1968. YSM Outstations - the best job in the Dockyard, although the job wasn't actually in the Dockyard at all!

I reported to my new boss Alan Hills, in the MCO (Maintenance Control Offices) as instructed on the agreed date, to take up my promotion. This was to be as the Technical Supervising Officer (TSO) in charge of the YSM Outstations.

I admit to being more than a little apprehensive with 'first day nerves', as this was a new section, new people, and my first responsibilities as a line manager on a permanent basis; so I suppose this was quite natural.

Alan worked from the Inspector's Office on the ground floor of the building, alongside his colleagues Dennis Jordan, Jim Race, Bill Bogie, George Stapenhill and Ron Jones. The building also had the Foremen's offices - Bill Aston, Ken Manley, Ron Barnes and Frank Lewis - and the upper floor was occupied by the Maintenance Control Planning and Estimating staff.

Alan introduced me to Ron Barnes, our Foreman (line manager), and between them they outlined my new job's requirements and responsibilities. Ron then suggested that Alan should show my where my office was, and explained in more detail the requirements of my new role.

The concise job description was 'The Installation, Maintenance, Testing and Disposal of 'functional' MoD equipment in the (Navy's) Southern Command (South East England)'.

This basically meant that all the equipment purchased by the MoD for the Navy Department at these Establishments was looked after by a small mobile workforce from Chatham. These items usually had (and were supposed to have) a 'Yard Number' identification plate attached.

Additionally we were required to be in attendance on site when contractors were carrying out Statutory Requirements (testing & inspecting) equipment, eg Felco-Moores, who were the main contractor for periodic testing of mobile cranes and fork-lift trucks.

My office was located above the 'Loco Shop', only a short distance from the MCO building. Alan took me over to introduce me to Roger Putland, the guy who had been doing my job (on a temporary basis) since the unfortunate demise of the previous job-holder, Arthur Brookman.

I could tell from Alan's demeanour that he was more than satisfied with Roger's efforts in the post and was not completely happy about me coming in and taking over (although this was the way the system worked - Roger was doing the job on a temporary basis). I was going to have to prove myself. Fair enough.

My other concern at this stage was the reaction of Roger himself and the workforce. How would they react to the change?

First things first; I had no problems with Roger, he understood that he would be replaced by someone, if not me, and could not have been more helpful. He explained the setup of the section, comprising two mechanical fitters, Alan Wenham and Peter Harris, and three electrical fitters, Johnny Peak, Colin Shultz and John Wright. A skilled labourer/slinger, Des Terry, and a labourer, Dave Lee, completed the entitlement.

Roger said his thoughts on a handover were that our first day would be spent in the office, to cover the management essentials, and the rest of the week would be spent visiting some of the outstations. On some of these visits we were to be accompanied by Alan Hills (the Inspector), which we could agree later. Sounded good to me.

Admin requirements included preparing and collecting travel warrants for personal or staff use, although most of the time we would use our own cars, as stores and equipment needed to be collected from Chatham and taken to the outstation sites. If we used our private vehicles, motor mileage could be claimed at an agreed rate per mile (another form). This motor mileage form, Form 305, was also used to claim subsistence - an allowance to claim for extra meals if over 5 hours (lower rate) or 10 hours (higher rate) was worked out of the Dockyard or away from home.

A weekly report was required by the Foreman (title MFO – Maintenance Foreman Officer), Ron Barnes, which detailed a brief account and progress report of all significant work carried out by the detached staff from the Dockyard during the past week. Probably the most important task was to allocate the duties of the workforce for the following week (they obviously already had their duties for this week).The duties allocated would depend upon requests received into Chatham from the outstations, testing and maintenance schedules already in place, and any reported breakdowns.

I soon discovered that a significant job on the Monday visit to the dockyard was to collect the stores and spares required for the team already located at the various outstations, and to collect stocks of the consumable stores that were required for our workshop base at Deptford. These would include items such as fastenings (nuts, bolts, washers, split pins etc), emery papers, cleaning materials, paints, solvents, small quantities of oils & greases, replacement hand tools and the myriad other assorted items require to support an engineering workshop.

Most Monday evenings when I left the Dockyard, the boot of my car, and sometimes even the inside, was crammed full of stores and equipment. It was always a lottery when I got to the

Pembroke Gate exit and handed in my 'gate note' (the list of stores/equipment that I was authorized to remove) to the police constable on duty. When I opened up the boot to show the items the officer they would usually be shocked at seeing a bootful of items rather than the odd one or two. I would then have to explain who I was and what I was doing. Having recovered from the shock, the constable would either attempt a detailed check (which was a waste of time really, as it was unfair to expect him to know what he was looking for – especially in the case of equipment spares) or would stroke his chin and say 'Well, you had better get on with it old son, off you go!'

Roger and I decided that a priority visit should be to our workshop base at Deptford. The workshop was located within the 'convoys' yard, just off the Deptford High Street. The workshop itself was well situated as a base for the outstations staff to have quick access to most of our depots (outstations), with both Greenwich (the Royal Naval College) and Woolwich (Inspector of Naval Ordinance) depots within a few miles. Deptford also provided easier access (rather than travelling from the Dockyard) to the outstations at Brentford, Teddington, Slough and West Drayton.

The workshop was fairly small but well equipped. A full-size roller shutter door allowed access for large equipment such as mobile cranes and fork-lift trucks, a large pit was located centrally, and there were workbenches at one end. To the side a small office, doubling as a stores area, and a telephone just outside the door were the main features. At the east end a double door led to a small machine shop housing two lathes, a power hacksaw, a pillar drill, a double-ended grinder and a workbench with vices attached - all the necessary requirements for first-line servicing and repairs.

The next morning (Tuesday), I collected Roger from his home and we travelled the 30-odd miles to the Deptford workshop. Roger had arranged that all of the outstations staff would be there, so we would have the opportunity to meet. The journey to the workshop, which was on the London outskirts, gave me my first indications of the volume of traffic that I would encounter on my travels to the various outstation sites. It was busy - very busy. The journey through heavy traffic was no fun, and you certainly needed your wits about you on the A2 during the rush hour; the immediate impression was that the speed of the traffic was much higher than I was used to, and the lane changing to fill in any gaps was frightening! This would take some getting used to.

Having said all of that, it was still a nice feeling to be travelling to a new job to meet new people, and I felt a sense of freedom; although travelling to work, it was not the same feeling as having the constraints of the Dockyard walls dictating your daily environment. Yes, I really enjoyed the sensation of freedom, and this would stay with me the whole of my time on outstations.

We arrived at the Deptford workshop about 0900, and Roger introduced the staff. Alan Wenham was the senior man, at this time about 50 years old I would guess. He was of average build, thinning on top, and had quite a serious demeanour. He was a Londoner, which was to prove very useful to all of us on our travels as he knew the way through the 'back doubles' (short cuts), and would give us valuable travel advice. He was motor vehicle trained, conscientious and reliable.

Peter Harris was the other mechanical fitter. Pete was of average height and quite stocky. His outstanding features were his 'man-sized' moustache and his khaki dress. It soon became clear that Pete was in the TA (Territorial Army) and loved it. Pete was also very 'will-co' -(he would go almost anywhere, and try almost anything.) The mechanical fitters were a good pairing.

When the electrical fitters were introduced, I felt I already knew one of them, but couldn't put a name to the face. Once he said his name was John Wright, it clicked - I had known John's father when I worked in the engineering factory in the Dockyard, and had also come across John on the odd occasion, as he was also a motorcyclist. John was very quiet, and always gave the impression of being quite shy, which was silly really as he was a tall lad and quite good looking. He was also a very good electrician.

John's mate was Colin Shultz, and if possible they would choose to work together. This seemed to work very well, as Colin was almost the exact opposite of John in many ways.

Johnny Peake completed the trio of electricians. John was a funny little guy, fairly short and very animated in his gestures; he would easily have passed for an Italian! A very competent electrician, and very neat and tidy. If you wanted a job done with no mess, John was the guy. The first time I saw him running cables, I was surprised how careful he was to ensure that all the cable-clips were level and exactly evenly spaced. Always when he finished a job he would leave the site as he found it, clean and tidy. This was often remarked on by our 'customers'. John was just the man to have working on a clean inside environment.

Des Terry was the section's joker. He had an ever-changing repertoire of jokes, and once he got warmed up would keep us all in fits of laughter. I often saw Alan Wenham begging him to stop as he was crying with laughter! Des was the skilled labourer, which meant that he often assisted the fitters on their duties, and was a qualified slinger when required.

Completing the line-up was Dave Lee, the section's labourer. Not much to say about Dave really, he was very quiet, not a good mixer, and always (to me) gave the impression that his mind was elsewhere, where his priorities lay perhaps.

So, introductions made, and first impressions taken.

On the week's handover we visited Woolwich, Greenwich, Slough, West Drayton, Dover and Deal; quite a lot to take in on the first week, it just flew past. On the Friday we went back into the Dockyard, as Roger had various admin tasks that he needed to do before he left the Dockyard service and took up his new job with the PSA (Property Services Agency). I was very grateful for all of his assistance, and told him so, explaining that I thought he had done his best to ease me into the new job.

New starts are usually either exciting or foreboding - this one was exciting. I was looking forward to going to the various outstations, seeing what happened there and meeting my contacts.

One of the early visits was to the AOL (Admiralty Oil Laboratory) at Brentford, which was about to relocate to

CHAPTER 1

Cobham (Surrey). I was to take my boss Alan Hills with me. We arrived at the site, just past the Hammersmith flyover on the M4, not an easy place to get to mid-morning, and made our introductions to the two Technical Officers in charge, Bill Eggington and George Tidy. Alan stayed in the office with Bill, chatting over a cup of tea, while George offered to show me around and identify some of the equipment that we would be taking to the new site for them. Part of the working area was in a poorly-lit basement, and as we started to inspect the equipment I was almost overpowered by a very strong perfume. George was carrying on with the tour, but I was now very worried that I might have been snared into a dark area with a rampant poofter!

We carried on (me with a wary eye on George) through the lower level area and into a large laboratory, when again this pungent aroma hit us. On this occasion (perhaps because he had seen the look of panic on my face) George explained that the 'works' next door (the adjacent factory) was Coty, the perfume manufacturers; and that periodically their automatic extraction fans would expel these fumes to the outside (and into this site if the wind was in that direction). George also explained that they had got so used to it that they hardly noticed it any more. Whew! I sighed with relief, and relaxed more than a little.

During the next few weeks I visited the various outstations that would be my responsibility (in terms of husbandry of their equipment), most of which were previously completely unknown to me. Almost from the start I felt that the job was primarily one of liaison. I felt that regular visits to the contacts at the various outstations were a key requirement. Some of these contacts had expressed a feeling that they were too far detached from the Dockyard, in both senses, which made any assistance that they required difficult, and they would opt for contractor action if this was possible.

The other consideration in coming to this conclusion was that my team needed only minimal technical guidance; this was especially true in the case of the electrical 'boys', as I was not fully qualified in that area anyway. Technical support/guidance in electrical matters if required was available through Alan Hills, the Inspector, and/or Ron Barnes, the Foreman.

I soon established a routine which could be flexible enough to make any necessary changes, but would provide a useful basis for short term planning. A typical two week 'plan' would be as follows:

Monday (1st week)

In the Dockyard. Arrange travel warrants, submit travel claims for self and staff.

Collect stores and spares, arrange gate note.

Submit weekly report to Ron Barnes (Foreman) through Alan Hills (Inspector).

Discuss any problems, and next week's duties, with the Inspector and Foreman.

Contact the various outstations with details of proposed visits, and collect details of any work proposed.

Arrange any necessary work that was to be done in the Dockyard. (For example: lifting equipment – (wire ropes, slings, and shackles) would be brought in from the outstations for inspection and test in the Chain Test House, if required on an urgent basis.)

Most of the larger outstations would have two sets of lifting equipment, to cater for one set being away for testing; but this was not the case for the smaller depots for economic reasons.

Tuesday

INO (Inspector Naval Ordnance) Woolwich; RNC (Royal Naval College) Greenwich; & RNSTS (Royal Naval Stores & Transport System) Deptford.

Only occasional visits were made to Woolwich, as the Depot was towards the end of its closure programme, and we had few responsibilities there. However, some of the testing equipment in the laboratories (e.g. Izod hardness and tensile testing machines) were still being tested and calibrated by specialized contractors, and these would need to be checked for payment purposes.

Greenwich College provided a lot of work for the outstations section, particularly the electricians; one major project early on was to completely rewire a new laboratory and install multi-level power supplies throughout the laboratory.

The normal contact at Greenwich was Jimmy Glenton (on the scientific staff). He was a cheerful character who always made our team members very welcome, and invariably sent grateful messages back to the Dockyard for completed work packages. He drove a battered old Standard Vanguard car which was his pride and joy.

The Deptford workshop was our main base. Although I would make a point of contacting the Stores Officer in charge (Mr Smith) to be advised of any breakdowns or problems, usually they would have been sorted out as soon as they happened. So the visit was academic, mere courtesy really.

Apart from the in-house equipment at Deptford, which included mobile cranes (various) fork-lift trucks (various - diesel for external work, and electrical or Calor gas for inside the stores buildings) and conveyancers (for baggage handling), the workshop was used as a base to bring in equipment for repair, where the necessary facilities were to hand.

The prime example of this was the agricultural machinery programme. At the end of the grass-cutting season, most of the outstations would send their agricultural machinery back to the Deptford workshop for the annual overhaul/repair. This would be primarily lawn mowers (all types: sit-on, gang mowers, rotary and cylinder types, self-propelled and hover.) Other equipment included rotovators and chainsaws.

Because Deptford stores facility was so busy, breakdowns on the older equipment were fairly frequent, and normally at least one item would be in the workshop for repair. However, equipment sent in from the other outstation depots provided back-up work for the quieter periods.

Most of the outstations had been given the workshop's telephone extension (on the MoD Net) and could phone direct for help if the problem was urgent.

Wednesday

ACO (Admiralty Compass Observatory) Slough & AEL (Admiralty Experimental Laboratory) West Drayton.

The Compass observatory at Slough was a small unit run by serving naval personnel, where compass testing and calibration facilities were available. We had infrequent work at the station (which was fairly hush-hush) other than contractor visits, for their dedicated expertise (we organized this and paid the bills).

West Drayton was another busy unit. If possible I would visit on a Wednesday, as the traffic was marginally lighter on that day. I would call at the ACO at Slough in the morning, have an early lunch break and get to West Drayton about 1 to 1.30. This usually gave me time to do whatever was required and to get back on the road home by 3.30 or 4 at the latest. Any later than this meant heading right across London in the rush hour, which wasn't good!

My main contacts were Mr Harper (Senior Engineer) and Mr Nugent (Electrical Foreman). However invariably these two men were busy or elsewhere, so my day-to-day contact was Jack Flint, the workshop foreman. Jack was a larger than life sort of guy who seemed to run the place.

Thursday

Deptford Workshop. I would have one full day at our workshop (not the same day each week) to carry out my normal supervisory duties. I didn't feel the team needed technical guidance as much as moral support, to show genuine interest in what was going on, and to really get to know my team's strengths and weaknesses.

This was also the opportunity to discuss the next week's duties and their allocation.

Friday

BDO (Boom Defence Officer) Dover & RMB (Royal Marine Barracks) Deal.

After several long trips during the week, a visit to Dover and Deal on a Friday would be like a bonus. The traffic in East Kent was very light compared to the depots in or around London, and in that respect would make the day less stressful.

The BDO was a small unit situated in the Eastern arm of Dover Harbour. The contact here was Mr Bloy (ex-Navy - full beard), a nice guy on the Harbourmaster's staff. Our commitment here concerned two mobile cranes, a fork-lift truck, extensive lifting equipment (shackles, slings, eye-bolts, etc, which were all subject to periodic testing/inspection at Chatham) and of primary importance was their decompression chamber. This was one of only two in the Southern Command area, and if it was out of service for any reason (such as when the Chatham boilermakers were in attendance doing the periodic pressure tests) HQ Southern Command had to be notified by signal. Then checks were made to ensure that the alternative decompression chamber was in service before the Dover unit could be withdrawn from its 'available' condition. The decompression chamber was primarily used to treat divers who had been subjected to higher than atmospheric pressure whilst under water, in a controlled pressure-reducing environment to prevent the onset of the 'bends'.

The Royal Marines depot in Deal was less than 10 miles away, and was at this time a very large site. I would initially contact Mr Wilson in the admin block, where he acted as a focal point for any requests for assistance.

Effectively most of the work done at the barracks was organized from the instrument repair workshop, run by Sgt. Tony Bowles. The outstation 'visitors' had always got on very well with Tony and the other Marines working in this workshop, and as Tony and the others always made us so welcome (cups of tea etc), the instrument repair workshop had become our unofficial base when on site.

Deal was obviously a nice place to visit, and if the circumstances were right a nice brisk walk along the sea-front at lunch time was a real treat in the summer. And the local fish and chips weren't bad either!

Monday (2nd week)

In the Dockyard. I would do the normal admin duties: reports, travel warrants, stores demands and gate notes, and discuss major work packages for the forthcoming week with Alan Hills and Ron Barnes. I would deliver any items collected from outstations requiring urgent repairs/tests/inspections and collect items prepared in the Dockyard for return to the parent outstation.

Tuesday

ARL (Admiralty Research Laboratory) Teddington & AOL (Admiralty Oil Laboratory) Cobham.

The Teddington outstation was split into two sites. The HQ housed all the experimental workshops, and for the most part was restricted to visitors (in common with some of the other outstation sites). One building I did need to visit contained an enormous water tank (like an above ground swimming pool, but with glass sides), which I believe was used in ship's hull development and design. This building took pride of place when visitors were shown round, as it was these tanks that Dr. Barnes Wallis used in some of his bouncing-bomb experiments, when he was designing the 'Dam Busters' bombs.

My contact here was a Mr De May, who usually gave me the impression that he was far too busy to talk to me, even if he had wanted to. However, we got on sufficiently well to conduct business without any problems.

The other half of the site was the Lodge in Bushy Park, a couple of miles away. This was a royal park full of deer, and it was always a good idea to be very careful when driving through the park (I had no wish to have to go to see HRH to explain why she was a bit short of venison). In the summer the park was a really nice place to take a lunch break; however, it was a place to be avoided if at all possible when the stags were rutting, as they could be very aggressive.

The man in charge of the lodge was Wally Comfort, a real old 'country boy'. He wasn't much of a talker, but he really impressed me with his ground-staff skills and kept the park neat and tidy. Chatham's prime concern at this site was the agricultural machinery, mowers mainly, but they also had a few rotovators and chainsaws.

The road from Teddington to Cobham goes right past Hampton Court, and I always made a mental note to visit it one day, as it always looks very impressive. I haven't made it yet!

AOL Cobham had been successfully relocated from its original site at Brentford. What a wonderful new setting! Cobham (Surrey) is a very nice part of the world anyway, and the site located in an old manor house grounds just outside Cobham village was beautiful. The entrance was off the A3, up a tree-lined drive leading to the (old) Manor House with several outbuildings to the side. These outbuildings had been converted, and were now the workshops/offices/stores and laboratories for the new facility.

To the rear of the main buildings there were large, well-kept allotments, and on more than one occasion, after business, I was offered some really nice tomatoes or a lettuce free of charge!

The Technical Officers, Bill Eggington and George Tidy, were obviously delighted with their new work environment (who wouldn't be?) and it was always a pleasure to visit this site. I frequently used to pull George's leg about being trapped in the cellar with him at Brentford, with the fumes from Coty next door giving me cause for concern!

My preference after leaving the Cobham site was to return to Chatham via the A25 rather than go back through London. Although the traffic could still be very heavy (depending on the time of day), it was a change of route that I enjoyed.

Wednesday

HMS *Ganges* - this was the naval training establishment situated near Ipswich. The first thing you noticed when you visited was the massive mast on the parade square (Quarterdeck). This was where when parades/demonstrations were held the chosen lad (the 'Button Boy') had to climb to the very top and stand on the button, a small round platform at the very top. Bloody hell, was that high! Better him than me.

My contact at Ganges was Lt. Arnott, who was officially retired but was allowed to continue wearing his uniform. He was a typical serviceman, polite and welcoming. After the usual pleasantries and a most welcome cup of coffee he handed me over to his Chief Petty Officer, who would be my day-to-day liaison.

Amazingly, on my third visit to HMS *Ganges* Lt. Arnott introduced me to the newly-arrived chief, CPO Tim Wraight. As soon as I saw him I recognized him as the brother of one of my school friends, Joe. It transpired that Tim lived in Upchurch, the next village to me, and we had independently travelled about 120 miles to *Ganges* to meet up again. What a small world!

I remember one of the major tasks that we had to do at *Ganges* was to overhaul the davits (a type of fixed crane) along the sea wall. The guys loved it, it was summer and they could work alongside the water's edge, shirt off and catching a few rays, just like being on holiday. They did get the job done though, I saw to that. I always enjoyed my trips to *Ganges*, more so after the appointment of Tim Wraight as the unit's Chief Petty Officer, in spite of the distance to be covered to and from the depot. Tim was a smashing guy and always made our trips and the work in hand a pleasant experience.

Thursday

Greenwich and Deptford. Most weeks we had work ongoing at the Naval College. This was primarily the repair or servicing of the instructional equipment in the laboratories/classrooms (training aids) and the machine tools, or electrical installation or maintenance packages. If no work was currently in progress I would often still make a visit to discuss any problems they had, or the details of work that was being proposed for acceptance in the near future. Jimmy Glenton was the main contact and always seemed happy to see anyone from Chatham and make us welcome for the 'statutory' cup of tea.

Onwards to our workshop in Deptford, where invariably several major tasks would be going on at the same time. Periodically (at three-monthly intervals) Felco Moore, the contractors who would test and certify our lifting equipment, would be in attendance and would require our assistance. Their normal three-monthly visits would essentially be a visual examination, combined with a calibration check of the 'safe load indicators' and alarms. (These checks were obviously very important to prevent overloading the device, which in turn could result in damaged equipment, damaged loads, and in extreme cases the tipping-over of mobile cranes, with possible loss of life.) Being MoD, we were very careful to ensure that all the safety checks were done in accordance with their schedules, and the equipment was kept in tip-top working condition.

It was a frightening experience when I first observed the Deptford depot's own cranes unloading barges on the river wall. The mobile cranes were intermittently working at (and beyond) their 'safe working limit', where if the crane is subjected to any more weight it is likely to topple over. Alarm bells would be ringing, alarm indicator lights flashing, and one or both of the rear wheels would lift off from the ground. The drivers seemed to be unconcerned, and carried on lifting the heavy loads out of the barges, which when the tide had fallen could not be seen! It was quite possible that any of these cranes could become so overloaded that it would topple over into the river, or more probably straight onto the barge it was unloading. Probable loss of life, and a lost barge and mobile crane, were more than likely! By the way, this was 'piecework' and they were on bonus. The sight frightened me.

Months later, when I visited the same wharf area whilst the cranes were operating, it seemed to be much quieter, no bells and alarms ringing; I commented on this to Alan Wenham, my deputy, who was with me, and he explained that he believed that some of the drivers had disconnected the alarms on their cranes as they were too noisy. I was so glad that this was not an area of my responsibility!

This visit would constitute my 'supervisory day' of the week, when I had the opportunity to assess at first hand the progress that had been made on the equipment repairs being undertaken, and also a chance to get to know the staff to a deeper level. When the workshop wasn't busy (eg when the agricultural machinery repair programme was in hand in the winter months) it still had sufficient tasks to keep the workload ticking over. Ad hoc repairs to the Deptford depot's equipment (which was worked very hard to say the least) were an almost daily occurrence, and an infinite variety of equipment could be 'shipped in' (once approval had been sought) from the outstations. This included mobile cranes and fork-lift trucks (if the work was too major to be tackled on site at the outstation), back-up or spare agricultural machinery, in fact a diverse range of equipment, as long as it was purchased through the MoD and therefore the responsibility of Chatham.

One of the usual problems for the outstations guys was that a significant amount of the equipment looked after had no handbooks (for repair/test details) or spares list, so often the first task was to obtain these, if available. Additionally we had no 'library' facilities at the workshop, so care had to be taken to ensure that you were working to the latest specification, and not outdated information.

I feel that one of my personal successes on the outstations was to introduce a planned maintenance schedule for the section's workload. This took into consideration the routine inspection visits by contractors, the winter overhaul of the agricultural machinery, the specialist skills of the staff, the importance of the work packages, and to some extent the preferences of the workforce. This was initially greeted with some reservations from the staff, but when they realized that they knew where they would be in the forthcoming weeks, and could plan accordingly, it was taken on board and worked very well.

Friday

Deptford workshop. If no urgent or necessary visits had materialized during the week, I would often return to our Deptford workshop on Friday, sometimes calling in to Chatham (Dockyard) first if there was anything to collect or deliver. This was useful, as it gave me extra time at our busiest work area (ie the Deptford workshop) and also on a personal basis; it was an easier trip home from Deptford than from most of the other outstations, particularly if it had been a week involving long journeys.

I was now quite used to the trials of road travel to the outstations, but it soon became clear that my faithful old Wolseley car was not going to be able to cope with the new demands that were going to be placed upon it. The A2 was always very, very busy, with three lanes full of traffic trying to beat each other and be the first into or out of town. That was almost acceptable in terms of driving, but as I always said - once you get to Falonwood, London traffic starts; forget the Highway

Code and put your foot down!

The old Wolseley had given sterling service for many years and would have continued to do so, but the speed of the traffic, requiring fast pull-aways from traffic lights, left the old car struggling. It was just too heavy to match the power/weight ratio of the vehicles it was competing with, and at its age and mileage it was just a matter of time before the wonderful old car gave up the ghost. A great pity, but no option – a new car was needed. So I reluctantly sold the Wolseley to a mate in the Pattern Shop (Alan Gardiner) for £75 and brought a year-old Vauxhall Viva SL90, in white, MKL 659F.

Those first two weeks saw me visit the outstations that would form the basis of my duties on the section; although some other outstations were still operating (just, in most cases), they would not commit us to any significant work packages. I did visit the outstations at Harlow (Essex) and its 'sister' at Baldock (Herts): the first visit was with Ron Barnes, when we went to both sites to introduce me to the sites' representatives, and the second (and last) time I visited Harlow alone. This was just prior to the closure of the depot, and I was tasked to survey their machine tools prior to disposal. (When Ron Barnes allocated the job the week previously I felt obliged to volunteer the information that I had never before surveyed machine tools and therefore felt that some sort of guidance was necessary!) He advised me to speak to an in-house fitter on the machine tools repair section in the engineering factory, and after a 15-minute chat I was a fully qualified machine tool surveyor (delegated)!

Some of the smaller outstations seemed only to come out of the woodwork when they were in trouble. I remember visiting an RNR (Royal Naval Reserve) establishment at Ipswich, after they failed a fire inspection due to their extinguishers being out of date. They requested help from Chatham and I was tasked to take a bootful of (in-date) extinguishers to the depot as replacements. Problem solved.

Another unusual task was when I was asked to go to a service establishment to survey their flagstaff (I can't remember where the unit was). I had never surveyed a flagstaff in my life, and knew slightly less about them than I did about brain surgery. However, having learnt a lesson when dealing with the survey of machine tools (ask an expert), I sought advice from the Dockyard section, who had expertise which they passed on sufficiently for me to do this one-off survey.

If the specialist task was of sufficient magnitude, it was usual for the appropriate expert to visit the outstation to carry out the examination/work, assuming of course that the equipment could not be conveyed to Chatham to have the work done. This applied mainly to very large items, like mobile cranes, fixed items such as wall or traveller cranes and items in everyday use which could not be taken out of service for an extended period, such as special shackles, eye-bolts and other items of lifting gear.

One of the specialized tasks which necessitated site visits by experts was the result of an accident involving a fork-lift truck. An accident had happened where the heel of a fork had failed and subsequent examinations had revealed that forks on other trucks had signs of significant cracking. An instruction was issued that all fork-lift trucks would have their forks non-destructively tested on an annual basis.

I had compiled an Equipment Register for all outstations, so we knew where the visits would be necessary. The next step was to explain the problem to the boss of the NDTC (Non Destructive Test Centre – a Mr Gullick) and he readily agreed that one of his staff would accompany me to an outstation to carry out these tests using a 'permanent magnet' procedure. You clean the area of the fork heel to be tested, cover the area to be tested with white paint and then coat with a solution of paraffin which has iron filings in the mixture, then scan the area with a strong magnet. The iron filings will be attracted to the cracks, if any, and show up clearly as lines between a 'valley' of iron filings.

It was agreed that as the outstation visit was something of a perk, so to keep things fair a different member of the NDTC team would accompany me on each visit. This worked very well, and the NDTC boys did a good job and enjoyed their day out. I particularly remember taking Mick Russell, Mick Cooper and Chris Wood on the visits.

Other specialist visits involved the Chatham Boilermakers, who were required to witness deflection tests on cranes and carry out pressure tests, including the decompression chamber at Dover.

One of the outstations that I had heard of but never visited was HMS *Dauntless*, a Wrenery (WRNS base) near Reading. When at last I did visit the place it did not end well. When we (Alan Wenham was with me) were leaving the Establishment to make our way back, I did not see a dwarf wall behind me in the car park and reversed into it.

Of course, as we were at a Wrenery when this happened, you can guess the remarks that were made (with some justification) about eyeing up the Wrens and not concentrating on my driving. No major damage was done to the car (in contrast to my pride) and I managed to do the necessary repairs myself, although the replacement spray paint I used (supposedly the official one) did not match exactly. This was bloody annoying, as it compounded a problem concerning damage sustained a little while previously when the car had been parked outside our workshop at Deptford. I had seen what had happened; one of the stores staff was using a fork-lift truck towing a conveyor (a large roller platform used for luggage crates etc), and had misjudged his turning circle such that the rear swung round and dented the rear wing of my car. I was not too pleased. The driver seemed completely unconcerned, and stank of beer.

I reported the incident to Mr Smith, the Stores Officer, who arranged to make good the repairs; respraying, mostly. Unfortunately, although the repairs weren't too bad, the paint was not an exact match, probably due to the original paintwork changing colour with age. So I now had a car which was at least three different shades of white!

This was the other side of my duties on the outstations section. The high mileage on the car under loaded and fast conditions took a toll on its expected life, and the journeys made and places where I had to park meant that some sort of accident damage was inevitable. In a couple of years I had done about

65,000 hard miles, and the Viva was knackered. Time for a car change again, and this time it was a beauty.

I brought a lovely MGB GT in teal blue, LKO 381F. This had wire wheels, twin spot & fog lights, leather upholstery and overdrive in third and fourth gear. Although at first glance this didn't look as if it was a suitable car to transport big loads of supplies around, in fact it was ideal. With the rear seats folded down, the hatchback allowed large items to be carried, or alternatively masses of stores could be accommodated.

Alan Hills' wife, who I had got to know quite well by now, used to take the mickey about the car and suggest that she would buy me a 'flat hat' to complete the image. She let me down - I never got the hat!

The Planned Maintenance Schedule for the outstations section was already showing important benefits, and taking into consideration the routine inspection/tests visits by contractors, the winter overhaul of the agricultural machinery, the maintenance schedules that covered the equipment we 'husbanded' (eg fork-lift trucks and machine tools), it also left a little 'float' time to allow for unforeseen work commitments. The schedule also took into consideration some of the work staff preferences, as some of the depots were more popular with some of the staff than others! Also the most distant outstations like *Ganges* and *Dauntless* really needed to be reached by car, as rail access was difficult and very time consuming.

The outstation boys were a great lot. I learnt a great deal in terms of man management, communications and supervisory skills in this, my first job as a supervisor.

Sometimes the odd indiscretion would rear its ugly head, and usually a cautionary word was sufficient, but on one occasion when one of the staff persisted in late attendance, and was obviously intent on 'taking the piss', a written warning was necessary.

I was well aware that not all the work undertaken in our Deptford workshop was bona fide, and this small percentage fell into two categories. The first category was 'unofficial' items from one of the outstations which were in addition to their authorized entitlement of equipment, and not purchased through naval funds, therefore not our responsibility to maintain. Provided that this was a small or inexpensive activity, it was a favour to the Depot and I could live with that.

The second category was 'rabbits'. These were private jobs, done in works time. Additionally the job might also consume MoD resources (material & spares). Sometimes it would be difficult to identify, as 'private' items could be of identical equipment to service (authorized) items. It took me a little while to wise up to checking the item serial numbers!

This category can be acceptable in small, infrequent measures, but is obviously illegal and dangerous for all concerned. Active surveillance was essential to ensure that this activity was very closely controlled, and even more closely restricted!

All too soon my time on the outstations was finished. I was at the Deptford workshop when a phone call from Alan Hills gave me the news that the results of the 1970 inspectors' examination had been announced, and I had qualified for promotion.

Good news and bad news. The good news obviously was that I would now be promoted to PTO 111 (Inspector) grade; the bad news was that I would have to leave the outstations section after a comparatively short time. I remember explaining the situation to Alan Wenham, my deputy, who was confused regarding the procedure for promotion in the Dockyards, as many other people were. I explained that often when you took promotion it was on a 'temporary acting' basis, which meant it was a short-term appointment which was not expected to last. A good example was when I was doing 'deputy chargeman' duties, covering for sick and annual leave periods.

If a vacancy occurred it was often filled on an acting basis until the person concerned qualified (officially) for the post either through an interview (for PTO1V vacancies only), or via an academic Qualification (ONC [Ordinary National Certificate], HNC Higher National Certificate) or the 'Inspector of Trades' examination for higher grades PTO 111 & PTO 11 etc.

Understand? No? Well, I'm not surprised!

Anyway, as I explained to Alan, I had been promoted to Supervisor (Chargeman) on outstations because I had passed an assessment interview. This had been confirmed by my successful position on the 1968 inspectors' exam. My higher qualification on the 1970 exam meant that I was now 'Qualified' (List 2), and would be offered promotion to the PTO 111 grade (inspector).

CHATHAM DOCKYARD YSM MAINTENANCE AND UTILITIES SECTIONS

This was promotion – but at a price. When I was first notified that I would be promoted, I was told I had been appointed to the post of 'Assistant Refuelling Director' in the nuclear site. Nice title – but I was not entirely happy. I had always had considerable reservations about working in an environment which would mean being exposed to (possibly large) doses of radiation. This was due in part to a dockyard-wide briefing I had attended where the speaker (a senior Dockyard official) had pooh-poohed the idea of any problems of radiation poisoning, and even explained that we (the Dockyard workers involved) would be unlikely to be in contact with more radiation than that omitted from a luminous wristwatch!

Incidentally, I don't blame this official, even if he was talking out of his ass, as he was probably conned or being naïve concerning radiation treatment at that time. This is what I would like to believe; as the management stance was to get the boat done and back into service at almost any cost, and the health of the workforce concerned was almost incidental. I firmly believe that the possible effects of radiation contamination were well known to the Dockyard management from our American Navy counterparts.

I think I fully appreciated the vitally important need to get the boats out to sea. I also felt, perhaps unfairly, that some of the younger element were offered promotion with a 'posh' title, eg Assistant Refuelling Director, and a substantial increase (possibly double) in wages (through allowances and overtime) as a bribe to enter the nuclear site with not too many questions asked. How could they refuse? It would be very difficult to turn down an offer like that.

However, the decision as to whether to accept the job on the nuclear site or not was taken out of my hands. Apparently one of the requirements before taking up the job was to pass a medical. When I enquired at the Dockyard surgery what the purpose of the medical was, I was told that it was strictly routine and nothing to worry about. Not satisfied, I persisted. 'Yes, but what is it for?' I asked. It was explained to me, reluctantly I thought, that a satisfactory 'blood count' was a prerequisite of taking up the job (a check to ensure that sufficient white blood cells were present in the blood). When the results of my blood test came through, my blood count was too low and unacceptable. I was told not to worry, as this sometimes happened if the person being tested had recently had a cold, or some minor infection. A repeat blood sample was taken. To cut a long story short, I had three blood samples taken over a period of a few weeks, but still could not reach the required standard in terms of the blood count.

I was then notified by the Personnel Department that I was to take up a different appointment as the Inspector (PTO 111) of the Maintenance Section on the Yard Services Department (YSM). At this stage I discovered what was in fact common knowledge (though not to me), that a lot of wheeler-dealing had been done by other dockyard personnel to take this (my) Refuelling Directors' job, as the money was irresistible, and the knives were out.

For my part, I did not mourn the job loss. I always felt that exposure to high levels of radiation could lead to serious health problems later on. To me it depended on your unique metabolism, and I always felt concerned about the risks. So no problem- perhaps even relief!

YSM Maintenance

On August 10 1971, I was promoted into the MWO (Maintenance Workshop Officer) Section on YSM, (the department I was already working on). This was not entirely good news, for two reasons. First of all, as previously indicated by my phrase 'promotion at a price', I was worse off financially to begin with. This was because on outstation work, the allowances for mileage and subsistence left a small 'profit' after the expenses were paid, which obviously was not available to me now. Additionally the pay scale in the promoted grade showed little pay enhancement, as I went from a middle pay grade PTO 1V to an almost bottom pay grade PTO 111. Not much incentive there!

The second reason was that I was about to (unknowingly) enter an area of responsibility which was run down, under-resourced and largely out of control, and was trying to maintain obsolete equipment with inadequate staff, and with no technical literature. And that was just the good bits!

However, flushed with the success of my promotion, I was determined to do the best I could and suffer any necessary short-term pain to achieve my long-term career goals.

When I joined YSM my immediate boss, Frank Lewis, was on the point of retirement. The previous incumbent in my post, Ron Jones, was still there for a supposed handover, but he was completely 'bombed out' and of no help whatsoever. (Perhaps this is unfair, because he was certainly unwell.)

I was introduced to my staff, three very senior (in terms of age) PTO 1V Supervisors; Cyril Holmes, Bill Norris, and Harold Rowan. Cyril's real Christian name was Sherlock - I suppose it had to be, with the surname of Holmes. He was very energetic for a man in his late 50s, a staunch Trade Unionist, and was very protective of the rights of his workforce; more of that later on. His area of responsibility was as follows:

The Ringmain Boilerhouses. These were the five major boilerhouses which were located at strategic points around the

Dockyard to provide steam to the workshops, offices and ships for heating, cooking, air conditioning, and for any process requirements (eg galvanizing tanks). These boilers provided steam to the whole of the Dockyard, with the exception of the area north of the ships' basins (the Boathouse to No 9 Dock area).

The steam 'ringmain', and its associated condensate returns systems. The various boilerhouses were interconnected by pipework so that every building south of the ships basins could be connected to the steam supply. It was a massive system covering many miles, running almost from Gillingham gate to the Main Dockyard gate and over to No 9 Pumping Station.

These supply pipes were for the most part located in steam trenches, which also carried other services (hydraulic pipework, electrical cables, and possibly air and water supplies).

The Locks Pumping Station and hydraulic system in the locks area. A dedicated gang based in the locks workshop maintained the hydraulic pumps and accumulators in the pumping station, the hydraulic hauling engines for the caissons and the (water) hydraulic system which operated them.

The locks equipment was subject to an annual overhaul (refit) when hauling engines previously refitted at 'leisure' during the year would be installed, and the replaced engine would be taken into the workshop as a repair by replacement item for next year. Every four years the hauling chains were subjected to a detailed inspection and replacement links fitted, dependent upon use and corresponding wear over the previous period.

These duties constituted an enormous amount of work for

Cyril Holmes, the Chargeman, and over the years he had learnt how to best exploit this.

Bill Norris's area of responsibility was the heating systems inside the buildings, workshops, offices, stores etc. The heating was usually done by radiators, mainly of the old cast iron sectional type, but radiant panels and plenum plants were also used (blowing air through a radiator to create a warm air supply).

Bill's section also maintained the 'dispersed' boilers, which were the smaller boilers not connected to the steam ring main in outlying areas, north of the ships' basins. These were generally solid fuel fired (coal & coke) and usually of a very old design. They operated in a very dirty environment and were very inefficient. They were operated by stokers who ideally were ex-Navy and did not mind working on their own and in dirty (coal dust etc) conditions. In a way these boilers were more dangerous than the larger and slightly newer ring main boilers because of their very simple, almost antiquated, design. They did not have automatic safety devices fitted, and were very reliant on the stoker-operator.

Bill used to like looking after the canteen equipment, as often a free lunch or some cakes would be on offer. The equipment included the ovens, blenders, mixers etc that would be found in any industrial catering establishment.

Harold Rowan completed my trio of chargemen. His responsibilities were:

The ropery equipment. This equipment was (and still is) very basic engineering, but although it is of a great age (mostly) it is still in fairly constant use, and reliable.

CHAPTER 2

The sail/colour loft equipment - sewing machines, mainly used to manufacture flags, sashes and bunting as well as sails. A wide variety of materials were used in their manufacture (cotton, nylon, canvas etc). A significant amount of work undertaken in the sail/colour loft was on a repayment basis, ie it was work done for and paid by an external request. For example, the 'Miss Bowaters Beauty Queen' sashes!

I had heard before I started this new job that Cyril Holmes was a very strong personality who wanted to 'do his own thing' and would resent any form of control, and this soon became apparent. I don't think he resented me any more than he would have done anyone else of my age who was coming into the section, trying to exert an element of control and aiming to undertake our tasks in a controlled and planned way. It just so happened that I was the 'lucky' guy. Cyril had pretty well been left to his own devices and allowed do his own thing for some little while, so he was not about to appreciate anyone or anything that threatened this.

Cyril's immediate boss (whom I had now replaced) had severe health problems which no one wanted to discuss, but I believe they were in the nature of a nervous breakdown. In the period when I was working alongside him and taking over, it was immediately clear that he was unwell. He had a permanently vacant facial expression and slurred speech, and it seemed that his main efforts were confined to seeing how loudly he could fart (which he really enjoyed) and trying to touch up the tea lady! (She didn't mind too much.) When he saw Cyril heading towards the office he would make a bolt for the toilet door, lock

250

himself in, and would not come out until Cyril had left. Not much of a hand-over for me then!

My boss, Frank Lewis, was on the point of retiring. He got on well with Cyril in general terms, so he didn't want to rock the boat. Who could blame him?

Cyril for his part was conscientious, but equally he was determined that his efforts would be fully rewarded. He was a very active trade unionist and never really saw himself as part of the management structure, except on very rare occasions when it suited him. It was common knowledge that he 'manufactured' the need to work weekend overtime (Sundays preferred - double pay) by manipulating events and ensuring that breakdowns to essential equipment would be done on an overtime basis, rather than during normal working hours.

The senior foreman on the department, George Tapson, was also about to retire and got on well with Cyril (probably because they were both also freemasons), so he had little interest in insisting on unpopular and difficult methods to implement changes to the work practices that had developed.

George Tapson retired quite soon after I joined the Maintenance Section and was replaced by Johnny Bubb. Johnny and Cyril did not get on, and I don't believe they liked each other. That was a problem insofar as it was the senior foreman (Johnny) who authorized overtime working, and as he knew what was going on he tried his best (without much luck) to curtail excessive hours. It became a battle of wits, and guess who was piggy in the middle?

I tried very hard to explain to Cyril that his efforts in securing overtime for his men were commendable, and if we worked together we would arrive at the same conclusion (no dramatic cuts in overtime - because there was always going to be a need for this). I did have limited success, but I believe his attitude was coloured by seeing other departments apparently on continuous overtime without doing too much work, as was believed to be the case in the nuclear site, and he felt that his fitters deserved the same remuneration.

I believe Cyril eventually saw the light, as his team of fitters burnt themselves out. They would work all week, then overtime on Saturday and Sunday, but would then take a day's leave in the week to give themselves a break, so Cyril found himself short of staff mid-week.

We did have several rows before I settled in fully and we found some middle ground area from which we could work.

Let me give an early example of one of Cyril's least co-operative moments. I attended a ring main boilerhouse to do my first boiler test - it was a safety valve operational test under steam conditions, necessary to ensure its safe operation. (NB: I was the nominated person to sign the boiler test certificates, which are a statutory requirement, and the boilers could not be returned into service without this document.) I had received no formal training to do this at this stage. (Or later on for that matter!)

I met up with Cyril at the boilerhouse and the conversation went something like this:

Me: "OK Cyril, as this is my first boiler test, perhaps you would talk me through the procedure?"

Cyril: "Well, as you're the bloody inspector, perhaps you would talk ME through it!"

This was the stage at which I thought, this is going to be difficult at times!

For information: We (the section) had no technical literature on these boilers. All the handbooks and technical information available to me at that time referred to ships' boilers, which generate superheated steam and are completely different to the 'land' boilers we were testing.

However, things did eventually get better in terms of a working relationship, and although we had strongly contrasting views, I finally had a lot of respect for Cyril.

At this point Frank Lewis (the foreman) retired, and was replaced by a Don Francis. He was posted in from Rosyth I believe, and appeared to be quite rigid in his approach; he clashed almost immediately with Cyril (chalk and cheese, personality wise). I believe Don Francis took a good look at the job and realized what a nightmare it would be. Whether that is true or not I don't know; I do know that he only stayed in the job for a very short time, perhaps a couple of months, before he transferred to Bath.

I had worked with Bill Norris when I had been an apprentice and he a fitter on the crane repair section alongside No.7 Slip. By this time Bill was in his late fifties, and sometimes it showed. His biggest downfall was that he would take the word of his workforce that they had completed a job, and wouldn't bother to check it. I remember one occasion when this came home to roost. Bill told me that one of the dispersed boilers that his men had refitted was ready for test, and we arranged to meet on site at the appointed time. A boiler test is a joint exercise between the fitters who do the refit and the boilermakers who do the actual pressure testing. When we got to this boilerhouse and the boilermakers started to fill the boiler prior to applying the pressure: water pissed out everywhere. The fittings had not been put on correctly, and had not been tightened up. I was not amused. It was not only that I looked foolish, it made us engineers look incompetent in the eyes of the attending boilermakers. I bollocked Bill big-time, when we were alone. It didn't happen again.

Bill wasn't very dynamic, but he did try his best. He did not have the best of fitters, as the younger and more interested ones were usually poached for the nuclear site, and he was left with the older, and often green card (somehow disabled) fitters.

Harold Rowan was quite a character. He looked after the maintenance of equipment in the south end of the Dockyard, his main task being the Ropery. Although the equipment was very old, a surprising amount of spares were available or could be manufactured, so ordinarily no major long-term breakdowns were experienced. The equipment itself was very basic engineering and there were few major problems.

Harold was old school, very opinionated and set in his ways. He too had been left to his own devices to run his section as he wished, with little control or even interest from his line managers. This can be explained in part by the fact that the ring main boilers and the steam heating supply system (Cyril's section) were top priority and this was also where the main and recurrent problems arose; therefore this area was where the management activities were concentrated.

Having said that, Harold ran his section very well; he kept the machinery running and presented few problems. However his section was relatively lightly loaded and most of his work was on routine maintenance tasks, which are obviously much easier to deal with than breakdowns. Harold also ran his section in the old way, where the chargeman was omnipotent; his men did as they were told or else! But it worked for him.

I remember two funny stories regarding Harold. The first was when he had to complete an apprentice's report for a lad who in Harold's eyes had not come up to scratch. Harold did not like apprentices anyway, and only took them into his section for training under duress. His stance, having had some experience, was that if you gave an apprentice a job to do he would probably mess it up, and if you didn't give him a job to do he would get bored and cause mischief. Unfair really, because certainly the biggest part (the apprentice's work standard, and his subsequent behaviour) was determined to a great degree by his 'skipper'.

(When apprentices left a section after their period of training a report was raised by the chargeman and sent back to the Personnel Division via the inspector and foreman.)

This particular apprentice had not impressed Harold at all, and at the end of his report concerning the overall assessment he wrote: 'This apprentice is not up to the required standard. He has demonstrated no basic skills or even interest in his period of training in this section. My overall opinion is that with a little more practice this lad would make a fucking good statue!'

I explained to Harold that this comment was neither constructive nor acceptable (although there was a certain black humour and even a lot of truth in the remark). Harold refused to change his comments, so we agreed to disagree, and referred the report to the Foreman for arbitration. Charlie Willis was now 'in the foreman's chair' having just taken over from Frank Lewis. He did convince Harold that the report was unacceptable and a revised and more meaningful edition was produced.

The other amusing story regarding Harold goes as follows:

Harold came to work one Monday morning rather subdued, swearing more profusely (he liked a good F & B) than usual, and was obviously in a black mood. When asked what was wrong, he eventually opened up and said that he was being ostracized by his wife 'big-time', and it wasn't his fault.

'What wasn't your fault?' we enquired.

It transpired that Harold's wife was a regular at their local church (some cynics would say that being married to Harold, she would have to be), and the vicar would regularly ask Mrs Rowan to bring her husband along to the Sunday service. She would explain that Harold was committed elsewhere on Sundays due to his special hobby - winemaking. (It should be explained at this point that Harold was a very experienced winemaker who had won major awards, judged events and advised winemakers on the local radio.)

'Wonderful!' said the vicar. 'I must call on him sometime and congratulate him on his achievements.'

So the following Sunday evening, after church, the vicar jumped astride his trusty push-bike and rode over to see Harold.

'Come in' said Harold, 'and bring your bike in as well, the bastards around here will pinch anything that isn't welded down.'

Harold took the vicar down to the cellar, his inner sanctum, where the serious winemaking magic was performed. The vicar was amazed at the quantity, variety, and in due course the quality of the stock.

It all started off quite harmlessly.

'You see vicar, a delicate wine like this elderflower is more of a challenge to perfect than some of the coarse reds that are shovelled out by the supermarkets' explained Harold. 'Please try a little.'

I suspect you know what happened next. The vicar was amazed by the quality of Harold's home-made wines, and enthusiastically tried quite a few. Quite a few too many, actually.

Mrs Rowan had been out visiting her sister, and as soon as she opened the front door she knew that something was wrong. She heard giggling, then singing – hymns! From the cellar? What on earth was going on?

When she entered the cellar she could not believe her eyes. The vicar was riding his bicycle in a very tight circle around the cellar, red in the face, singing the Lord's praises. Then crash, he fell off with his bicycle on top of him in a giggling heap, and was heard to swear in no uncertain terms concerning the inadequacy of his 'bloody bike'.

Mrs Rowan was shocked. The vicar was a giggling wreck. Harold was in the shit.

Harold and the next-door neighbour managed to pour the vicar into Harold's car and took him back to the vicarage, where he remained, unseen, for two days. Hence Mr and Mrs Rowan were not on speaking terms, and Harold was all wrinkly-lipped.

This inspector's post on the YSM maintenance section was a poisoned chalice. First and foremost, it was a task that was impossible to do well. This was because the steam heating system had over the years 'grown like Topsy', having consistently had heating systems added on to workshops and offices at the end of the steam system with minimal increase in boiler plant to satisfy the increased demand. Additionally when new boiler plant was made available it was installed in a boilerhouse which had the space available and not in the most suitable location.

But the principal problem was the inadequate design of the trenches which carried the steam supply pipework. These trenches were usually crammed with other services, which could include gas, mains water, dockyard water, air, condensate returns and pump lines, and demineralized water. This meant that whilst in principal it was a good idea to 'collect' all of these supplies into one supplies trench, to actually work on any of these services was an absolute nightmare, with no space between the various pipes. It was often the system at the bottom of the trench that had failed, and this meant the removal of all the other pipes on top before any repairs could be attempted. This meant that these other services would need to be shut down also.

Another major flaw with these service trenches was that they had inadequate drainage. The drains that were installed were usually blocked, and in the winter months, when rainfall was at its highest, these trenches would invariably partially fill with water, with the immediate effect of cooling the steam pipes (through saturated lagging) and reducing the steam pressure inside the pipes.

Looking back now, I can see that because the steam heating system had been added to in an ad hoc manner, most of the boilers were aged and inefficient, and it was not in the interests of some of the maintenance staff to eliminate breakdowns (and reduce/lose their overtime), it didn't have much chance of working!

As previously explained, I would not blame anyone for this situation, which had evolved over a period of years. Lack of resources was a major problem, and most of the staff available were 'fighting fires' and did not have the time or inclination to look at the overall problems.

It was certainly hard work on YSM, and we earned our corn - such as it was. My particular job was busiest in the run-up for the new heating season, when all the boilers had to be pressure tested, after their annual refit, and a certificate produced before they could be put into service. This was done in conjunction with the boilermakers, who provided the test pumps and gauges, and were obliged to be present at all of these tests. Often the adjacent boilers would be operating in the boilerhouse, so there would be very hot conditions to work in. Directly after the test it was often necessary to go to another boilerhouse, and it was a good idea to ensure that you had cooled down again before going out in winter weather, unless you were desperate to get pneumonia!

This was especially important if the boiler test had included the need to 'set to work' the boiler safety valves, under steam conditions. What this basically means is that one of the safety valves is gagged (they are a dual unit) and the steam pressure in the boiler is increased until the safety valves 'blow' (the valves lift to allow steam to escape and prevent any increase in boiler pressure). This is a hot, noisy, horrible job; when the valves lift to vent the steam they do so with quite a bang (you'll need to change your underpants on the first couple of occasions). These valves are on the TOP of the boiler and it's quite a tricky job to do any adjustment particularly in that heat, and when the valves lift - steam and dust everywhere for a few minutes, glasses steamed up, can't see a thing! The procedure is then repeated for the other valve.

In truth, it was not absolutely necessary for the inspector (me) always to be adjacent to the fitter doing the test in the worst area or conditions, but I always felt that I was showing faith in the team who had done the work, and it encouraged a feeling of teamwork.

Complaints would pour into the office regarding poor heating, especially on Monday mornings after the weekend shutdown, when the 'phone would be red hot, and I never had enough staff to put matters right, so not much job satisfaction. On the other side of the coin, most of the guys on YSM tried really hard to provide a good service, and they were a conscientious lot.

For my part, one of the worst aspects was that I was expected to be on call, unofficially and unpaid, 24/7. If there was a breakdown, and sometimes even if someone had just forgotten to put in a request and was therefore without heating, they would contact the duty officer, the 'Control Engineer'. I believe that originally this position was for emergency problems with electrical supplies, but it quickly morphed into a handy number (dockyard extn. 2535) which almost anybody could phone with complaints about steam supplies in 'silent hours' (outside normal working hours).

The control engineers were of the electrical persuasion, so they were often unable to answer the queries presented to them - so guess who they contacted? Yes, that's right, yours truly. I didn't mind this too much if this happened occasionally and the situation warranted an urgent solution, but in the end it became ridiculous. I was being phoned up almost every evening, and when it got to three times in a night or at 3 am and 4 am, I decided that enough was enough. My wife was pregnant, and her mother was very ill at this time, and these persistent phone calls started waking us up in the early hours. She was being woken up in a panic thinking that her mother had been taken ill again, and I was obviously having a disturbed night's sleep as well.

I told my boss that I was not prepared to accept this situation as on ongoing routine. He was less than impressed, and considered that it was my duty. So I suggested he should try it. The good news was that my stance engineered a change such that a duty officer was nominated (on a paid rota basis) to cover problems outside the normal working hours.

It was at about this time that I was informed out of the blue by my boss, Charlie Willis, the foreman, that a compassionate move had been arranged for an inspector called Stan Sargent from Rosyth and he would be taking over my post. I asked, quite reasonably I thought, what was going to happen to me. 'I don't know, that hasn't been worked out yet,' was the piss-poor answer I received. They (the powers that be) had decided that I would be moved, for no reason connected to my ability/performance, and didn't know what I would be doing next! Charming, bloody charming. What a way to inspire your staff and create team building and job satisfaction!

A couple of weeks later Stan arrived from Rosyth. Charlie Willis brought him into the office and introduced him, and explained that I should start a handover. When I started to explain the structure of the section, Stan stopped me and said that he had no intention of taking over from me, as the job he had requested at Chatham was in the apprentices' training area, and that he had no intention of landing himself in a section as busy and stressful as this!

Over the next couple of weeks Stan would come into work alongside me in the office, but show no interest in proceedings and would often look preoccupied for long periods, saying very little, but looking desperately miserable. In this period he had locked horns with Cyril Holmes, as almost from day one they had decided to dislike each other.

After a couple of weeks, Charlie came into the office early morning, as usual and Stan was sitting alongside me, feet up on desk, as usual. Charlie commented, 'You had better start showing some interest Stan, you'll be in charge soon'.

Stan exploded. Glaring at Charlie, he snapped 'If you think I'm staying here working my bollocks off, and at every bastard's beck and call, you're a bigger prick than I thought you were!'

Charlie was somewhat taken aback, and was obviously

unsure as to what he should do. Stan then stood up and opened his shirt front. 'Look at this' he shouted and revealed an angry and horrible-looking scar about eight inches long, running down his stomach. 'This is what I got for doing a job like this' he continued, 'Fucking ulcers. No more, no more, you bastards are not going to kill Me!'

It all went quiet. Charlie turned and went back into his office. Stan did up his shirt, and slumped back into his chair; he was now ashen and trembling.

Stan was quiet for the rest of the morning and sat at the desk brooding. After lunch he moved close and almost whispered 'Sorry about that this morning old friend, but I had a flashback to my old station.'

He then explained some of what had happened shortly before his transfer to Chatham. He had worked in the nuclear site at Rosyth. It was a very busy and demanding task. It was a job that demanded 24-hour commitment, due to the importance of the job, the unrealistic time schedules, and the continual problems they were experiencing in new work areas. Stan and his boss were under continual pressure, culminating in each taking a notepad to bed with them so that when they awoke during the night with work-related problems they could make notes before going back to sleep!

Stan got on well with his boss, a very nice person who he respected workwise. But the constant stress had been taking its toll on Stan's health and he had become more and more disillusioned. The final straw came when quite suddenly his boss had a massive heart attack and died, at home, over a weekend. Stan was devastated to lose such a good colleague and friend. When he went to work on the Monday morning he reported what had happened to his 'big boss'.

This man's reaction amazed and angered Stan beyond belief. The big boss's reaction to the news of Stan's colleague's demise was to say, 'Christ, that's buggered it, I'd better get in touch with Bath [headquarters] for a replacement'. He made a dive for the phone, and requested a replacement engineer! No 'How did it happen?' or 'Is his family OK, what can we do for them?' Stan was speechless and disgusted. He never really recovered from that experience.

Stan had opened up, so he now dropped the other bombshell. He had just that week been advised that his wife had been diagnosed with cancer, and it was probably terminal!

I didn't know what to say or do.

About two weeks later Stan got his posting notice, and off he went to be an instructor in the Apprentices Section (Chatham), as he had been promised.

I had been on the Maintenance Section for about 18 months when George Stapenhill, the inspector on the Utilities Section, was transferred into the engineering factory, and I indicated to his new foreman that I would be interested in transferring to that job. I transferred into the Utilities Section with Ron Dawe, UMO (Utilities Maintenance Officer), as my boss. This section was very labour intensive, averaging between 80-100 staff and comprising three discrete sections.

CHAPTER 2

YSM UTILITIES

Ernie Goddard ran the fitters sections. Ernie was a bit special; he had been in the Dockyard for many years and was one of the senior chargemen. He was technically sound, very experienced, always showed common-sense, and was greatly respected by his staff, hence his nickname 'Daddy Goddard'. He was short and tubby and it always appeared that his short legs were struggling to keep up with him. Never without his cheese-cutter hat or favourite pipe, he was always ready with a smile and advice. His workshop base was No. 3 Well, where the maintenance team, fitters and labourers, would base themselves when not working on the breakdowns and maintenance tasks of their concern. These principally comprised the following:

The compressed air ring main and its compressors (situated in Nos. 3, 5, and 9 compressor stations).

The hydraulic main, which operated the locks, caissons and most of the dock penstocks.

The dockyard well pumps, No. 1 and No. 3 wells, maintained for the hydraulic main, fire main, some toilets, and emergency use.

The main dock pumping stations, No. 5 and No. 9, were operated by fitter operators in attendance (Fred Wilby and Len Sym were two of them). These guys operated and maintained the main and drainage dock pumps, and at no 9 pumping station they would run the air compressors in the adjacent bay.

Ernie ran a tight ship, with very few problems, and although minimal overtime was worked, the staff were happy and well-motivated.

John Eldridge, and later Fred Hayward, ran the stokers' section. Although still referred to as chargemen, they were officially PSG V grade (Process and Supervisory Grade 5).

The stoker teams operated the five main boilerhouses, the dispersed boilers, the portable boilers and package boilers. The five ring main boilerhouses were as follows:

No. 1 Boilerhouse: 5 boilers in three sectioned building (2-3 stokers required).

No. 2 Boilerhouse: 6 boilers. Old ex-coal-fired converted boilers (2+ stokers required).

No. 3 Boilerhouse: 3 boilers (2 stokers required).

No. 4 (Central) Boilerhouse: 5 boilers in two sectioned building (2-3 stokers required).

No. 5 Boilerhouse: 6 boilers. (2-3 stokers required).

The exact number of stokers employed varied with availability and was also dependent upon how many boilers were 'on line' (operational) in that boilerhouse.

The dispersed boilers were at:

MTE (Maintenance Training Establishment) North Basin 1.

2 boilers (1 stoker)

Boathouse. 2 boilers (usually only one in service, 1 stoker).

Locks Boilerhouse, 1 boiler (1 stoker).

Optical Shop, 1 boiler (1 stoker).

Package boilers. (stones vapour - steam generators) These were diesel fired; they could be transported to dock and basin-side sites, mainly for 'steam to ships' requirements, where no ring main steam was available. Stokers were made available as required.

Portable boilers. These antiquated boilers (which looked like Stevenson's Rocket) could be used in remote areas. They were coal and/or coke fired and very inefficient. Stokers were made available as required.

A couple of stoker 'floaters' were required to enable the single station (ie one man) stokers to take 'comfort breaks'. Stokers were forbidden to leave their boilers when operational until an adequate relief was available.

Johnny Eldridge was a lovely guy who had been on the section for many years, man and boy, and knew all the stokers (and their strengths and weaknesses) very well. He did a good job running the section before he died prematurely - not reaching retirement - and Fred Hayward took over.

Fred 'Ginger' Hayward was a mate of John's; he ran the section well. Fred and John were colleagues who I believe both started their working lives in the Dockyard as 'yard boys'. This was a scheme where young boys on leaving school entered the Dockyard as general (trainee) labourers, until they decided which jobs they wished to train for. These would include stoker, crane driver, locomotive driver, slinger and others.

Tom Jewiss ran the crane drivers' section, and was on the point of retirement. It was not an easy job, because he never had the luxury of enough drivers to operate all the cranes. This meant getting the drivers to split their tasks and drive two and sometimes three different cranes (at different locations) on the same day, something that they did not like.

The drivers preferred to operate 'their' crane only (for obvious reasons - it meant that they didn't have to travel to and from cranes, in all weathers, and keep climbing up the access ladders). Also of course, if they worked from one crane they could make it their 'home' by installing a few personal items such as a radio or items of cutlery. Additionally, if a crane driver worked from one site he got to know his 'customers' and usually established a good working relationship with them.

The nuclear site had priority over all the Dockyard craneage, and this used up most of the section's resources. The nuclear complex spanned No. 6 and No. 7 Docks and each dock had dockside cranes on each side (ie east & west of 6 Dock, and east and west of 7 Dock; additionally the main refuelling crane, Yard No.12570, was located centrally to span the majority of both dock areas. This meant that at peak times the refuelling crane and two of the other dockside cranes could be operating on shiftwork; the two other dockside cranes operated on a daywork plus overtime basis.

This meant that often fourteen crane drivers were required to operate these five cranes! This always seemed excessive to me, and I believed that good planning could have reduced this number considerably. However, when I voiced this opinion to my line managers it was regarded as heresy. The nuclear site was sacrosanct, and what they wanted they got.

Unfortunately, when this situation arose, poor old Tom

Jewiss was denuded of crane driver numbers for the rest of the Dockyard. As I said, Tom was on the point of retirement and we only worked together for a relatively short time. He was replaced by Derek McGuinness on promotion from the Bosun's party, and Derek struggled almost from day one. A lot of the drivers were quite senior and knew all the tricks, and it was always going to be a challenge for such a young man in this environment to establish his authority. The timing of his appointment was unfortunate too, as the nuclear site was gearing up for a busy period (two-stream re-fuelling), the Tower crane (a new and completely different type of crane) had just been installed (which required extra training for its drivers) and there was a new safety requirement introduced which necessitated that all the dockside cranes had to be anchored ('dogged down') when high winds were expected.

This requirement came about when during a period of strong winds in the South Dockyard area a dockside crane had been caught by the sailing effect of the wind and driven along its rails. Gathering momentum as it went, it hit the rail stops at the end of the track with an almighty wallop, and the crane almost jumped the track and toppled over. It could have ended up in the dock! The story goes that the watchkeeper on board the ship in the adjacent dock watched this happen in disbelief, mouth open, wide-eyed, and nearly (or possibly did), fill his pants, (understandably). Anyway, all hell was let loose, and the new procedure was implemented.

Ron Dawe (the new foreman) was tasked with obtaining

technical information covering the equipment and machinery which we operated. I believe that this urgent requirement was probably triggered by an unfortunate experience concerning Prince Charles. HRH was serving in the Royal Navy as skipper of one of the coastal minesweepers and came in to dock at Chatham. Unfortunately, this was the precise moment when a small hydraulic pipe joint on the locks operating equipment decided to fail, causing a locks system failure. A significant delay (hours) was caused until repairs were made, the locks returned into a serviceable state, and the ship could enter the Dockyard.

This was not good on several levels. First of all, the heir to the throne does not expect to be kept waiting to enter one of his mother's dockyards (he wasn't amused). Secondly, docking can be a tricky process, depending upon tides, currents and winds, and any complications in this procedure are not welcome.

Last but not least, but an important revelation to the Dockyard management (who were made aware of the locks problems in very short time), was that:

(a) Very few people knew how to operate the locks, and some of these were not available when this breakdown occurred (at or shortly after the end of the normal working day).

(b) There was no quick back-up means of operating the locks in the event of a failure of this type. The back-up operating equipment needed to be assembled, was slow, not regularly tested, and few people knew how to operate it!

(c) There were no drawings, handbooks or operating

instructions for any of this equipment. Operating instructions had always been handed down by word of mouth, and this was always considered to be all that was required. Until now!

Incidentally, after this failure, a modern system was installed in an attempt to ensure that this problem did not recur. This system employed several 'power packs' (oil-operated hydraulic units) to operate individual lock caissons. I understand that the new system was not completely satisfactory, and barely capable of its designed purpose; it was also probably an unnecessary expense, as the breakdown problem could have been resolved in a more effective way. Perhaps politics played a part in the installation (to demonstrate that some positive action had been taken?) Perhaps also the fact that the new system was not going to be a successful long-term solution was not too much of a consideration if the tenuous future of Chatham as a dockyard was already known?

The new system caused problems almost immediately when a hydraulic oil leak vented into the river Medway - not good. The Medway was being cleaned up at that time, and any spillages which were likely to cause pollution were taken very seriously by the Environment Agency.

Meanwhile Ron organized copies of drawings and handbooks when they were available -bearing in mind that some of this equipment was installed nearly 100 years previously - and arranged for Drawing Office support in helping to produce schematic diagrams and systems of work where possible.

Another example of the need for this operating information was after a stoker had burnt himself quite badly by opening up a valve on a pipework system painted in green (most of the other pipes in the Boilerhouse were also painted in this colour). The stoker believed the pipe was carrying water, as the one next to it was, and that was painted green too. However it was a steam pipe, and he was badly scalded. After that accident a colour-coded chart was installed in all the machinery spaces, and the various systems, eg water, steam, air etc, were identified by the British Standard colour code.

The locations of a lot of the underground services (air, hydraulics, dockyard water etc) were largely unknown. No installation drawings were made (or if they were, they had been lost) and the installers had long since gone. We overcame this problem in part by walking the route and producing our own schematics. On Wednesday afternoons Ron, Ernie Goddard and I used to trace the route of the systems against a large scale map of the dockyard; Ernie would be identifying where the system was buried (he and/or his gang had installed or worked on these systems in the past) and I would mark it on the map using fixed reference points and taking additional notes. (It must have been handy to the contractors when they took over, as it showed the location of miles of copper pipework, up to 8' in diameter, with brass flanges - worth a fortune in scrap metal!)

It was hard work on YSM, and the lack of job satisfaction often made it worse. As explained, the equipment we were maintaining was certainly obsolescent, if not obsolete. This meant breakdowns were inevitable. We were always short staffed, because the elderly staff were retiring faster than we could replace and train their replacements. Replacements were not easy to find, as generally the money was poor without the additions of overtime and allowances, which were not always available. Most of the 'better' staff (younger or better trained) did their best to get into the nuclear site, where the money was much better and regular. Therefore a large percentage of the YSM staff were elderly or green card (restricted on medical grounds) or both. Crane drivers in particular, after finishing their training in the dockyard, would leave to work 'outside' on much better money. So, no matter how hard you tried, you could never do a 'good job', and were pilloried on a regular basis for the inevitable cock-ups.

Ron Dawe now left the department, and was replaced by Dickie Gomme. Dickie had been transferred down from Rosyth, and seemed an OK sort of guy, but I found it difficult to form an effective working relationship with him, and I think we both struggled to adjust.

My gripe with Dickie was that I had been left to run the section with just the occasional 'nudge' from my previous boss (Ron Dawe) as required, but that was not Dickie's way, and he insisted in micro managing (in my view) my section. Secondly, Dickie was very much a management man. He seemed to agree with any directive from the head office, even if it was obviously seriously flawed, and would not effectively argue his point, which was often to the detriment of his own staff. Being newly arrived, I suppose that this was understandable.

By this time I felt wrung out by my efforts on YSM, and

decided that it was time to move on. I applied for a transfer and was offered a job in the Planning Division (where I had not previously worked) and was posted to Planning Manager . 6 (PM 6).

CHATHAM DOCKYARD: PLANNING MANAGER'S DEPARTMENT (PM 6)

Christ, what had I done? The PM 6 section was not busy, in fact there was very little to do. Coming into this from a section where we were 'fighting fires', it was very difficult. We had no major projects in the section and Len Peacock, the foreman, was dishing out the sparse work packages in a drip-feed fashion. This made the days very long and the other members on the team were all pissed off about the situation. Not much fun to be had then!

The members of this group I remember were Rob Copplestone, who came from Maidstone and emigrated to Australia, Norman Jackson, the electrical guy, and Tommy Taylor, mechanical like myself, and a self-confessed 'rabbit king'. For the uninitiated this means that he was an expert at getting unofficial jobs ('rabbits') done for himself and others: he knew where the work could be done and had the contacts there who would help.

The other significant thing I remember about Tommy was that he was desperately keen to return to Devonport (Plymouth Dockyard) from where he originated and had trained and spent his early years. Unfortunately he made the mistake of letting the Personnel Department know of these aspirations, and they made sure that his transfer back to Plymouth did not happen. Rightly or wrongly, the official stance was that a transfer should only be in the interests of the service, and that there should be no advantage or personal gain by the transferee. Tommy somewhat naively had said that he wanted to retire 'back home' in Plymouth, and that as the government had paid for him to come to Chatham they ought to pay for him to go back to Plymouth. This did not go down well. Any attempt at a move at public expense was blocked. A shame really - if Tommy had kept his mouth shut he might have got away with it, but he didn't, on both counts, and he was very bitter.

Tommy used to walk me around the various workshops under the pretext of assessing work progress, and invariably he would collect some item which had been made or altered for him or one of his friends.

In terms of jobs done whilst I was on this section I can only remember arranging a few boats' or ships' badges (ships' badges are the big ones) to be manufactured in the Pattern Shop, and even these small requisitions for work were eagerly snapped up as a job to do when the foreman handed them out. This was not a time I recall with any pleasure, as the days seemed endless trying to find something to do, and of course morale in the section was at rock bottom. Because (mainly) of constant complaints about the situation the section was granted three hours overtime per man per month. Whoopee!

The good news was that even this pittance in terms of extra earnings was welcome, as we were on flat rate (basic pay); the bad news of course was that we had to enjoy doing nothing for an additional three hours a month!

My other memory from this section was of the tea lady. She was a miserable piece of work even on a good day, and she didn't have many of those. It should have been the highlight of the day when the tea trolley came round, a nice cuppa. In reality the tea was usually made about half an hour earlier, nicely stewed, and by the time it got to us it was barely lukewarm. And the taste! I heard it described in various ways, but the nearest by far was that it tasted like very, very slow drying varnish laced with dog poop! To enjoy this delicious treat we were only expected to pay £1.50 per week; needless to say, I didn't stay in this 'tea boat' after the first month. I then realized why the others were not members!

I could not stand working under these conditions, and after sticking it out for approximately four months I approached the Personnel Department and requested (begged for, even) a transfer. I explained that I had qualified in the top ten percent of the Inspectors' Exam, and did not believe that my talents were being fully utilized, if at all, in the present job. My pleas were answered, and I was transferred to the Fitters Afloat section FA1 as the inspector in charge of the refit of HMS *Plymouth*.

CHAPTER 4

CHATHAM DOCKYARD: HMS PLYMOUTH INSPECTOR OF FITTERS (FA1)

This move did not work out well; in fact it was probably the least successful of my time at Chatham. I was appointed as a result of requesting a transfer from my job in the Planning section (PM6) and my predecessor leaving under something of a cloud. Ted Robinson was a friend of mine, and a good engineer, but he had badly upset one of his senior line managers, who ensured that he was transferred out.

The section comprised of three PTO 1Vs; Ron Connor, Pete Clark, and Dave Rogers. As with most of the afloat sections at this time a culture of heavy drinking prevailed. I kept well clear of this, not on any moral grounds, but simply because at home my wife had just had twins and sleep was at a premium. I found that getting home late with a skinful of beer invariably meant another disturbed night - torture! So I tended to steer clear.

Another significant reason for my caution was that I found working on ships again to be a very dangerous environment, where it would be easy to have a nasty accident when you were fully sober, and in my mind you were just asking for trouble if you were pissed!

My reluctance to join in on the piss-ups was probably one of the main reasons why it was not going to be easy for me to fit in. Another reason was the completely different culture which existed on the afloat gangs to that of the YSM, or other sections for that matter.

Of course, it was always going to be difficult going into an environment I had been away from for about 20 years, and learning the new equipment and systems that were of my concern, but I don't think my staff disguised the fact that they were not going to help me too much. This was partly because I believe they had got on so well with Ted Robinson and would have resented almost any newcomer, and also that they wanted to do their own thing without too much interference, initially anyway. I soon found that one of my major problems was that it was not going to be an easy task to get the support trades interested; the coppersmiths, who promised the earth, but never delivered, and the shipwrights' support, where I experienced intermittent enthusiasm, or none whatsoever. The (Navy) Chief Petty Officer, who would be in charge of engineering aspects of the ship on the completion of the Dockyard refit, was also transferred out at this time, taking his considerable expertise of the ship with him.

All this may sound like making excuses, and perhaps it was. All I can say is that it didn't work out for me here, so I applied for a (mutually agreed) transfer.

The post I was allocated to was in another planning area

(PM4), which would be concerned in part with the planning aspects of HMS *Plymouth*. Another planning job, I thought – here we go again. However, this job was not like the previous planning job in PM 6 - this time there was a real job to do!

CHAPTER 5

CHATHAM DOCKYARD, PLANNING MANAGER'S DEPARTMENT (PM 4)

This would be the last section I would work on in the Dockyard at Chatham, although of course I did not know this at the time. The section was run by John Mills, and later by Jim O'Kane. Staff at the time were Dave South and Norman Funnel (Electrical), Paul Broom and myself (Mechanical) and Chas Baker and Bill Willis (Constructive – Shipwrights). Several projects were ongoing, but certainly the most important were the refit of HMS *Plymouth* and the installation of a new Sonar system on HMS *Phoebe*.

The group seemed to get on with each other, and at least on this planning team (bearing in mind that a job in planning is not usually one which people are fighting over), we had real work to do, and could do our bit in progressing the ships' refit.

The main problem was that by now the realization that the Dockyard at Chatham, if not a certainty to close, was a firm favourite, and this thought and its implications hung over us all like the proverbial Sword of Damocles.

Time moved on. We were reaching the end of the sonar installation on HMS *Phoebe* and it was time to look ahead at her sister ship, which was due to dock at Chatham as a follow-on for a repeat task. The project was to install this new system on a squadron of four ships, two to be converted at Chatham and two at Plymouth. As was the accepted convention, a pre-refit visit was arranged to Plymouth, where HMS *Cleopatra* was berthed; she was to be the second sonar installation at Chatham. Most of the team, including myself, went to Devonport Dockyard to discover the extent and detail of the work which was expected to be done at Chatham.

We returned to Chatham fully briefed on the expected work packages, and optimistic that soon this work would be in hand at Chatham, at least delaying any closure for the immediate future. Work details and the experience gained in the sonar installation on HMS *Phoebe,* coupled with the advance information we had acquired from our visit to Plymouth Dockyard, made us all confident of a successful work programme on the *Cleopatra.*

The arrival date for HMS *Cleopatra* came and went - not a good sign. Worried, we petitioned our team boss (Cdr. Dawe) to investigate feedback concerning revised docking and programme dates, without success, as he was given answers which ultimately proved just to be delaying tactics. HMS *Cleopatra* never arrived at Chatham.

After several months of rumours, during which time the morale throughout the Dockyard hit an unbelievable low, we were told by the Commander that he and most senior Dockyard managers were to attend a meeting, at which any Dockyard closures would be formally announced. At last. At least after months of rumour and counter-rumour we would have our futures confirmed, one way or another. To say that most of us had severe trepidation doesn't come anywhere near to describing the situation, as our whole futures were in the balance.

A significant number of the older staff working in the Dockyard were totally convinced that it would never close. They would repeatedly say that he Dockyard had proved a mainstay of refit expertise for the Navy for almost 450 years, and provided an excellent service for the Navy; and wasn't this where Lord Nelson's ship, HMS *Victory*, was built? All true of course, but in the end, none of it mattered.

When the boss came back from this historically significant meeting, he looked pale and shocked. Two 'yards would go - Chatham and Portsmouth!

There was no more work coming in, and it was the worst possible news concerning the closure at Chatham. You can guess what it was like going to work in this environment for many months after the closure announcement.

Our group was transferred into the nuclear site, which I believe was a purely political move, as there was no work that was available or suitable that we could pick up straight away, or even in a reasonable time span.

I mention this time in the nuclear site to relate one of the things that should never have happened. After we had been in the site for about a week, we were told to assemble in the centre of the main control room floor, along with other men from other reallocated groups. I would estimate that there were about 40 guys present from all the trades. The 'big boss' of this group, Pete Hygate, told us to introduce ourselves, and give a précis of our experience. Not so bad so far, but in most cases, after each person had explained what they had done (by this time severely intimidated and almost apologetic), Pete Hygate just said 'Well, you're no good to me then, you can bugger off and find something else'.

I remember that I was extremely embarrassed when it was my turn, and some of the more senior men, a few of whom had worked with him before, were even more distressed, as they were having to explain and justify themselves. None of this would worry Pete Hygate though. He was, in my opinion, a ruthless bastard and a nasty piece of work. Needless to say, I was glad that I was not one of his 'chosen few' - how could you work for a man like that? We all felt as if we were trying to justify ourselves to all and sundry present (the rest of the staff on the control floor), and being lined up and interviewed in this manner was more like an Arabian slave-market! So much for 'Investors in People' and 'Man Management' techniques!

I spent the next few months, along with most of the other Dockyard staff, scouring the vacancy notices (VNs), for likely future employment. This was not easy; after 24 years of working in the Dockyard at Chatham, it was going to be quite a wrench to pack up sticks and move the family to parts unknown. I think all of us felt a certain trepidation, anticipating going into a completely new working environment in a different geographical area. Also it was not going to be easy, because about 5000 of us were now looking for a job!

However, I was determined to seek my own salvation if at all possible, as I knew that if I did not find a job for myself I would be posted to Devonport Dockyard, almost certainly in the Nuclear Department. No thanks, not for me; I was determined to find a job myself, rather than wait for the Personnel Department to do their stuff.

I applied for several jobs over the next six months or so and went for several interviews, sometimes with other guys from Chatham who had applied for the same job, and we would occasionally travel together. My work-change happened after a successful interview at the Royal Aircraft Establishment (RAE) Bedford, to which I would be transferred as the Section Leader on the Plant Services section, on promotion.

On my final day at Chatham I carried out the administrative duties that came with the termination of employment, returning 'on loan' items to the stores and saying goodbyes before reporting to the Personnel Department to hand in my Dockyard entry passes (personal and vehicle). A very nice young female (temporary) clerk at the personnel reception desk took my passes and checked my name off against her list.

'Oh, you're Mr. Smith' she said, 'and you're off to Bedford; well, good luck'.

And that was that. I felt more than a little let down. I had just served 24 years in the Dockyard, and to be discharged in two minutes by a complete stranger (however nice she was) seemed to me to be completely wrong.

Granted, the old days when a collection for a leaver was done on the section and often elsewhere, for a little present or memento to mark the occasion, were long gone. So many people were leaving, with others were being shuffled around in the Dockyard to new areas as their sections closed, that it was impossible to keep up the old traditions. In fact in the end nobody knew who you were. So no collection then, and no exaggerated (and often untrue) nice words from your boss to send you off, but it still hurt. Twenty-four years is a long time. Surely something better could have been organized to mark our exit?

And was the closure the right decision anyway? Looking back to the closure of the Dockyard in 1983/84, it was a devastating blow to the Medway Towns, one from which they have still not fully recovered - as it had been to Sheerness earlier.

The engineering industry in particular (Blaw Knox, Wingets, Berry Wiggins, Metal Box, Elliotts, etc) progressively shrank and eventually disappeared, greatly exacerbating the unemployment situation and having a hugely detrimental effect on the area. The dockyard employees who were now required to transfer to another work station discovered that due to the Dockyard closure there was now a glut of houses on the market, possibly up to 2000, and prices and sales were being prejudiced. I experienced this on a personal basis, with people trying to take advantage of the situation by making unrealistically low offers on my property, because they thought that I was desperate. In actual fact I was devastated that I had to move, as I had only been in my property for about two years and in that time I had spent substantial time and money in making it my dream property.

All the above is fact, but the other side of the argument is that the closure or at least some major restructuring of the Dockyards was essential. Traditional three-year refits could not be continued with a significantly reduced fleet, and the transformation which gas turbine units, refitted by replacement, significantly contributed to rendering the whole context of the existing Dockyards obsolete, not least of all because major work packages would now be done by contractors.

NOTE 4
A balanced view

It must be understood that the dockyards were in many ways a type of insurance policy against a sudden urgent requirement to prepare and repair the Navy's warships and submarines. This meant that a 'captive' workforce of fully-trained and highly-skilled tradesmen and their associated requirements in terms of tools, workshops and materials had to be readily available.

Most of the dockyard workforce earned very low wages and relied on bonus payments and overtime to make a reasonable wage. This money was often earned in extremely poor working conditions, particularly on board the ships and submarines while they were under refit.

There was also a moral, if not mandatory, requirement by the Navy to employ war-damaged and other disadvantaged personnel.

Although the dockyard pay was poor, it gave its workforce the dignity of a regular wage, and a chance to improve themselves. The vast majority were conscientious, loyal and extremely hard working, some even to the detriment of their health, and they should be applauded for their efforts.

When a balanced view is taken, I can now see that the apprenticeship system was an invaluable stepping stone to a multitude of managerial, technical or scientific opportunities, if you made the effort and were interested and determined.

I now believe that there was a lot of truth in what my old dad (himself a 30+ years dockyard workman) used to say: 'The dockyard apprenticeship is the finest in the world, and if you stick to it, the world is your oyster.'

I'm not sure the world was my oyster, and engineering fitting *per se* was never going to be my preferred long-term employment, but my apprenticeship left me with excellent skills and helped me to achieve most of my long-term career prospects and eventually a reasonable standard of living.

In common with the other Services, the dockyard was an excellent trainer. Apart from its own internal training centre covering management skills, scheduling, planning, effective speaking etc, a multitude of technical training was available. Establishments such as the DoE (Department of the Environment) training centre at Cardington taught plant engineering subjects, including air conditioning, boilers and electrical topics, while the naval establishments, mainly at Portsmouth, ran excellent courses by top-level trainers on in-service equipment.

A particularly good area was the weapons, where almost every equipment was covered by courses at HMS *Excellent, Vernon, Collingwood* or *Sultan.*

On reflection it is perhaps not surprising that this training was available and necessary for the dockyard workforce, as they were required to install, repair and maintain such diverse equipment, including:

Main engines, in various forms – steam, diesel, gas turbines and nuclear.

Auxiliaries: turbines, pumps, compressors, air conditioning and refrigeration.

Underwater fittings: propellers, shafts, rudders, bearings, valves, sonar, hydrophones and torpedo tubes.

Weapons: main and secondary systems.

Electrical and electronic: supplies, radar and radio.

Associated services: dockside cranes, pumps, lifts, transport, laundry and rope-making equipment, canteen equipment, etc.

With all those skills under our collective belts, we really were the unsung heroes. Weren't we?

CHAPTER 6

BEDFORD: ROYAL AIRCRAFT ESTABLISHMENT: (RAE BEDFORD)

On 13th April 1982 I was off to start my new job in Bedford. The personnel department at Chatham had arranged 'digs' for me for the first week, as was the custom, so that was one problem resolved (possibly). I reported to the Admin Department at the Tunnel Site on my first morning, and they 'ferried' me up to meet my new boss Brian Tucker. I then realized that I had met him once before - he had been one of the board members when I had attended the site for the job interview. Brian was quite young for the PTO 1 grade, about mid-30s, but being a university graduate this was not unusual in the MoD engineering area. He always reminded me of Kenny Ball, with the same dark hair and trademark moustache. I hit it off with Brian straight away, as he tended to be a cheerful sort of guy, and tried to be considerate and fair to his staff in his actions. He outlined the job, and what would be expected of me.

The establishment was split into two discrete areas. The Tunnel Site was where the working wind tunnels were located;

mainly the 8' tunnel and the 4x3 tunnel, along with the required associated auxiliary plant rooms. These wind tunnels required enormous amounts of electricity to operate (RAE Bedford had its own gas turbine electrical generating capacity for back-up purposes), the main drive and auxiliary equipment (evacuators etc.) and very large cooling towers/equipment, which was where the consumption was highest.

The main admin block, various workshops, a central boilerhouse and an MT (motor transport) section were among the diverse work areas within this large site.

The airfield site was the other part of the establishment, located about three miles away. This airfield was actually nearer to the village of Thurleigh than Bedford, and was invariably referred to locally as 'Twin Woods', the old name for the airfield.

Any local discussing the airfield would very quickly tell you two things about it. First of all it was believed to be the longest runway in the country, and this is why the Americans earmarked it for emergency use during the Second World War. Secondly, it was the airfield from which Glenn Miller took off on his fateful last journey, never to be seen again.

Obviously the most striking features on the airfield were the aircraft hangars, but an almost infinite variety of test and experimental equipment could be found on this huge site. Naturally the site had its own control tower (the airfield was operational as required), crash and rescue, fire-fighting and runway-sweeping facilities. The major user of the site for its testing of new or improved equipment was historically the Navy.

Among the experimental equipment being operated at this time were two aircraft catapults (one steam and one cordite-propelled), the 'rolling platform' (used for testing/training of pilots for landing aircraft on ships decks under steaming conditions), and ongoing trials to the 'ski-jump' equipment used and newly introduced into service on the aircraft carriers.

My job was Section Leader on the Plant Services Department, and I would have responsibilities for sections on each site.

The section at the tunnel site was run by Tommy Cesar. Tommy was a shortish chap, smart, conscientious, and Irish by birth. He had a wicked sense of humour, and if he got the chance he would like to pretend to any unsuspecting victim (visitor) that he was an IRA bomber/extremist. Eventually he was nearly taken seriously by a visitor to the site, so that particular prank died a death. Tommy's remit was to maintain the mechanical service systems in the site (steam, air, water etc) through the efforts of his chargeman, Gordon Wright, and the maintenance of machine tools and welding equipment, which was the task delegated to Dave Godfrey.

One of Tommy's major tasks while I was at Bedford was to oversee the replacement of the boilers and all the associated auxiliary equipment which supplied the steam for heating and processes work at the tunnel site. Tommy also provided the operators and maintenance cover in the pumping station located a couple of miles outside of the site near Sharnbrook. This took its water supply from the Great Ouse and pumped it up into the

RAE site for production purposes (cooling water, fire main, toilets etc).

My second in command at the airfield site was John Hudson. John was from the North Country, quietly spoken, very experienced (he had been at the site for many years), and took a real pride in his work and the efforts of his workforce. He had been doing 'deputy' duties for about six months, in the job which I had now been posted into, so it surprised me that he was not promoted in post. I believe the 'party line' was that the Management at RAE were looking for some new blood to come into the site, so this was possibly a consideration.

However, I was promoted instead of John, and I wondered if he might show some signs of resentment. In fact it was completely different; he was most helpful and straightforward, and an excellent and reliable deputy.

I used to split my week so that I had almost equal time at both of the sites. In practice this usually meant that I would be at the airfield site on Monday and Friday and the tunnel site on Tuesday and Thursday, with a 50:50 split on Wednesday. This was the best situation for me as it meant that if I was held up on the journey back from Kent after the weekend at home, it was not quite so important and obvious, as my permanent office was on the far side of the airfield site. Although in the winter months, before I had moved house to Bedford and was travelling at weekends, I would often return to Bedford late on Sunday night so that I would be ready for work early on Monday, and I would not have to face a nightmare journey with heavy Monday morning traffic in dreadful weather conditions.

A big advantage of the airfield set-up was that I was usually able to get away early on Friday afternoons. I used to make a point of working longer days Tuesday, Wednesday and Thursday and taking short lunch breaks, so I honestly did more hours than I was expected to and was paid for.

Fridays were a real treat, especially if the sun was shining; the airfield was a very pleasant place to work, and my office was on the airfield perimeter, next to an exit gate which led me across country to the A1 and a direct route home.

There was only one downside; Fridays were often the day when trials would take place on the rolling platform, which was not far from my office. Starting mid-morning, Harrier jump jets would practise landing and manoeuvring on this platform, and you had to hear the noise to believe it!

The guys at Bedford were great. When in conversation I mentioned that my hotel digs were not very special (although my room was tiny, it was still cold, and the small black and white 'telly' was unreliable), the PTO 111 on the electrical section next door, Tony Golder, said he might be able to help. Tony had been transferred to the RAE about six months earlier, from Bath. After the first few weeks in a hotel, he had been staying with the mother-in-law of one of his chargemen, Basil Green. He said that this lady, Mrs Bletsoe, might be prepared to let me lodge with her as he had done. Sounded good to me.

I visited Mrs Bletsoe and explained that I was looking for somewhere to stay until I could find a property which I could buy so that I bring my family up to Bedford to live. I said it would be for a minimum of three weeks (how naïve was I, to think I could arrange anything so quickly?) She replied that this was no problem and I could stay as long as I pleased. Just as well, as in the event I was to lodge with her for the next eighteen months or so!

Her house was a pretty semi-detached in a quiet road in the centre of Sharnbrook village. Mrs Bletsoe herself was very nice, a widow perhaps in her early 60s, but very spritely except for a troublesome hip. She was a little strait-laced and rather posh, but for some reason she took a shine to me and I believe she really enjoyed me staying with her.

After I had lodged with her for some time I discovered that her husband (her second husband) had been a professional jockey and was quite well to do. (Bletsoe is a small village nearby, and she used to joke that it was named after her husband.) Apparently he won the Grand National, in 1908 I believe, on a horse called Rubio, and she often spoke of this with great pride. This explained why the highlight of her television viewing was the Horse of the Year Show, when everything stopped, and the evening meals that she prepared were much simpler, although still quite acceptable.

On the subject of evening meals with Mrs Bletsoe, two things come to mind. The first was that on Wednesdays we used to have fish and chips from a van that travelled around the outlying Bedfordshire villages in the evenings. We used to have plaice and chips, and it was really delicious. I used to look forward to it all day at work on Wednesday, and couldn't wait for it to be served up with some of Mrs Bletsoe's favourite Hellmanns' mayonaise.

The second was something that happened one night when I had got down for dinner a little earlier than usual and was sitting in the dining room talking to Mrs Bletsoe through the partly closed kitchen door. All of a sudden a fearful commotion broke out, with the landlady banging about and shouting at her big black Labrador dog, Heidi.

'Naughty Heidi, put it down, give it to me now!' she shouted. There were sounds of scuffles, then all quiet. During dinner Mrs Bletsoe announced that she was sorry that the pork chop I was enjoying was a little smaller than usual, but Heidi had snatched it off the kitchen worktop, and it had taken all of Mrs Bletsoe's determination to retrieve my dinner. She said that when she had retrieved the chop, she had trimmed off the bit Heidi had been holding in her mouth, so the rest was untouched! I wasn't sure about that, and it took the shine off my appetite for the rest of the meal! I used to wonder afterwards how often this happened, but best not to dwell on it!

Most evenings were spent watching the TV in the lounge (obviously Mrs Bletsoe chose the programmes), especially in the winter months when a nice walk in the pretty surrounding area was out of the question. I tried the pubs in the village, but they were very quiet or even empty most week nights, and anyway I had got out of drinking practice, so that after more than two pints to drink I felt sluggish for most of the following day. Drinking was already becoming very expensive anyway, and I thought it would be all too easy to become a regular in one of the local pubs, which was something I did not want to happen. I did used to visit the local football clubhouse occasionally, where the steward (Albert) and his wife were very friendly, and the club was used as a regular watering hole for some of the younger lads from the airfield site, so we could pass a pleasant evening with a game of darts.

A special night that I always looked forward to was a visit to the Bell at Cotton End, on the outskirts of Cardington village. My friend Pete Barnes was living in Arlesey at this time and about once a month, usually on a Thursday night, Pete, his wife Val and I would arrange to meet up at this smashing pub. It was a quaint old building with a thatched roof and pictures on the walls of the old airships which were built or housed in the massive hangars at Cardington, just down the road. Their dark mild was to die for!

Incidentally, the Cardington site was an outstation from the RAE at Bedford, so occasionally I would visit that site if they requested assistance from us, usually connected with their range of machine tools. These visits were always a pleasure and full of interest, especially if the hangar doors were being operated. These massive doors would take 20 minutes to open or close! Always an impressive sight. I knew the Cardington site from my dockyard days, as I had attended several technical courses at the Department of the Environment (DoE) Training School located there, which covered plant engineering subjects including boilers, air conditioning/refrigeration, water treatment and electrical power and distribution, but these massive hangars still impressed at this much later date.

I should explain why the house move to Bedford took so long. First and foremost it was not a move I relished, as it meant moving away from my roots and all that that entailed, and I must admit a confidence problem. Would I fit in? Could I do the job? This was probably even more difficult for my wife, as we had three small children to look after, and also - something that I had not considered earlier - when I went to work at the new site, I would soon (by necessity) make friends and settle in. It was a different problem for my wife, as she would have no friends or family and would have to start from scratch making new friends.

Our parents were of concern; my mother was over 80 and not in good health, and she relied on me a great deal. My wife's mum had heart problems and was quite ill at times, so both needed support in varying degrees. However, both of us had no alternative. Although we proceeded with the relocation, it was fraught with worry and major reservations.

The main problem however, was housing. As so many properties were on the market due to the dockyard closure, house prices were static or falling in the Medway area, and many of the prospective buyers thought they were onto a good thing and would cash in by making stupidly low offers.

At the Bedford end, it was not easy either. We had discussed our requirements and came up with a shortlist which included the following wish list:.

(1) It must be in a village location.

(2) It must have a local school.

(3) It must have a local playgroup.

(4) It must have a doctor's surgery within reasonable striking
distance.

(5) It should have shopping facilities within reasonable access.

Most of the above were necessary because my wife was not a
confident or experienced driver.

With the list of requirements in mind I started my house
search, planning to select those which I thought offered promise
to view in the evenings; a shortlist could then be made and my
wife could visit so that we could check out the properties
together.

Not all of my selections went down terribly well. One of the
properties on my shortlist was a modern property in the village
of Denford. This property seemed ideal to me; it was very
modern, and I liked the location. There was a good school in
the village. I confess that one of the considerations in my choice
was the fact that the vendor, a USAF airman, was prepared to
throw in his nice BMW to clinch the house sale. Couldn't be
bad, could it? The car wasn't new (about four years old) but still
in nice condition, and I needed a new car.

However, it was soon pointed out to me that the property
was not for us, because:

(a) It had a tiny kitchen (the owner had designed it himself;
and he was a bachelor).

(b) The furnishings being sold with the property were
inappropriate (white shag-pile carpets, white leather sofas
etc - not the best with young children).

(c) It was too far from my place of work.

(4) The property was accessed by a steep hill - tricky when it snowed.

(5) She didn't like it.

So I didn't get the car. But she was right – it wouldn't have done, (this house).

The next property we looked at was a small detached house, as yet unbuilt but part of a new development in Thurleigh. A small close, Vicarage Close, comprising about 30 houses, was being built almost outside the airfield site gate, which made it an ideal location to get to work. The village had the other requirements we were looking for so we made a reservation and placed a deposit (buying off-plan).

Sorted, or so we thought. We explained to the estate agent that our house in Kent was on the market but not yet sold, and were told that this did not represent a problem as the property in Thurleigh would take between 3-4 months to build. Once we had paid our deposit the new house would be ours when it was built. Good, I thought, I can now concentrate on getting to grips with my new job without the overarching worry of finding somewhere to live in the near future.

As I had agreed, I kept in touch with the estate agent selling the property in Bedford, updating them on viewings held in Kent, and things seemed to be progressing well. About four months after we had placed our deposit, I received a letter out of the blue from a new estate agent informing me that they had taken over the sales of properties on Vicarage Close, and that they required me to exchange contracts on the sale within a week, or the property would be put back on the market. My solicitor in Kent who was dealing with my sale and purchase was amazed, as he had never come across such high-pressure sale tactics before. His advice was short and sweet. It was extremely unwise to exchange on the property in Bedford when I did not have a firm buyer for my own property. It would be madness. I should tell them to poke it. (He did not say that, but that's what he meant.)

So I was not able to continue with the purchase of the Thurleigh property and it was subsequently sold. I had in the meantime discovered that this new estate agent was very aggressive in its sales tactics, and presumably had another buyer who could proceed in my place. Also, I suspect, at a higher price! So it was Property 1 down the pan.

The second property we decided on was on a small development just starting in Sharnbrook, the village where I was lodging. These were very nice houses being built by a local builder, so we bought a really nice property 'off plan'. Again all seemed to be going well, and progress could be seen on the property almost every day.

When the property was nearing completion, the site contractors started to erect the boundary fences to the properties. Bloody hell! The boundary fence to the rear of our prospective property was only ten feet from the patio door. It transpired that some reorganisation had been done on the layout of the plots since the site drawing we had seen. An additional plot had been incorporated into the development by moving existing boundaries. I was doubly miffed, as ours was the plot most affected. We had lost most of our garden, and no one had bothered to tell us about it. We cancelled our reservation on the plot, and it was back to square one.

Almost immediately we found a nice house which suited most of our requirements in a pleasant village called Ravensden. That was the good news. The bad news was that other people were also interested in this property, so it would amount to a race as to who could sell their property first and put a deposit down.

We were still unable to sell our property in Kent. We had lots of people to view it, but several were either just time-wasters or were chancing their arms and putting in really low offers (almost insulting to someone who had spent a lot of time and effort to make their place just right). The housing market was unfortunately still very sluggish as the final dockyard closure drew nearer.

Not altogether surprisingly we lost this last property, beaten to it by the other couple, who were in a position to proceed. I find it difficult to describe this latest disappointment to both of us, as I was living out of a suitcase, and was missing my kids growing up.

This situation was made worse, as later that week when I was explaining the latest set-back to Brian Tucker, my boss, he said he wondered if I was really serious about a house move or was just making excuses! I was not pleased, and thought this was a most unfair remark. Brian was somewhat taken back by my reaction, and explained that he was being pressurized from headquarters (who were paying my subsistence allowances whilst I was on detached duty) to bring my move to a conclusion ASAP. Thanks, headquarters.

A couple of weeks later we had a bit of luck at last. We had a serious prospective buyer for our property in Kent and the builder in Sharnbrook had just announced the release of the next phase of development. We placed a deposit on a nice plot that had now become available and made a reservation, once again 'off plan'.

This time fortunately, things progressed in a reasonably straightforward manner. I was lucky in that because I lodged in Sharnbrook, and the development was less than a mile away on the other side of the village, I was able to walk down to the site and watch the house being built. It was for me a pleasant walk in the evening to visit the development and to discover what progress had been made on the property.

Soon the property was almost complete and it was time to make the legal, domestic and various other arrangements arising from a house move. Now I would need help from the headquarters finance department (located in Bath) to provide the finances for the house move, but that was never going to be straightforward - how could it be?

The major problem I had (and needed help to resolve) was that although I had exchanged contracts on my property in Kent, I could not arrange completion to match the Bedford builder's requirements, and would therefore require bridging finance for about two weeks, until I could complete contracts at the Kent end. This was not a unique problem and one that was often catered for by the MoD, but the assistance was extremely slow, and offered grudgingly and only as a last resort. I was continually phoning Bath for confirmation that bridging would be in place, but could not instill any urgency at the other end and was told that the delays were due to staff sickness or shortages. Nothing changes, does it?

This worry continued all through the week before completion was required. On this Thursday night it was a pre-arranged meeting with Pete Barnes and Val at the Bell in Cardington, and I must admit that the worry of the inconclusive moving arrangements was a dampener on the evening's enjoyment. When I explained to Pete that I had not been granted the bridging finance, and therefore the whole move was in jeopardy, he offered to lend me the necessary money so that the move could go ahead! More importantly, he meant it; he really would have lent me this money if I needed it. Not many people would have done that, and I have never forgotten it.

I ended up phoning Bath from a phone box near my home in Kent (my phone had been disconnected as part of the house move) the day before I needed the money to be made available by the MoD, still seeking confirmation that this would be arranged. Stressful or what? In the event the finance was made available at the last moment, and the move went ahead, but what a struggle!

CHAPTER 6

I now realized that I had another problem. I had been visiting the building site on a regular basis, and three weeks before the projected house move was planned it was obvious that the property would not be completed on time. I could see this for myself, but to make sure, I had an unofficial chat with the workforce (who by now I knew quite well), and they confirmed my suspicions. I had also seen two other couples move into the site, and neither house had been finished properly on the move-in date.

I contacted my solicitor and explained the situation to him, and we decided that officially we would be moving in on the date given, but really I would defer moving out from Kent until two weeks later. Thank goodness we did this. On the day we were supposed to move in at Sharnbrook I went to the property mid-morning, and the first thing that I noticed was that the painters were trying to paint the stairwell, but the plaster was so new that excess water was running down the walls! Somewhat tongue in cheek, I asked if they were using underwater paint, which fortunately they thought was quite funny as well. I asked for a truthful completion date (other work was still required to be done), and was told it would be at least a week before the house was finished.

I did get in touch with the builder, Mr Docherty (a very good builder, but a lousy organizer), and said that my family were half way up the M1, expecting to move into their new house, and that the property was not in a habitable state. He apologized, said that he had been let down etc etc, and suggested that I arrange accommodation at the Swan Hotel in Bedford at his expense until the property was completed - he estimated a couple of days. I explained that I appreciated his offer, but this situation should never have arisen, and that I did not think living in a family room in a Bedford hotel for an unknown period was acceptable, and I would get my family to return to Kent pro tem (They hadn't left really). Finally, two weeks later, we did move in (house complete now), and we all said goodbye to Kent.

It was much better at work now, without the worry of wondering if all was well at home, and not having to do the return trip each weekend. It all seemed to be good to be true.

It was.

By now I had a good understanding of the site, the equipment, and my staff. I was on one of the airfield management committees, so I had met most of the senior managers and colleagues. I was happy in my job, I liked the area, which was great for the kids to grow up in, and I hoped I would be settled for the next few years. Ha-ha - some chance!

At the sister (tunnel) site they were often short of tunnel controllers (the man in overall charge of the safe operation of the wind tunnel), and they had a vacancy that they could not fill. This post was confined to PTO 2 level, or above, and was not popular. The job was highly responsible, as very large machinery was operated, sometimes in critical conditions, absorbing massive amounts of electricity (liaison with the grid supply authority was often necessary) and high levels of co-ordination were essential. When trials were being conducted it was often necessary to run the tunnel continuously for extended periods, which meant either shift work or extended overtime working.

The job, once the tunnel was running, could be routine for many hours, and in common with the others, I found it very difficult to maintain alertness over these extended periods, routinely monitoring gauges and instruments on massive control panels but always being ready to act if an emergency situation arose. In essence this was not a job that appealed to me in the slightest. I enjoyed the freedom of my plant services work in a work area in which I was fully experienced and in a job which I had applied for. None of this mattered. I was told that I would be trained as a tunnels controller, this being the 'priority of the service'.

So I was transferred to the tunnels site to train as a controller. I tried to make a go of it, and in fairness the job had its lighter moments, but it was not a job I really enjoyed. Most of the scientific staff who were carrying out the testing seemed aloof and uninterested in forming any kind of working relationship; I was never quite sure if this was because they did not want to associate too much with the technical grades (like me) because they felt that we were inferior, or because they were so engrossed in their experimental deliberations that they were locked into a world of their own.

The hours of intent gauge monitoring drove me potty. Sitting in front of massive instrument panels waiting for something nasty to happen did nothing for me at all. I had the recurring nightmare that when/if a disaster struck I wouldn't instantly remember the emergency procedures. I was told that this was normal, but it didn't help.

At this time my mother-in-law was suffering heart attacks back in Kent and my wife was very concerned. We discussed the possibility of a job relocation, if anything suitable materialized, and a job with the Army Department at Woolwich was advertised shortly after. I applied for the job, was interviewed, and was subsequently successful and posted to take up my next job as OIC (Officer-in-Charge) Equipment Tables Section, Workshop Technology Branch, REME.

CHAPTER 7

WORKSHOP TECHNOLOGY BRANCH REME: OIC EQUIPMENT TABLES SECTION

A transfer to Woolwich seemed to be a sensible option, as it would reduce the domestic problems related to our sick and aged parents and we could be living back in Kent, where it was much easier to keep an eye on them. Secondly, the writing was on the wall at Bedford, as the MoD's move to contractorise the site's activities was moving quickly ahead, and I felt that redundancies were just around the corner. It would probably be 'last in, first out' and I was still a relatively new boy, so future plans would have been uncertain to say the least.

The Army site at Ha-Ha Road was the location for several resident REME (Royal Electrical & Mechanical Engineers) Groups, and at this time several Maintenance Advisory Groups (MAGS), mainly staffed by serving personnel were on the site also. I and 14 MAGs dealt with weapons, and 15 MAG was the medical and dental specialists, co-located on the Woolwich site.

(Although I did not know it at the time, I would be transferred into 15 MAG, which would be relocated to Ludgershall and redesignated the Medical & Dental Equipment Supply Group, as its OiC later on in my service.)

The boss of 15 MAG and 2iC of the Branch was Major Jim Stanyer, who had progressed through the ranks (a ranker) and was both a gentleman and an excellent boss. Unfortunately Jim Stanyer was killed in the *Herald of Free Enterprise* tragedy in 1987, which was a great shame and loss, as he was one of the few people in the branch you would want to be associated with.

Other facilities in and around the Ha-Ha site were a small laboratory, a workshop, an HQ building, the REME data centre and the REME Codification and Scaling Authorities (ACA & ASA). The branch into which I was transferred was the Workshop Technology Branch REME. The CO was Lt. Col. Kirby, and his main concerns were the Workshop Processes Group, the Workshop Equipment Group and oversight of the Army's Staff Suggestions Scheme.

His 'right hand man' (clerk) was Connie Harwood, a miserable person on a good day. Whatever assistance you required was always problematic, or took forever. For example, if you had the temerity to ask for a new pen or other minor item, she would invariably look at you as if you were completely mad, and then advise you that she had run out of said item and was awaiting resupply.

When Connie went on leave her fellow Clerical Officer (Ros) from the Workshop Processes Group upstairs would deputise. Ros did not like Connie (few did), and she would hand out the stationery items like there was no tomorrow. The problem was that the stationery cupboard (always securely locked) was next to a large radiator in Connie's office, and due to the excessive heat most of the stationery was useless. The heat had completely dried out the pens, felt tips, correction fluids etc, and they all had to be discarded. We had a field day with the other items though, and stocked up sufficiently to last us until Connie's next leave period.

The Workshop Processes Group (our 'sister' group) was run by the PTO 1, Roger Moore, known for reason you can guess as the Saint. His group were the Army's advisors on welding techniques and maintenance of the 'Approved Welder' system, chemical cleaning procedures and production of specialized technical literature EMERs (Electrical & Mechanical Engineering Regulations) for Army use.

Stan Hand was Roger's senior PTO 2, and a remarkable character. Stan was well built (quite chubby in fact), a Brummie with an highly amusing asthmatic laugh. He smoked a 'radioactive' pipe and had developed meanness to a highly specialized art form.

A few examples of this. The other members of the section used to say that Stan refused to pay 50 pence a week to join the 'tea boat', and when he was working late he would recycle the old, used tea bags (left in a dish at the side of the tea-making table), and the milk residue in used cartons and if possible scrounge sugar, or go without and drink it unsweetened. He was also credited with owning a static caravan, which he used whilst on detached duty, saving him outlaying money for proper digs. Perhaps his best 'little earner' was the flat which he had purchased in Woolwich and sublet to a colleague; Stan meanwhile lived nearby with his girlfriend, rent-free I should imagine.

He had a beaten-up Ford Cortina with a blue nylon fur cat stuck to the window, in which he used to travel to the various Army sites on advisor visits. This really annoyed my boss, Brian Clifton, who felt that this did not put the Army's technical specialists in a very good light. But Stan worked for the Roger's group, so there wasn't much Brian could do about it.

Others on Roger's group included Mick Russell, who was a non-destructive testing expert - his key task was testing the 9lb artillery pieces used in Trooping the Colour - and John Boyne, who was I believe a science graduate and advised on adhesives, among other things.

My group (Workshop Equipment) was run initially by Gerry Thompson, but he was replaced almost immediately by Brian Clifton. This group's three main sections were:

The Hand Tools Section, run by Les Haddock, with a staff of three PTO 3s and a clerk. They were tasked to evaluate new-to-service hand tools, investigate defect reports on in-service tools, compile Equipment Table scales (used in equipment accounting), and processing the stores release of special tools and test equipment (STTE), which was done in conjunction with the authorizing PTO 3 from my section.

The Machine Tools Section was run by John Coe, again with 3 PTOs who were the army's advisors, evaluating new machine tools, arranging procurement specifications and investigating defect reports. They were involved in some high-profile machining requirements on the Challenger Main Battle Tank drive equipment. The desk officers in the section were encouraged to visit the machine tool exhibitions and manufacturers' works to be aware of new machines and technology. Likewise, occasional visits were made to firms when large orders had been contracted, to confirm that quality standards and delivery were as agreed. This was until Brian Clifton arrived and decided that the high profile visits to Germany and Italy should be done by him as first choice!

The Equipment Tables Section was the area of my immediate concern. It had a PTO who was the authorizing officer for the allocation of special tools and test equipment for REME (STTE), Dennis Neville. This specialized equipment was procured by an equipment manager at Andover headquarters, and was earmarked for dedicated repair units, until released by us at Woolwich in accordance with an authorized list known as a 'WEST Scale' (Workshop Equipment Special Tools). This equipment was known as the 'Part R' in the unit's Equipment Table.

Two other PTOs working for me, Reg Grover and John Langford, were responsible for producing new or amended Equipment Tables (AFG 1098 or 1198). These tables were an accounting document which listed all the equipment requirements necessary for the unit to perform its role. It included weapons, ammunition, vehicles, clothing and tools among the essential list of requirements. The document was renewed every four years and was subject to amendment at any time, but not usually within six months of its production.

My first impressions of the site at Woolwich were that they were a miserable crowd, and that first impression stayed with me for all my time at Woolwich. It was perhaps not too surprising, as almost all the staff had been transferred in as a result of their original workplace's closure, and they felt they had been shoved onto the scrapheap. After many years of working at their former establishment and believing that they were doing a good and important job, they found themselves in a new, uninspiring environment, mostly where the work to be done was strictly routine and presented little or no challenge.

As for the ex-Navy guys, we felt that the Army's set-up (organisation & procedures) were ten years behind the Navy's. To say that most of the staff had chips on their shoulders was completely inadequate - more like the entire Brazilian rain forest, and miserable with it. Happy days ahead!

My first day in the new job set the scene quite nicely. When I got to the office on the first day Colin Simms, who had been doing the job on a temporary basis, was waiting to hand over to me. The handover consisted of Colin pointing to a ledger on his desk and remarking: 'That's where all the incoming work is booked in by your clerk (if you had one), so that's it. I'm off to a meeting now, and I 'm not fucking interested in this lot any more, as I was promised this job by the lying bastard management'. With that he left to join his permanent section in the hand tools area, located downstairs. Thanks, pal.

The work was quite difficult at first. This was because my boss, Gerry Thompson, seemed to be desperate to get away from Woolwich, as he was commuting to and from the Stowmarket area at weekends and staying in the mess during the week. He had little interest in proceedings or offering advice (I would understand why in the fullness of time!) My colleagues, in general, did not understand what my section did, and they weren't overly interested - they had their own part of the 'ship' to run, so they were unable or unwilling to offer advice.

The section worked very closely with (in fact with the delegated authority of) an engineering branch at Andover Headquarters (EME 2), and it was assumed that they would train me (remotely) on the job. My staff had no interest or intention of telling me anything, unless I specifically asked. Even then I might or might not get an answer, depending on how they felt!

Dennis Neville and Reg Grover were mates with Colin Simms anyway, and thought he had been badly treated, so there was no way they wanted to co-operate with me. However, I wasn't going to go away, and gradually we gravitated into a reasonable working routine.

A new Clerk (Jean), and Reg Grover's replacement (Harry Getliffe) arrived, and on a personal note I began to understand the structure and requirements of both the branch at Woolwich and where it fitted into the Army's role. Things were starting to look up.

Ron Selwood (ex-Army) was my opposite number at the headquarters in Andover. Most of my work was channelled through his office for approval and prioritization, with the exception of the release of 'special tools', which we controlled at Woolwich. As I was new to the Army department he felt it essential that I should see how the Army operated at first hand, and was instrumental in arranging a liaison visit for me to HQ BAOR (Headquarters British Army of the Rhine) at Rheindahlen and to visit some of the major Army workshops in theatre. This proved to be an excellent visit. My contact in the HQ Germany, Ken McGuckian, shepherded me around the massive Army workshops (37 Rhine and No 4 Armoured Workshops) and we also visited the intermediate and 1st line units (Field Workshops and LADs - Light Aid Detachments), to give me a complete insight into the Army's repair capability and strategy. I think I learnt more in that week than I would have done in six months at my desk in Woolwich.

Gerry Thompson left and Brian Clifton, my new boss, arrived. He made things, in terms of staff morale and job satisfaction, much more difficult than necessary, almost from day one - in fact at times bloody near impossible.

Brian was a complete Jekyll & Hyde character. Outside the site gate, say on the rare occasion when you were invited to join him on a trip, he was good company, but once inside the site, he was a completely different character. The biggest problem we all had with Brian was that he was so greedy. He seemed to believe that the allowance for the group's travel and subsistence was for his personal use only, and openly resented anyone else making official visits and therefore spending some of 'his' money, which he seemed intent on spending single handedly, and practically succeeded.

This led to rock-bottom morale, as it made major projects significantly more difficult for the desk officer doing the work. Secondly, as trips out were looked upon as a perk and something of a reward for a job well done, when this option was closed down it was a big disappointment to the workforce, who had little else to look forward to. This was especially true in the case of my section, because whereas the other sections had contact with firms' reps, and at Christmas little gifts were brought in (minor stuff such as calendars and pens usually, but small tokens of the year's efforts), in my section we had no contact with contractors, so even this little perk was unavailable to us. When the other sections displayed their 'goodies' it caused a lot of resentment.

None of this worried Brian at all. He seemed to have very little interest in the concerns and welfare of his staff. All of the above was clearly known by the branch boss (the Lt. Col. at Chertsey), but he was not sufficiently unhappy about it to interfere and rock the boat.

I did visit most of the Army workshops in the UK, and some of those in Germany, but this was probably to be expected, as I was working from Woolwich for over seven years, and most of these trips Brian could not prevent as they were instigated by the HQ at Andover, and usually involved doing workshop equipment audits.

The job itself was quite interesting. The Equipment Table was the Unit's accounting document, showing their entitlement to all the equipment which was considered necessary for them to perform their role. Their holdings should be as shown in the Equipment Table unless supported by 'surplus' (extra) or 'deficiency' (reduced holding level) forms showing these authorized changes (both plus and minus figures had to be approved by the Sponsor at EME2 Headquarters Andover). Normally changes were approved by written amendment requests, supported by the Technical Quartermaster or his staff, except in extreme cases, when site visits for confirmation were sometimes necessary. In the seven years I was in this post, I was tasked to visit most of the UK workshops (mainly arising from the implications of the Static Workshop Review (SWR), a major re-organisation of the Army's workshops, for and on behalf of HQ Andover, and even got to the Benbecula site in the Outer Hebrides! I really enjoyed this aspect of the job, as it was an opportunity to meet (and hopefully help) some really great people.

After I had been in post for about two years a significant change was implemented to the accounting procedure for the Special Tools and Test Equipment (STTE), known as Part R in the Table. The REME Data Centre was tasked to provide a computer-based accounting system using a stand-alone 'Equinox Meridian' computer. Barry Harris had joined the section, transferred from Plymouth Dockyard, and the part R was his area of responsibility. In conjunction with Les Mohegan from the

Data Centre, a relatively smooth transition was made from the existing paper based forms to a computer-based account, and there was a massive improvement.

For example when 'Op Granby' (the first Gulf War) was in full swing, some of the operational units needed urgent replacements or additions to their special tool holdings . The new system enabled us to interrogate the database, identify where holdings were and often transfer them from a lower priority unit (for example one of the training establishments) to the site of operations.

'Op Granby' was a very busy time for my section in particular. Major redeployment was taking place for units in BAOR (Germany) to move into the war theatre, and because some presence was still required in Germany it meant that most units required additional equipment (in our case special tools) on an urgent basis. I had been called back into work several times in the first few weeks of hostilities to arrange urgent redeployment of equipment, and I recall two such occasions really well.

The first time was when we had an alert for extra equipment and Brian Clifton, Barry Harris and I had returned to the Woolwich site at about 8 pm to raise the required authorizations. This was during the Easter period and a fair was in full swing on Woolwich Common. Only about 50 metres from our office, just outside the perimeter fence, was the worst possible fairground stall - a hot dog stand!

As the evening drew on (we had had our evening meal several hours ago by now) we were all starting to get a little peckish, and the tantalizing smell of hot dogs was wafting over continuously in our direction. Absolute torture. We had no catering facilities on this site, and if we had they would have been closed anyway, so we just had to grit our teeth and soldier on for the next couple of hours, finish the job, and get off home before rampant malnutrition set in!

The other unusual night was within a few weeks of the above occurrence, when again we were working late, having been recalled back to Woolwich. This time it was Brian Clifton and me; Barry Harris had been in earlier and had returned home. On this particular day it was the third time I had been to work that day! I had been to work as a normal working day, but had only been home for about half an hour when I was 'asked' to return to cover an urgent requirement. I did this, and got back home again about 9 pm. This time I had been home for about two hours before I was asked to go back, as an emergency had arisen. Back again to Woolwich - I knew the way by now! - arriving just before midnight, when I worked through for another couple of hours. I was feeling pretty knackered by this stage!

Brian and I left the site (again) shortly after 0130 and started back home. I was following Brian down Shooters Hill when suddenly a police car materialized from nowhere and pulled me over. The police officer asked me if I realized that I was speeding. Shooters Hill has a 30 mph speed limit, but it is difficult to keep below this as it is a steep slope which tends to build up your speed unless you have a foot on your brakes. I replied that I did not realize that I was speeding and apologized. The officer asked where I had been, and then said that as I had committed a moving traffic offence he was going to breathalyse me. As I had just left work on a call-out for the Army, if the breathalyser test was negative he would let me off with a warning. Needless to say the test was negative (I had been to work all day and most of the night for Christ's sake), and I went off home unscathed. I told Brian next morning, but he didn't seem really interested. However, my extra efforts to provide the necessary equipment to the Operational units was noticed at HQ, and I was awarded a bonus payment to reflect this.

As time passed, rumours persisted of our relocation to another site; Chertsey, Andover and Christchurch seemed to be among the favourites. This would not be very popular, as all the staff in my section were fairly newly appointed, Barry Harris and Dickie Dukes (from Devonport) who had replaced Dennis Neville and Reg Grover, and Harry Gettliffe and Rose Forrest, who had replaced John Langford and our section clerk Jean. This was obviously a very unsettling environment, but it was probably going to happen as our building, 10/20, and others on the site were in very poor condition anyway. In winter Barry and Harry used to make up a form of temporary double glazing from polythene sheets to cover the gaps around the old steel-framed windows. Additionally, a unit move had always seemed likely as it had always been stated that the long-term intention was that the site would revert to common ground. Also, with the latest reorganization we had been 'taken over' by the Vehicles and Weapons Group at Chertsey, and it made some sort of sense to have us co-located with them.

Occasionally I was asked to represent Brian at the commanding officers' conferences which were held monthly at Chertsey. All group heads or their representatives gave a short prepared brief in turn to the CO, Colonel Steel. On one particular occasion Roger Moore was also unable to attend and he asked me if I would present his brief as well. No problem, I thought, so I agreed. On the train to Chertsey I read through Roger's notes to me, and all was well until I came to the section which Stan Hand had included. Talk about gobbledegook! Well, too late to change it now, even if I could.

When it was time for me to present Roger's section brief, and in particular Stan's entry, the inevitable happened; I waffled on through this unintelligible list of chemical formulae, products and procedures, noting that most of the members around the table had glazed over after about two minutes. At the end of this brief, which ended something like 'which could mean acrylic-oxidisation culminating in polymer de-stabilised anti-crystalline tetrachlorinates,' the Major sitting on my right said 'Well, it would wouldn't it?' to everyone's barely-concealed mirth. I felt a right plonker, and didn't volunteer for that particular duty again!

When the Equipment Tables were produced or amended they were sent to the Equipment Tables Publication Centre (ETPC) for final editing and production. Initially the ETPC , which was primarily staffed by the military, was co-located in our building on the ground floor, and this was ideal as any queries could be resolved by a quick visit downstairs. The ETPC had a major advantage over us when doing the ET compilations in so far as they had direct access to the main computer systems used in stores management (ISIS and OLIVER). However, probably due to the overarching relocation of the Woolwich units, they were relocated to St. Mary Cray, which put a slight delay in the production chain. Actually this worked out quite well for me as I could sometimes take any new work over to St Mary Cray on a Friday afternoon, resolve any problems, and usually manage to get away on my home journey at a reasonable time, which in any case was easier than the journey home from Woolwich. Of course, this didn't please Brian Clifton.

After about four years at Woolwich, I started to look for a different job. This was because the work environment at Woolwich was always depressing, I felt I was no longer challenged in the work, and I thought that a little job satisfaction would be nice for a change.

A new job opportunity was never going to be easy. I did not really want to move house again, so openings would be scarce. Brian was not keen for me to move, so I would have to play a waiting game. I applied (rather naively) for a couple of jobs, one at the RSME Wainscott, and one at 44 District Workshop Ashford, in the next year or so, not realizing that although they were advertised as vacancies, they had in fact been earmarked for other people. (The 'old boy' network reigned supreme; especially in the Army Department at that time.)

Early in 1992 it was formally announced that the branch would be relocating to Chertsey. To most of the staff at

Woolwich this meant either a very expensive house move or a nightmare commute. This would be either daily (almost impossible to imagine travelling round to junction 11 on the M25, and home again in the evening) or staying in the officers' mess at Chertsey Monday to Friday, and doing a weekend commute. This option was also dependent upon the Officers' Mess Committee agreeing to a PTO 2 civilian staying in the mess. (Although a PTO 2 and sometimes PTO 3s were accepted into the majority of officers' messes, Chertsey had tried to restrict entry into their mess to PTO 1 level (Major/ Lt. Colonel) or above ranks for Civilians.)

A vacancy notice (VN) appeared early in 1992 advertising a vacancy at 44 District Workshop Ashford for the post of Production Controller. I applied for the job, along with one of my colleagues from Roger Moore's group, Dave Botting. We were both interviewed, but I realized that Dave would be advantaged as he knew the outgoing post holder (Captain Sargent) from previous work encounters; and Dave did not have to say that he would be the preferred choice. At the end of the interview I was asked if I would be interested if the post of Quality Engineer became vacant in the near future. Of course I was. I said yes, and so the die was cast. It should be explained that available posts at Ashford were not so desirable as in some other areas, as that workshop's future was in grave doubt, and it was really a case of when it would close, and not if.

However, Dave and I knew that we could expect at least three years' employment there, which gave us time to review our options, and equally important, it would get us away from that terrible place in Woolwich. Looking back, only a few occasions can be recalled with any pleasure from my time at Woolwich; perhaps the Christmas carol service in the beautiful garrison church and the sports days which were held at Chertsey were the exceptions.

I knew some of the staff at Ashford who would be working for me if I got the Quality Engineer's job. Bill Stevens (who I knew from Chatham) was the Senior Examiner, and I had met John Wells when he was on the management services team and we had liaised on Equipment Table matters. John was now working as the Quality Audit Officer, and would be my 'right hand man' if I was in the Quality Engineer's post.

I was called for interview and subsequently invited to join the workshop as the Quality Engineer. It was now September 1992.

44 DISTRICT WORKSHOP, REME ASHFORD, QUALITY ENGINEER

44 District Workshop REME was administered by the Army to undertake 'base overhaul' for all Land Rover and some Bedford engines. It had repair facilities for vehicles, communications equipment and weapons (with a resident armourer). The dependency included a variety of Army and TA (Territorial Army) units throughout Kent and the neighbouring counties, for which they carried out recovery and repairs.

The Commanding Officer was Colonel Hunter; the 2iC Major Ted Sargeant. Other staff/ management at this time were:

Workshop Services: Ron Hendy (Ex Lt. Col.) and Bob Wright, PTO 3.

Production Control: Dave Botting (+ Control Office staff).

Apprentice's Training: Brian Pack, Kevin Lancaster and Mick Rutherford.

Workshop Management Accounts: Caroline Boydell and Margaret Rye.

CHAPTER 8

IT Support: Les Oliver and John Fraser.

Quality: Bob Smith (yours truly) and John Wells.

Assessors' Office: Barry Lawrence, Tony Towning, John Salt (ex-Chatham) and Jock Brodie.

The production PTOs at this time included Dennis Packham, Steve Hawkins and Geoff Lambourne. They were supported by and subject to quality checks by a team of examiners. This team was run by Bill Stevens (PTO3) and included: Ken Stanley (later Dickie Holtum) as chargehand (vehicles), Steve Kingsnorth, Dieter Bass, Dickie Lane and Brett Wright. The engine line chargehand examiner was Eddie Wicken, who could be assisted by one or more of the examiners on a rotational/requirement basis.

This was my first foray into the wonderful world of quality. I had of course been involved with quality control in various previous tasks, but this job was to achieve a 'total quality' standard, a different thing altogether. The Army had committed itself to updating the quality assessments in its workshops, updating from the current requirement, British Standard (BS 5750), to the new International Standard - ISO 9002. The new standard was much more complicated, all embracing, and subject to ongoing external auditing.

The quality assessment to the new standard was to take place in October 1992, three weeks after I started in the new job!

This was a case of hitting the ground running, if ever there was one, but it was a pleasure to work with these people at Ashford, who had a very positive approach to the quality assessment, and understood its possible implications regarding the workshop's closure. (The workshop would be in great danger of an early closure if the quality standard could not be achieved; of course a 'pass' did not guarantee a continued future, but it certainly helped.)

We worked bloody hard, John and I, in the time available to us, to provide all the necessary requirements to meet the standard. (This took the form of an audit team - two assessors from BSI (British Standards Institute) auditing for three days.)

Well, we passed our assessment and achieved the ISO 9002 certification with only a few deficiencies (non-conformities) to work on. This achievement was down mainly to the efforts of John Wells, a quietly-spoken, unassuming but excellent Quality Audit Officer. He had a unique way of shaming, encouraging or using other devious skills to ensuring that any deficiencies that he uncovered were dealt with properly and quickly by the person(s) involved.

Within six months of my tenure at the workshop, the Army's role in the command of its workshops was taken over by an agency, the Army Base Repair Organisation, (ABRO), so the workshop would now be known as ABRO Ashford. Technical grade civilians would now be responsible for operating the workshop for the Army. The Commanding Officer was replaced by a Workshop Director (PTO 1 Grade), Carl Floyd, and a new chapter in the workshop's life was about to begin.

The first task was to keep the workshop open. Easier said than done. Rumours had been rife for several years concerning the possible or probable closure of this workshop, and the reasons which governed this position. My strong belief is that Carl Floyd was given a brief as the incoming workshop boss to make the strongest possible case for the workshop to remain open, to prove its worth and viability. Actually he did both and more, but to little avail. He was stitched up like the rest of us, as the decision to close the workshop had in fact already been made.

However, back to the story. The workshop had a good and long-standing reputation for providing a valued service to the units in its dependency, but its main function was the Engine Line, and this would need to be proven to exceed a competitive contractor's service in terms of quality, time and cost.

My main concern was the satisfactory outcome of the quality audits which were done at six-monthly intervals and the longer term target of 're-accreditation' of the updated ISO 9002 quality standard in three years' time.

It was always my belief that if the workshop failed to achieve this standard its future was in grave doubt, although of course even if we achieved all that was required of us, it was still not a certainty that the workshop had a future.

The basis of the quality accreditation was to produce a quality manual which identified the key requirements necessary to achieve the quality standard. This obviously depended on the establishment concerned and its function, but would include the following key data: the function of the establishment, the head of the establishment's policy statement, its structure, a 'family tree' showing areas of responsibility, its commitment to quality and its future plans.

The quality manual would be supported by the Workshop Standing Orders (WSOs), which detailed what was done, where it was done and how it was done. In other words, 'Tell me what you do, and how you do it'. It would also show how supplies were ordered and monitored, describe any testing of products necessary and give training details.

The whole of the workshop procedures and processes were subject to review and periodic audit, to confirm that all operations were being undertaken correctly and in accordance with the stated regulations. These tasks were monitored by the Audit Plan produced and implemented by John Wells, the Quality Audit Officer (QAO).

One of our colleagues, Bob Wright on the Management Services team, was a fan of real ales and often at weekends he would visit the nicer rural pubs around the area to sample the guest beers, and then on Monday give us a full report. I didn't know the area too well, so I suggested that Bob show John and I some of the better pubs he had visited when we were all free, on a Friday lunchtime. We started going to the Swan in Great Chart, as we found they were offering four pint jugs of 'Speckled Hen' for a fiver! Too good to pass up, especially as they also did a mini steak, chips and peas for about £3.50.

Another nice pub locally was the Hooden Horse, where they did very nice lunchtime 'specials' at reasonable rates. We also visited the Tiger, a beautiful pub overlooking the Downs, and a gloriously sunny day when we visited; the Tickled Trout at Wye and the Farriers at Mersham,- happy days!

The workshop was a happy place to work. Most of the workforce had either been apprenticed there or had worked there for many years. They took a pride in their work and were good at it. They could not believe that 44 District Workshop (as they still referred to it) would close, especially as the Chief Executive of ABRO (Army Base Repair Organisation), Brigadier Drew, had described this workshop as 'the jewel in my crown'.

I tried to soften the blow when the closure came up in conversation by explaining that Chatham Dockyard (where I was previously employed) was a vital cog in the Navy's defence capability, undertaking two-stream nuclear submarine refitting, when it was closed in 1983/4. Therefore if the political will was there to close the Army workshop at Ashford, that was what would happen. I did temper this statement by saying I believed that the best option for us employed at the Ashford workshop was to demonstrate the workshop skills and facilities in the best possible way, to prevent the closure or try to make it as difficult as possible.

We did - but it still closed.

Although the workshop again achieved the required quality standard (ISO 9002) and proved that it could compete favourably with contractor competition in terms of cost, time and quality, but that still wasn't enough!

The workshop carried on as usual for a few months after the announced closure. By now we had had our interim quality reviews and it was time for a full-blown re-assessment. I felt that this was a critical time to get any necessary actions done and plans in place in preparation for our assessment, as I was convinced that the morale of the workshop staff was about to roll down a downward slope. People would say, 'Why bother knocking ourselves out getting the renewed quality standard when we are going to be closed anyway?'

To me, the answer was simple; if we failed in our assessment, the powers that be would say, 'They cannot achieve the required standard, therefore they must close'. But it was also important to me to ensure that the workforce had a difficult but realistic target to focus on, which would counter the ever-present worries and concerns arising from the workshop's closure. Anything that would bolster morale was vitally important.

So, thankfully at least in the short term, the workshop carried on doing what it always had, producing high-quality refurbished engines for the Army's Land Rovers, and my team of Examiners continued their efforts to ensure that the work standards remained at high levels.

All too soon we had a team of consultants at the workshop in an effort to find employment solutions for the staff. (It was led by a Mr Bates – think about that one!)

On a personal basis I believed that I would be much better off finding my own job, so I started my own personal job hunt. This was easier said than done, as Ashford was not the only establishment closing, and jobs were getting scarce. I attended a couple of interviews, and was even offered a job with the RAF at Brampton. This was a good opportunity, but unfortunately it meant another house move, so reluctantly, I turned the job down. Shortly after that a post became available as head of the Medical & Dental Equipment Support Group, Ludgershall, part of the Electronics Branch REME, which was administered from Malvern. I applied for the job and was interviewed.

The interview itself was quite unusual. The journey down to the site was no problem as I had been to Andover (about seven miles up the road) dozens of times when I worked at Woolwich. I stopped in the tiny town of Ludgershall for a quick wee, and got to the site nice and early. After signing in at the gate, I was met by one of the staff, Barry Charles, who I knew from Woolwich, and escorted to the group's office (a large Portakabin). I was told that the Big Boss, a Lt. Col (an Indian Officer who was referred to as Col. Toshie) was travelling down from Malvern to do the interview, and he would be a little late. No problem so far.

The boys in the group made me welcome and we had a cup of tea and a chat. When the Colonel arrived about half an hour later, he went into to outer office and chatted to the staff and had his coffee. That was fair enough – he wanted to see his staff, but I thought that it was a little unfair that I was ignored (I didn't expect an apology for his late arrival) as I had travelled some 120 miles to get there and some sort of recognition (instead of being completely blanked) would have been appreciated.

The interview itself was, from my point of view, most unsatisfactory. I had been interviewed many times over the years, some good, some bad, and I knew what to expect.

I was asked if I had any in-depth technical experience on the equipments of the group's concern, and when I replied that mine was limited, the Colonel seemed to switch off, although my CV, which he had in front of him, made this quite clear. The other questions at the interview seemed irrelevant, and the Colonel disinterested. Needless to say, I later received a 'Dear John' and my application for the post was rejected. But I subsequently appealed against non-selection - and was offered the job.

CHAPTER 9

ELECTRONICS BRANCH (MALVERN) REME OIC MEDICAL & DENTAL EQUIPMENT SUPPORT GROUP (LUDGERSHALL, WILTS)

The Admin Section at Malvern had arranged initial accommodation for me at Ludgershall in Tedworth House, the Officers' Mess, and because I had been 'transferred in' on detached duty I was allowed to make this a permanent arrangement. This would of course mean commuting back to Kent at weekends, but this was on balance not a major problem for me, as it meant that my family would not be forced into another house/area move.

Tedworth House was a marvellous old building, a wonderful 17th Century manor house in extensive, beautifully-manicured grounds and a great place to live. Lots of my colleagues would complain about 'living in' in a service mess, but I always found it to be a very pleasant experience. Some would complain, 'You've always got to dress up in a suit for dinner, and all that posh Army talk', but I enjoyed the environment. I would normally respond by saying that in a service mess it is always warm, you are usually fed very well, and on a personal basis I have met some really nice people.

Tedworth was a case in point. When I went down to the bar (it was the usual custom to meet in there for a quick drink before dinner) on my first night in the mess, the bar was quite full and obviously I didn't know anyone. Within the first minute Dr Derek Wilkins came over and introduced himself and his immediate group and did his best to put me to ease.

Derek was a long-term resident, a Mess Committee member, and he sat on the Army Medical Appeals Board. He was always the first to welcome in new mess members, and was a happy, cheerful sort who was genuinely interested in meeting and talking to new people. Although he would be interested in whoever he was talking to, he never mentioned the fact that he had had an extraordinary life, including being shot down as a Second World War fighter pilot (and spending some time as a prisoner of war) he held the honorary rank of Brigadier in the Territorial Army (TA), and that some of his exploits had been recognized with the CBE (Commander of the British Empire). He also had half shares in a light aircraft and a Lotus seven!

Another of my colleagues in the mess was Derek Hockney. He was a PTO 1 (Professional & Technology Officer Grade 1) working in the Defence Lands Office; he was a few years older than me, and again he had lived in the mess Monday to Friday for several years. So we were the three 'tame civvies' in the mess, and often met up in the bar for a nice glass of red wine before dinner. Happy days!

We did do our bit though in contributing to the activities in the mess. Derek Wilkins was the Gardens member on the Mess Committee, Derek Hockney organized the refurbishment and matches on the previously unused croquet green and we all helped reinstate an unused sun terrace when the mess bar was moved to the west end of the building.

Derek was also very friendly with Fred de la Billière, the brother of Peter de la Billière, who was C-i-C British Forces during the 1990 Gulf War. Fred lived just up the road, and would often pop in for a quick drink and a chat. Fred was ex RN (Fleet Air Arm I believe), so he and Derek could talk at length about the old aircraft they used to fly. I think they flew nearly as many miles in the Mess as they did on active service!

Fred was good company too, a bear of a man with a handshake that made your eyes water, but we all used to enjoy his visits to the mess, when he would entertain us with stories about his early days in service with the Navy. I think he took a shine to me, as I had spent many years working in the naval dockyards and could easily relate to most of his stories; that, and the fact that I had become good friends with Dr Derek.

I had no complaints about my time in the mess; the food was very good as we had an excellent Scottish chef (Jock) who could conjure up wonders. My real favourite was deep fried Brie for the starter, beef Wellington for the main course and Crème Brûlée for the sweet. Jock excelled in all these dishes. Good job they were all low calorie and slimming!

The necessity to 'dress' for dinner sometimes became a chore, but when we were settled down in the lovely old dining room (candlelight and silver) in a wonderful setting with good and ever-changing company, and many interesting people passing through the mess, it was certainly worth it.

The Medical and Dental Equipment Support Group (MDESG) was located next door to the Medical Supplies Agency (MSA) in the Drummond Barracks site. It was basically two large Portakabins in a figure 'T' configuration. Although we were administered from the Electronics Branch Malvern (which soon evolved into the Army Technical Support Agency [ATSA]) we were fairly autocratic, and in fact worked more closely with the Equipment Sponsors at Andover. Perhaps it should be explained at this stage that the Army had for years been trying to decide where the Med. & Dent. Should 'sit' (how and where it should fit into the system), as the Equipment did not have guns or wheels, so the Army had problems trying to understand it!

The group was divided into two sections, each with a HPTO/PTO 2 (Higher Professional & Technology Officer) in charge of a small team comprising civilians (PTO 3) and serving Army and RAF staff at Warrant Officer levels. I tried (unsuccessfully - mainly for political reasons) very hard during my time in charge to recruit a Navy member into the group. Each section had dedicated equipment on which they advised.

The principle functions of the group were to assess equipment which it was proposed would be entered into service; to investigate 'defect reports' on in-service equipment, and to carry out 'ease of maintenance' tasks. These would ascertain the degree of difficulty in carrying out repairs; and identify any special tools or equipment which would be required to maintain the equipment in a serviceable condition.

Secondly, we had to produce the Army's 'Hayne's Manuals' for the equipment in or about to enter into service, known as AESPs (Army Equipment Support Publications). These AESPs formed the basis of a priority task for the group, as it was the Army's intention that all in-service equipment should have its own dedicated AESP available.

Often the equipment manufacturer would provide its own handbooks, which we could use as a basis for our instructions. The main adjustments which were needed related to how the equipment was to be used, the environment and conditions. In the civilian environment most equipment would be used in a surgery or hospital, in fairly 'civilized' conditions. This did not apply to the equipment that was to be used in a hostile theatre, as it would need to be resistant to shock and vibration, water ingress, contamination and extremes of heat and cold. Additionally, extra testing was required for service equipment to ensure compliance with all relevant service regulations. Some of the low population equipments had little or no technical information available, and it was then necessary to start from scratch to provide the basic technical information that would be required.

Although the MoD's policy was to procure equipment from British manufacturers whenever possible, this was not always an option, due to the need to go through the competitive tender procedures, opening up competition to European suppliers. Other equipments were only made by a single manufacturer or their product was so superior that it was (as an exception) possible to buy from them only. Most products purchased from European suppliers had adequate technical information supplied with them, usually in several languages, but this was not always the case, and sometimes the information supplied was difficult to follow. In fairness, this applied more to equipment predominantly from Asian companies.

One major equipment which did present this type of problem was the GIAT. This was a French designed 'mini-hospital' built into expanded ISO containers, providing a purpose-built field operating theatre or a four-bed intensive care unit. These were excellent and proven units supplied at short notice for an operational requirement. The initial problem was that the technical literature (operation and maintenance) was only available in French. This problem was quickly overcome and all seemed well, and the GIAT was deployed. It was then discovered, on commissioning the unit, that it was not possible to connect the in-service BOC oxygen cylinders, as the connecting threads were incompatible!

This was not a major problem as the fault had been identified in good time, and purpose-made adaptors were made and fitted. It just goes to show that millions of pounds' worth of technical (and important) kit can be rendered useless for the sake of a couple of £5 adaptors!

Another interesting project during this time was to evaluate an Australian-developed item known by the acronym of MIRF (Mobile Intensive Care & Resuscitation Facility). This was basically life-vital equipment (defibrillator/heart start, oxygen supply, etc) mounted on a compact but heavy duty trolley; the top half was utilized as a stretcher, and could be collapsed down onto the bottom platform, which housed the medical equipment. It was rumoured that this was the next big thing in the medical world, and that these units would accompany VIPs and royalty on state visits and the like. The trials were a success, as the unit did all that was expected, but for some reason it was not successfully adopted.

I have good cause to remember this equipment, as I was injured during the assessment.

One evening when the desk officer doing the assessment was packing up at the end of his testing I happened to be passing, and as it was quite heavy duty equipment, I offered to help. As we were both struggling to collapse the top half of the assembly (one side had become stuck) it suddenly became free, and crushed the last joint of my little finger on my left hand. It was obvious that the finger was badly damaged, and a trip to A & E was required. To cut a long story short, the joint was irretrievably damaged and is now immobile. I did investigate a claim through the MoD, but they more or less said that as I was the supervisor I should not have been helping. So tough luck!

I didn't expect a fortune in compensation, as I had been in the MoD far too long and know how things work, but a little more flexible approach and interest wouldn't have gone amiss! Lessons learnt there.

By the way, I still see the Desk Officer (Bill Asty) who was doing the assessment (and was completely blameless in this accident), and pull his leg concerning it.

Massive changes were taking place in the drawdown of the services at this time, and the effects were cascading down to us in the group. The medical facilities were drawing down in BAOR (Germany), as the troops were redeployed, and in the UK the military hospitals in Woolwich (Army) and the Naval Hospital (Haslar) in Portsmouth were going also. The RAF was affected likewise.

The majority of the work tasking for the Group emanated from the Equipment Manager/Sponsor (ES32e) at Andover. This section had been run for many years by Hugh (ex-Col.) Hind, and Mick Hayward, both of whom I knew from when I was working at Woolwich. Hugh was then at Andover, and Mick was the PTO in charge of the medical equipment support in the Queen Elizabeth Hospital just up the road from the Ha Ha road site. ES32 were the policy makers, and effectively controlled the majority of the projects that would be undertaken by my group.

Probably the single biggest project during my time in charge was the investigative project surrounding the potential implications of the 'Millennium Bug'. It was recognized that some computers might not be able to relate to the year 2000 in their memory/control chips; this could cause malfunction or shutdown of the medical equipment, which had the potential for disaster. For example a syringe driver, commonly used in most hospitals, has a chip which controls the dose rate and timing of injected fluids. If the control chip malfunctioned as a result of this Millennium Bug, it was conceivable that multi doses, or none at all, could result. Not good for the patient!

The group was tasked to identify every piece of medical equipment in service which had a computer chip installed, and confirm that there would be no repercussions on 'Millennium Day'. This of course applied to equipment already in service, home and abroad, and items currently held in store prior to issue. A big project taking many months.

We checked all the equipment in service, and prevented any major problems arising from this millennium change. OK now then, for the next thousand years!

Life in the mess continued as normal. As Tedworth House was a 'transit' mess, people were coming and going all the time, going into or returning from theatre, attending courses, on manoeuvres, end-of-service activities etc etc. One of the new mess entrants was Lt Col. Brian Eadon, who was the new pharmacist posted into the MSA; he was a football nut like me (he used to play for the Crusaders, an Army team for veterans), and we got on like a house on fire. I believe that in one of the first conversations I had with him I explained that I could watch any football, even the women's matches. He said he felt exactly the same.

Occasionally, if we knew that matches were being played in the evenings, we would take a trip to the various stadiums.

We went as far as Swindon (the match was cancelled!) and were almost regulars at the Salisbury City ground (they did nice burgers).

The mess functions were marvellous. I attended several dinners organized by the MSA and the Officers' Mess at Malvern (which held its functions in the Foley Arms), but the most memorable was the Tedworth House Summer Ball in 1997. The services really know how to organize a function, and this one was a case in point. The organization takes many months, but invariably it all comes together and makes for a great experience. Two bands (rock and ballroom), a disco in the main ballroom, and a bucking bronco and laser clay shooting in the grounds outside; and it was a lovely summer's evening! The evening was James Bond themed with a wonderful five-course meal and plenty of drinkypoos, what a night! I crawled into bed when the festivities finished shortly after 4 am and expected to feel pretty dreadful next day, but surprisingly, apart from feeling a little 'woolly' next morning, there was no major hangover, thank goodness.

Living in the mess was pleasant for me for the reasons stated, and provided different pleasures summer and winter. In the summer it was an ideal chance to either walk some of the surrounding area (the mess itself had extensive grounds, and the immediate Tidworth outskirts were very pleasant). Alternatively a short drive took me to some of the 'chocolate box' villages nearby, all of which seemed to offer delicious snacks and meals in idyllic surroundings. These trips would make a nice change from staying in the mess every night; no matter how good the company, a change of scenery was always welcome.

Winter was not quite so pleasant, as walks were often out of the question if it was raining really hard, very cold, or both. Fortunately the mess had Sky television, so usually there was a sports programme or a decent film on in the evening. I believe some of the mess members used to get fed up with football matches in particular, but it was first come first served, and often Brian Eadon or I managed to sneak in and book the TV for the match. Most of the mess members were more than happy about this, but I know that one or two who had no interest in football, or disliked it, were wrinkly-lipped from time to time.

The good news about staying in the mess is that there is usually plenty of good company. The bad news for me was that most of the mess members were young(ish) officers who spent a lot of their time in the bar. When I got involved in these nights (someone was always leaving, joining, or had just got promoted, it seemed) these younger guys could whoop it up till all hours and apparently it would not cause them any major suffering next day. But with me it was different. I was older, so probably my metabolism was different, and I wasn't 'in training' for drinking like these blokes. After a couple of disastrous mornings, I resolved to pace my drinking, to enable me to feel confident about surviving the next day!

I probably should have been grateful that I was not a mess resident a couple of years previously. Dr Derek and some of the other mess residents who were living in at that time often referred to a riotous period when several Royal Marines officers were on an extended detachment and living in the mess. Apparently, quite often towards the end of the evening when the Marines had been enjoying themselves for a couple of hours, one of them would shout 'nude bar!' and they would all strip off, to continue their evening drinking in the 'altogether' (except that they kept their boots on). At first one or two of the mess members were a little shocked, but as it didn't happen too often, it was considered amusing and tolerated. Well, they were Marines after all.

My only worrying experience was when one night some of the younger officers decided to get 'blotto' - really drunk. I can't remember what the occasion was, or if in fact there was any special reason. It may have been some of the bomb disposal guys who used to go away on a tour of duty for a couple of months, when they completely abstained from any alcohol due to the work circumstances. When they came back to the mess after these tours they really let their hair down.

However this night the 'boys' were getting drunk and over the top, and started to upset some of the others in the bar. One of the female nursing staff (a very nice young officer) asked them to 'cool it a little and behave'. The rowdies took offence at this and were abusive, so the young nursing officer (who was a close friend of the entire group) told them to get on with it and she went off to bed. It was now apparent that some sort of problem was likely later on, so several of us (me included) made our excuses and headed off to bed. The writing was on the wall, and before I got into bed I locked my bedroom door.

About 2 am I was woken up by banging and crashing in the corridor outside, stupid giggling noises, and someone trying the door handle. More laughter and people running up and down the corridor; then the all too familiar sound of a fire extinguisher being operated. More shouts, a bang, more laughing, then all went quiet. I went off into an uneasy sleep about 3 pm.

There were some very, very contrite faces next morning. The pack of offenders seemed to be going over the top with their apologies. Yes, they had woken people up, and yes, they had acted stupidly by letting off some fire extinguishers; but there seemed more to it than that. There was. At the height of their buggering about, one of the guys had fired off an air pistol (for no apparent reason and at no particular target) but unfortunately it had struck one of his fellow revellers and the pellet had penetrated his forearm. So that was what had quieted down the revellers last night, and this had the potential to be serious, not only for the officer who now had the pellet embedded in his arm, which would require medical attention, but because the actions would be seriously frowned upon by the Army authorities and disciplinary measures were most probable.

When they had realized they needed help they decided to throw themselves on the mercy of the nurse they had abused earlier in the mess. They woke her up, and all credit to her, she could see the implications if she did not help them. She not only removed the air gun pellet but wangled a couple of appropriate anti-infection injections for the victim the next day. So she had saved their bacon, no argument, and the lads had learnt a very important lesson.

We had a couple of amusing incidents during my stay. One morning about 1.30 am I was woken up by loud banging on the bedroom doors, coming along the corridor. This was accompanied by the shouts of the Security Police (it transpired) telling everyone to vacate the building and to assemble at the fire/emergency assembly point in the car park. We all exited the building in our dressing gowns (good job it was summer and it wasn't raining), and awaited further instructions. We took this incident in pretty good spirit as it was obviously in our safety interests. However after about an hour, and continual requests for information, it started to wear a little thin, and we were getting cold.

It was then explained to us that an intruder had triggered an alarm in the polo club which was located in the grounds a short distance away, and which was broken into fairly frequently, so a security alert had been triggered. This may have seemed over the top, but bear in mind that bomb scares were a way of life at this time, and this was a military establishment with security problems, primarily due to being such a large open site.

Possibly another reason for security vigilance was that Prince Charles had been a visitor to the Tedworth House mess from time to time. He would visit when playing polo at the adjacent club and would sometimes stay overnight in the mess VIP suite. He did not visit during my time as a mess resident, but I did get to stay in the VIP suite when my wife came to stay for my retirement presentation, so I've slept in the same bed as Prince Charles! I must admit that I was very disappointed - although it really massive dressing room adjacent to the bedroom, the furniture was old, dark and heavy and the bathroom was terrible. A big picture of his mum and dad over the bed probably made Charles feel at home!

One of the regular tales concerning Tedworth House centred on the resident ghosts. The most popular one was an old woman who used to appear regularly in the Green Room. She seemed to be someone who at one time had worked as a servant at Tedworth and usually appeared looking over someone's shoulder in one of the large wall mirrors, I couldn't find out any details (what she wanted, if she spoke etc), but the staff were convinced of her existence due to the regularity of her visits. In fact one of the recent staff had left her job allegedly severely distressed, and claiming that she had had a nasty experience when the ghost appeared, and it frightened her so much that she was unable to enter that particular room again. I must admit that although I never saw the ghost, the Green Room did have a very strange feel about it. It was a very large room, perhaps 50 feet square, and every time I entered there seemed to be a chilly atmosphere as soon as you went through the door, even in summer.

The other resident ghost was supposedly a Polish World War Two pilot. He had been sent to Tedworth House to convalesce, after taking part in a disastrous raid over France. The story was that he blamed himself for surviving the operation whilst all his mates that flew with him that night perished, and eventually, consumed with guilt, he shot himself. It was said that at times he could be heard berating himself and screaming for release from the anguish that he carried with him. Poor bugger, another casualty of war.

All too soon it was time for me to retire, to leave Tedworth House (and the MoD). It was now March 2000, and I had completed almost 42 years' service. As I was nominally employed by ATSA at Malvern, I was 'dined out' in the officers' mess (the Foley Arms) along with two retiring Army officers, which was a very pleasant evening, during which we were all told what a marvellous job we had done and how much we would be missed.

Yeah, right.

I did get a nice letter from the Chief Executive though.

I also had a farewell 'party' at Tedworth House, which was mainly for my colleagues at Ludgershall. It proved to be something of a disappointment, as the mess manager took my payment for the 'do', but forgot (?) to arrange for most of the drinks and food! (it was later established that he was a crook).

All over now then. I must admit that I was not going to miss the weekly commute, but the rest of it? Yes, I would certainly miss that.

CHAPTER 10

REFLECTIONS

Well; those 42 years soon went by, didn't they? It seems like only a few years ago that I was being shouted at by the police constable at the gate for riding my bike into the Dockyard instead of dismounting and pushing it in on my first day at work!

Fast forward a few more years (it was actually now 24 years since I had started in the 'yard) and off to the Personnel Office to hand in my passes and sign out. No farewell party, no flattering and no greatly exaggerated speeches. A young clerk new to the system said 'good luck', and that was that. Goodbye Chatham.

Onwards and upwards as they say, into the outside world, to follow the work wherever it sent me. I would be posted to Bedford, Woolwich, Ashford and Ludgershall as the MoD establishments continued to close, and I became a professional nomad.

Which was the best job? Hard to tell really. Does 'best' mean the best paid? Best colleagues? Best site/location? Or a combination, with all things considered? Also age must be taken into consideration, as when you are younger things are so very different.

The 'outstations' job was great. I was young and enthusiastic. I had the freedom to travel to a different site on most days, had a good team, and met some great people, and I loved it.

The Bedford job was also marvellous. Everything was different: new job, new site, new people and new area. Sharnbrook, where we lived, was a lovely typical Bedfordshire village.

At 44 District workshop, I worked with some really great colleagues who did their darndest to keep the workshop open and worked hard, but always with a smile on their faces.

John Wells, who worked for me on the quality team, was one of the most dedicated and underrated PTOs that I met. The workshop itself produced exceptionally high quality work right up until the closure.

My last job at the MDESG Ludgershall - was that the best one? I knew it was my last job, and that of course colours your thought process; also I had taken this post on promotion, which always helps! The life in the Officers' mess suited me very well. I always considered myself a privileged guest and tried to act accordingly. I was made very welcome, and I met some great and interesting people there.

My 'boys' in the MDESG group were second to none, all experienced technicians at Warrant Officer grade, and with a diverse mix of Navy (me), Army and RAF as well as civilian engineers, we provided an invaluable and recognized service to the MoD.

As the group head, it was necessary for me to visit some of

ther sites (Malvern, Woolwich and Andover in particular) to tend programmed meetings etc, and this obviously involved fairly regular travel, which I always enjoyed.

So which was the best job? I don't know. They all had their good and bad points, but I consider myself lucky that most of the time I felt I was doing a good job and enjoying it. Although I was trained as a mechanical (marine) engineer, those basic skills were only the bedrock of the management skills I would require when promoted.

The excellent training facilities provided by the MoD covered the techniques and skills I would require in future middle and senior management posts. These included planning, scheduling, communications, time management, performance appraisal/reporting procedures, quality and safety, alongside dedicated technical topics, computer training and many others.

The closure of the Dockyard had a disastrous effect on the Medway towns, from which they have still not fully recovered. Disregarding the emotional and psychological trauma, which caused a plethora of physical and mental problems (now largely forgotten) to the workforce and their families, the local environment has still to recover in many respects.

I believe that in many ways the health of the local high streets is a good indication of the wellbeing of the area. When the Dockyard was operational, Gillingham (as an example) had a high street which was a nice place to visit, with many excellent stores including Marks & Spencer, Debenhams, Tesco, Littlewoods, Burtons, the Co-operative and Currys. Not now.

The high street now, in my opinion, is dreadful. Fast food and low budget stores, and that's about all.

Perhaps this demise cannot be traced back directly to the Dockyard's closure, but I have yet to be convinced that this is not the case. Look what happened to Sheerness, if a parallel is required.

When the Dockyards closed, a lot of the older staff could not find alternative work, and not all the younger ones wanted to. I was very lucky, and had over 40 years' continuous employment. OK, the money wasn't great (contrary to the propaganda in some of the papers which says that all civil servants earn fantastic money and accrue enormous pensions). I made a respectable living, but I had to work bloody hard for it, and it was only because I achieved four promotions that I was able to maintain a reasonable standard of living.

The employment covered times when I was working in a wide range of very unpleasant conditions. On board ships it can be unbelievably cold during the winter months, and often you could be working in a dark, noisy, wet, noxious and fume-filled environment.

Testing boilers was a nasty job as well. On top of a working boiler it gets bloody hot and you would have to contend with clouds of dust (if safety valves were operated) and probably asbestos dust residue from the previous operations.

The dockside crane maintenance was no picnic either. The access ladders are vertical, and when it was wet or icy you needed to be quite careful. So all in all, working conditions would often cky, but at least I had the comfort of relatively safe job ctations.

My sons are now working in a completely different MoD environment. Job tenure is 2/3 years maximum - for the lucky ones. Pay rises are currently non-existent. They have, in my opinion, been insulted by an unfair and unworkable bonus scheme. No wonder morale is so low, and there is little or no job satisfaction. I am so pleased that I have now retired, and don't have the constant worry of job expectations.

While I feel sorry for the young men and women who are actively trying to make their way in the turmoil that currently exists in the MoD world, I also feel a sense of pride when I see their achievements under such difficult conditions, and have only admiration for them that they continue to maintain such an enthusiasm, and determination to continue their good work.

Well done, guys!